I0796802

WILLIAM BLIGH

Dedicated to all the team at the Robert White Centre,
Dorchester Hospital

WILLIAM BLIGH

That Bounty Bastard

Mike Rendell

PEN & SWORD HISTORY

AN IMPRINT OF PEN & SWORD BOOKS LTD.
YORKSHIRE – PHILADELPHIA

First published in Great Britain in 2025 by
PEN AND SWORD HISTORY
An imprint of
Pen & Sword Books Ltd
Yorkshire – Philadelphia

ISBN 978 1 39903 396 1

A CIP catalogue record for this book is available from the British Library.

Typeset in Times New Roman 11/14 by
SJmagic DESIGN SERVICES, India.
Printed and bound in the UK by CPI Group (UK) Ltd.

The Publisher's authorised representative in the EU for product safety is Authorised Rep Compliance Ltd., Ground Floor, 71 Lower Baggot Street, Dublin D02 P593, Ireland.
www.arccompliance.com

For a complete list of Pen & Sword titles please contact
PEN & SWORD BOOKS LIMITED
George House, Units 12 & 13, Beevor Street, Off Pontefract Road,
Barnsley, South Yorkshire, S71 1HN, England
E-mail: enquiries@pen-and-sword.co.uk
Website: www.pen-and-sword.co.uk

or

PEN AND SWORD BOOKS
1950 Lawrence Rd, Havertown, PA 19083, USA
E-mail: uspen-and-sword@casematepublishers.com
Website: www.penandswordbooks.com

Contents

Preface

In *The Island*, composed in 1823, the poet Lord Byron writes:

> The gallant Chief within his Cabin slept,
> Secure in those by whom the watch was kept:
> His dreams were of Old England's welcome shore,
> Of toils rewarded, and of dangers o'er;
> His name was added to the glorious roll
> Of those who search the Storm-surrounded Pole.
> The worst was over, and the rest seemed sure,
> And why should not his Slumber be secure?
> Alas! his deck was trod by unwilling feet,
> And wilder hands would hold the Vessel's sheet;
> Young hearts, which languished for some sunny isle,
> Where Summer years and Summer women smile;
> Men without country, who, too long estranged,
> Had found no native home, or found it changed,
> And, half uncivilised, preferred the cave
> Of some soft savage to the uncertain Wave —

Byron was writing about an event which happened in 1789 – the year of the French Revolution – and traces the path of the mutineers on board the *Bounty* as they flee to a South Sea island, 'their guilt-won Paradise'. The poem details the conflict between the mutineers (aggressive crewmen) and the resilient, hard-done-by leader, and accepts at face value that Bligh was the innocent victim ('the gallant chief'). That is not surprising, given that Byron had only read Bligh's own, somewhat one-sided, story of the mutiny, one in which there is never any suggestion that Bligh's conduct was anything other than exemplary.

But Byron is also attracted to the idea of the mutineers feeling driven to rebel in order to establish their own utopia in a tropical paradise, and the poem is full of romantic imagery. Byron wrote it without apparently knowing the fate of Fletcher Christian – even though by 1823 the story of Christian's escape to Pitcairn Island and of his eventual death had started to filter back to Britain. *The Island* deals with Byron's imagination, not with the reality of the situation. And that imagination was to some extent influenced by the same ideas as emerged in revolutionary France – ideas of personal freedom, of the right to free thought and freedom of speech, the right to rebel against oppression and cruelty. To the poet, there was the romantic appeal of building a life for oneself in a tropical idyll, free from outside controls. That is the great thing about being a poet – he can 'unsee' the poverty, the squalor, the sickness and the loneliness and just see the romance of paradise.

To Byron, the fact that many of the mutineers had at some stage during the voyage felt the lash, on the orders of William Bligh, was never a justification for what happened – Byron's generation (and particularly his class) accepted corporal punishment as being essential to naval discipline, whereas to modern eyes it is all too easy to condemn any form of corporal punishment out of hand. The fact remains: in the eighteenth century the navy was a flogging navy. Nelson flogged. Cook flogged. Flogging was permitted by the Articles of War. Every sailor on the actual *Bounty* was a volunteer, and every one of them knew that discipline was essential to onboard safety. If a sailor was negligent, or disobedient, he faced the lash and he knew that from Day One.

What has made the story of the mutiny on the *Bounty* resonate through the centuries is that it can be viewed from totally opposing angles; it can be seen through Bligh's eyes as a crime without any justification – a crime which led the miscreants to a well-deserved end when so many of them perished violently. For others, it can be seen from the perspective of the romantic rebel Fletcher Christian; he found love on a paradise island and gave up everything in pursuit of happiness and personal freedom.

Each generation has read something different into the story. What if Bligh and Christian had been in a homosexual relationship prior to an acrimonious split? What if Christian had been suffering from some sort of mental illness? What if Bligh was driven to intense jealousy because, alone among his ship's company, he felt obliged to stay celibate on an island where everyone else was enjoying 'free love' with the amorous 'summer women'? What if he was exhibiting what might anachronistically be called a 'Napoleon Complex' – a short man, below average height, trying to make up for his lack of stature by belittling those around him? And even – somewhat improbably – what if Christian did not die on Pitcairn, but made his way back to Britain?

It is a story which has inspired hundreds of books and several memorable films. And there is one central figure who lurks behind every scene: that of William Bligh. Who was he? What do we actually know about his life, about his behaviour? We may not like what we find – frankly, he wasn't a very likeable character – but he certainly wasn't the bullying tyrant portrayed on screen.

PART ONE

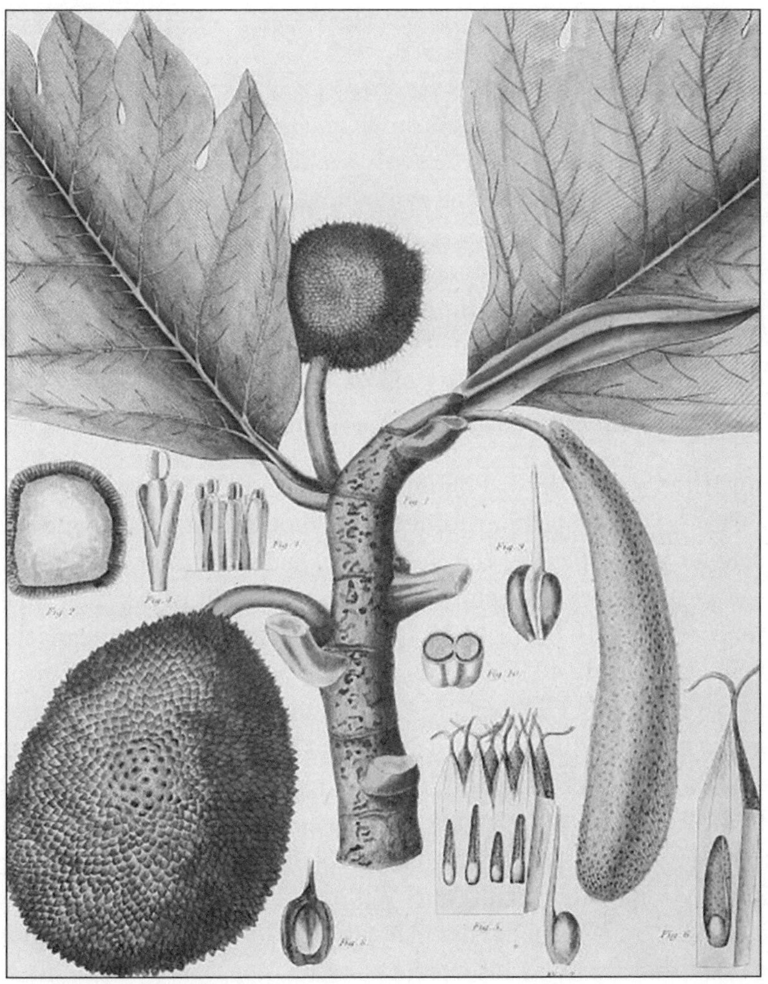

A detailed drawing of the different parts of the breadfruit tree, 1875.

Chapter 1

Family, Childhood and Early Career

The Western Prospect of His Majesty's Dock Yard near Plymouth, in 1736.

William Bligh was born in Plymouth, Devon, on 9 September 1754. His father, Francis, was a customs officer. His mother, Jane, had been married before, to a Richard Pearce, and she already had a daughter, Catherine, born nineteen years before William. Following the death of her first husband, Jane married Francis Bligh in 1753 and William arrived a year later. By then Jane was already 40 and William was to be the only child of the union. He was baptised on 4 October 1754 at Plymouth's St Andrews Church.

Later in his life William was to claim that he was 'a Cornishman', giving rise to some confusion because there is a record of a William Bligh being born at Tinten Manor at St Tudy in Cornwall. However, it is clear that this is a different William Bligh – but one who shared the same paternal great-grandfather (John Bligh) with 'our' William. In his later life our William's claim to be a Cornishman did not mean that he was born there – merely that he regarded the county as his ancestral home, not least because his father, grandfather and great-grandfather had all been born at St Tudy. And without insulting Devonians, let's just say that if you feel that you are Cornish, there is no way that you are going to call yourself a Man from Devon! The rivalry is still palpable.

Little is known about Bligh's childhood, but it is fair to assume that this 'only child' grew up as the apple of his parents' eyes. Without siblings to compete with, it seems that he must have become used to the idea of being 'the best' – always believing himself to be in the right, always ready to lash out at anyone appearing to challenge his desire to be 'top dog'. One suspects that from an early age he did not take kindly to criticism – and certainly these characteristics were evident throughout his adult life. He may well have been a mother's boy – or at least until Jane died when he was 14.

By then his parents had already marked him out for a career at sea. In fact, from the age of 7 years and 9 months his name had been entered on the muster rolls of the Royal Navy, attached to HMS *Monmouth*. On paper at any rate, he served as cabin boy and captain's servant between 1761 and 1763, but this may well have been a fiction – albeit a popular one at the time. Enrolling the boy in the navy was one way of ensuring that he would have enough years of service under his belt when he sat his exams to become lieutenant – but it did not mean that he was actually climbing any rigging or spending time at sea. It was a device used by Captain Cook, who readily put down the names of his own sons as being on board the ships in which he sailed – or at least, until he returned at the end of each voyage.

Bligh's association with HMS *Monmouth* almost certainly came with the help of Vice-Admiral Keith Stewart, who is often described as Bligh's first patron. Stewart was a friend of the family and is sometimes referred to as being a relative of William's mother. He may well have been the one to encourage the youngster to consider a life in the navy and to that end helped in his appointment as 'captain's servant'.

Bligh probably first tasted sea life onboard ship when he was 15, when he joined HMS *Hunter* – a small ten-gun sloop – as an Able Seaman. He was made up to Midshipman on the same vessel in 1771 serving under John Henshaw, before joining HMS *Crescent*, then under the captaincy of John Corner. He stayed on HMS *Crescent* for three years until the age of 20, when he got a posting on HMS *Ranger*, once more under the command of John Henshaw. The *Ranger* was busy patrolling the Irish Sea in the waters off the Isle of Man, then a centre of smuggling operations. It was during this time that Bligh would have met Richard Betham at Douglas on the Isle of Man – someone who, like his father, worked for the customs office. Betham was the Collector of Customs and it is highly probable that it was at this time that his daughter Elizabeth met the young Bligh. They were eventually married, but not until 1781 some seven years later.

During his time on HMS *Ranger* Bligh passed his Master's exams – an indication that he was a proficient sailor and, in all likelihood, a highly competent surveyor and chart-maker. On 30 September 1775, he was promoted to Master's Mate while still serving on HMS *Ranger*. Shortly after this, his career took an almost inexplicable upwards trajectory. In March 1776, after just six months in his new position, Bligh was approached by James Cook, then preparing for his third and final Pacific voyage, and offered the post of Master on board the *Resolution*. Bligh was just 21 years old and did not sit his lieutenant's examination until 1 May 1776. He passed, but by that time had already joined *Resolution* on 20 March.

What made Cook single out the young Bligh? One suspects that he must have heard of Bligh's abilities in surveying and mapping coastal areas and perhaps there is a parallel with Cook's own experience as a young sailor serving in the navy off what is now the coast of Nova Scotia. It was while walking on the beach at Kennington Cove near Louisbourg that James Cook had encountered a man called Samuel Holland, an army engineer, who was carrying out surveying operations along the coast.

It was a chance encounter which was to change Cook's life. Holland instructed Cook on the basics of surveying and took on responsibility for training Cook as his pupil. He never looked back. Years later, did the older James Cook see something of himself in the young Bligh? Whatever the case, he was prepared to act as his mentor, aware that the one thing needed on a voyage into the unknown, searching for the Northwest Passage, was a competent and highly motivated young Master, one who was willing to take a boat out day after day, recording the coastline, taking depth readings, and accurately compiling charts.

Cook had set out from Plymouth on his third and final Pacific voyage in July 1776; ostensibly, the voyage was intended to return to Polynesia a young islander called Omai, who had accompanied Cook when he returned from his previous voyage. It was, however, a cover to disguise the fact that Cook was to search for the fabled Northwest Passage. Previous attempts had been made by travelling westwards – past Greenland and then passing north of Hudson Bay. Cook was to try from the opposite direction, from the eastern coast of North America, up through the Bering Strait. To this end, two ships were involved in the expedition; Cook on board HMS *Resolution* and Charles Clerke in charge of HMS *Discovery*.

Having reached the Pacific after rounding the Cape of Good Hope and crossing the ocean south of Australia, Cook arrived at Ra'iatea, one of the Society Islands near Tahiti, and dropped off Omai. Poor Omai; he may have returned wealthy, but he was certainly not healthy. His fate was later described by George Hamilton when visiting Tahiti onboard HMS *Pandora*:

> Here we learnt the fate of Omai, the native of Otaheite, whom Captain Cook brought from England. On his return here he had wealth enough to obtain every fine woman on the island; and at last fell a martyr to Venus, having finished his career by the venereal disease, two years after his landing.

The expedition then headed into the North Pacific and, after becoming the first Europeans to visit the islands of Hawaii, proceeded towards the eastern coast of North America and set about mapping the coastline north of the Spanish settlements at Alta, California. On reaching Vancouver Island the two ships spent a month on a small island in Nootka Sound, which Cook named 'Bligh Island'. It still bears that name today. It was an unusual honour to bestow on William Bligh. Indeed, it sometimes looks as though Cook only wanted to name places 'Sandwich' – in honour of his patron and supporter at the Admiralty, John Montagu, Fourth Earl of Sandwich. It certainly was not common for Cook to name places after his crew and the name reflects the high regard Cook had for the mapping skills of his young lieutenant.

The expedition sailed through the Bering Strait and found their way repeatedly blocked by sea-ice and the decision was made to return to Hawaii to rest out the winter. Both ships had problems with water ingress – the planking opened up in the extreme cold, meaning that the ships' timbers needed constant recaulking.

It was back on Hawaii that Cook met his death at the hands of local islanders after what appears to have been a misunderstanding. He was killed on 14 February 1779, along with four of his men, in an attack which must have had a huge influence on men such as Bligh, as being an example of the perfidious and violent nature of the native islanders.

Instead of returning home, the expedition had one more go at locating the Northwest Passage, once more heading through the Bering Strait but yet again being thwarted by pack-ice and extreme cold. Eventually, they headed for home, via Japan, Macao and Cape Town. Frustratingly, they found that the weather prevented them from entering the English Channel and they ended up having to go all the way round the northern tip of Britain, reaching London via the Orkney Isles, before finally mooring up at Sheerness in the mouth of the River Medway on 4 October 1780.

Bligh certainly seemed to have a high opinion of himself on board. After Cook's death Charles Clerke had taken over command, but by then Clerke was already seriously ill. He was suffering from tuberculosis and was to die six months later. But according to Bligh:

> *C. Clerke* being very ill in a decline he could not attend the Deck, & th[us] he publickly gave me the Power solely of conducting the Ships & moving as I thought proper. His orders were 'You are to explore the Isles as much as you can & from thence carry the ships to Kamschatka & thence do your utmost endeavours to discover the NW Passage'.

That sounds something of an exaggeration – not only did Clerke remain in command until shortly before his death, but he could hardly have handed command to Bligh over the head of his Number Two, Captain Gore. But Bligh never was backwards in coming forward to claim credit. What is more, he was always infuriated if anyone claimed credit for what he reckoned was his handiwork. A case in point was the printing of the charts he had prepared during the exploration of the North Pacific. These were copied by Henry Roberts, using Bligh's original drawings, so that engraving plates could be prepared. The idea was that these drawings could then illustrate the official record of the voyage, which was prepared by Captain James King and published in 1784. Bligh obtained a copy of the published record and was furious to see that credit was given to Henry Roberts, angrily scribbling in the margin:

> None of the Maps and Charts in this publication are from the original drawings of Lieutenant Henry Roberts; he did no more than copy the original ones from Captain Cook, who besides myself was the only person that surveyed and laid the coast down, in the *Resolution*. Every plan & Chart from C. Cook's death are exact Copies of my Works. Wm. Bligh.

The annotated copy was subsequently added to by J.W. Croker, Secretary to the Admiralty between 1809 and 1827, with the words: 'This copy of Cook's last voyage belonged to William Bligh, Master of the *Resolution* who has made some marginal notes, which must be read with grains of allowance for his temper and prejudices. He afterwards became a flag officer.'

Those comments suggest that the Admiralty regarded Bligh as a boastful, arrogant officer and it is noteworthy that whereas many of the other officers on Cook's final voyage received promotions, Bligh did not. He had not got on with Captain Gore – or indeed with Captain King, which is presumably why King published his account of the voyage without involving Bligh, and certainly without crediting him for the charts he used.

The return of the expedition to Britain was followed by a plethora of published reports. The first was the journal of John Rickman published in 1781 as the *Journal of Captain Cook's Last Voyage*. Two botanists on board, Forster and Zimmermann, published their own accounts of the voyage (in German) in the same year. William Ellis, Surgeon's Mate on the *Discovery*, published his account the following year, and in 1783 the American explorer and adventurer John Ledyard, who had served on the expedition as a British marine, wrote his story of the voyage as *A Journal of Captain Cook's Last Voyage*, published in Connecticut. However, the 'definitive' account of the voyage, based upon Cook's own journal and supplemented by accounts written by James King and the surgeon William Anderson, was delayed until 1784. The three-volume set, published as *A Voyage to the Pacific Ocean*, was an immediate best-seller and the public appetite for news of adventures into the unknown Pacific sky-rocketed. Bligh had helped with the preparation of the account, and in recognition of his assistance in producing the detailed survey drawings Joseph Banks is believed to have been one of the people who recommended that Bligh should receive a one-eight share of the profits from the sale of the books. Subsequently, Bligh became a regular visitor to Banks's home and a committed letter-writer, as shown by the plethora of correspondence held in institutions such as the State Library of New South Wales.

Chapter 2

Lessons learnt

Detail from an engraving by Thornton of Captain Cook, artist unknown, 1784.

Bligh would have learnt a number of useful lessons from this, his first lengthy Pacific voyage. He would certainly have learnt about the overwhelming importance of preparing accurate charts of the coastline, and his meticulous style of mapping closely resembles that of Cook. Accuracy in observing the tides, the winds and the outline of the coast proved vital in the aftermath of the mutiny, when Bligh was to steer an open boat through the islands of the Pacific, through the notoriously complicated waters of the Torres Strait, and on to Timor in Indonesia. In this regard Bligh did not just see himself as an equal to Cook, he went so far as to criticise Cook's workmanship on at least one occasion. One of Cook's charts of part of the Bering Sea coastline was published after his death, and Bligh added these words:

> The opposite is from C. Cook's original survey, which agrees nearly with mine except in laying down Anderson's Island. Here is a gross mistake, for Anderson's and the East end of Clerk's Island is one & the same land, and how they have blundered to lay them down as two I cannot conceive.

It gives an inkling of the arrogance of the man; not content with merely pointing out a mistake by his commanding officer, but also calling it a blunder and a gross mistake, while at the same time deliberately drawing attention to the fact that his own records were accurate. It is, however, certainly true that Bligh's charts, particularly those made in the area of the Torres Strait, were incredibly detailed and well-drawn, forming the basis of Royal Navy maps of the area for well over a century.

Another lesson which Bligh learnt under Cook's leadership was the importance of maintaining the health of the crew, and it was a lesson which certainly impacted upon the way Bligh subsequently treated his men on board HMS *Bounty*. For centuries, scurvy had been the scourge of sailors on long voyages, decimating crews and killing literally thousands of sailors every year – far more than died in battle or from shipwreck. Early symptoms were loose teeth and bleeding gums, leading to haemorrhaging, hallucinations, anaemia and, ultimately, death. Back in 1754 Edinburgh surgeon James Lind had published his *Treatise on the Scurvy*, showing that 'anti-scorbitics' such as citrus fruits (and in particular lemon juice) could both ward off and cure the symptoms of scurvy. By the time of Cook's first voyage, little notice had been taken of the *Treatise*, but nevertheless the Admiralty had got it into its head that fresh vegetables had a role in counteracting scurvy and had ordered Cook to take with him on board HMS *Endeavour* some three tons of sauerkraut, intended to provide a ration of two pounds per person per week throughout the voyage. When Joseph Banks, the young botanist on board, started to exhibit signs of scurvy, he helped himself to a cup of lemon juice – and the symptoms promptly disappeared, However, Cook still did not appreciate the particular qualities of lemon juice, now known to contain large quantities of Vitamin C. He believed that all fresh vegetables were important, to such an extent that any crew member seeking to ingratiate themselves with their captain only had to return from a shore party brandishing a handful of herbs and greenery and then ask that these should be added to whatever soup or stew was being prepared.

Cook also encouraged the men to drink spruce beer, made using the young tips of spruce bushes found during his travels. On other occasions he directed the naturalists on board to identify edible plants, resulting in the diet being improved with delights such as scurvy grass, wild celery and the Kerguelen Cabbage (found in what is now known as the Desolate Islands in the sub-Antarctic). But above all he was convinced in the efficacy of the sauerkraut and on his return reported to the Victualling Board in 1771 that not a single sailor had died of scurvy during that voyage. It was the first time ever that this had happened on such a long voyage. On his second voyage there was just one scurvy fatality but by then Cook was attributing his success to 'mermalade of carrot', and to regular does of 'wort of malt'. On his return to England Cook delivered a paper to the Royal Society, stating that malt 'is without doubt one of the best antiscorbutic sea-medicines yet found out; and if given in time will, with proper attention to other things, I am persuaded, prevent the scurvy from making any great progress for a considerable time.' Ironically, Cook had been carrying quantities of what was called 'rob' – a highly concentrated concoction made from boiled oranges. Sadly, all of the Vitamin C would have disappeared during the reduction process…

Bligh must have been impressed with Cook's admiration for sauerkraut as he too set sail with vast quantities of it, along with the wort of malt and, like Cook, he kept a close and benevolent eye on what the crew consumed. To Bligh, any outbreak of scurvy was a sure sign of bad captaincy. So, when crew-member James Morrison reported that scurvy appeared on the *Bounty* on the run between the Cape of Good Hope and Tahiti, Bligh wrote in the margin of his manuscript: 'Captain Bligh never had a symptom of Scurvy in any ship he commanded.' Indeed, he may have been right – whereas the surgeon's log identified an outbreak of a 'disease of a scorbic nature', the surgeon may have been deliberately winding Captain Bligh up. It was just as likely to have been a deliberately misdescribed venereal complaint in order to put Bligh in a bad light.

For some years the Admiralty persisted with the sauerkraut and when HMS *Pandora* was dispatched to locate and bring back the mutineers, the doctor on board (George Hamilton) wrote saying:

> It may be remarked, the sour Crout kept during the voyage, in the highest perfection, and was often eat as a salad with vinegar, in preference to recent, cut vegetables from the shore. A cask of this grand antiscorbutic was kept open for the crew to eat as much of as they pleased; and I will venture to affirm, that it will answer every purpose that can be expected from the vegetable kingdom.

It was significant that Bligh was to follow Cook's practice of insisting on cleanliness on board, of airing clothes and bedding regularly, and of drying garments over a portable stove so that men were not required to go to bed in wet clothing.

Another health concern which Bligh learnt was the importance of identifying those members of the crew who were afflicted by venereal disease, of treating them, and of banning them from going ashore and infecting the islanders they met. In practice there was no effective treatment, because the cure – the application of mercury – was worse than the disease. Nevertheless, Bligh was to order regular inspections of the crew by the surgeon, requiring him to note down infection rates at regular intervals. He in turn recorded cases in his logbook.

There was one other lesson which Bligh learnt from Cook, and in particular from observing the captain being hacked to pieces: the importance of not offending the native islanders and of trying to understand their customs. It may be one reason why, when encountering islanders on Tahiti, Bligh invariably tried to get on the right side of the leaders by regularly giving them gifts. It was also Bligh's practice, when items were stolen by the islanders, to seek to punish his own crewmen for their negligence in permitting the item to be stolen, rather than trying to punish the thief. This may have helped keep the island chiefs on side, but it surely generated a sense of great injustice among the crew. Perhaps a more effective punishment was the one described by George Hamilton after the *Pandora* landed on Tahiti:

> A beautiful young creature, who lived at the Observatory with one of our young gentlemen, slipped out of bed from him in

> the night, and stole all his linen. She was punished for the theft, by shaving one of her eye-brows, and half of the hair off her head. She immediately ran into the woods, and used to come once or twice a day to the tent, to request looking at herself in the glass; but the grotesque figure she cut, with one side entirely bald, made her shriek out, and run into the woods to shun society.

Concerns about the hostility and unpredictability of islanders explain why, after the mutiny, Bligh kept out to sea in his tiny castaway vessel, unwilling to go ashore if there was any risk of coming up against islanders. He knew full well that in circumstances where he had no muskets with which to mount a defence – and no baubles and trinkets to act as bribes – he was extremely vulnerable.

But while Bligh may have learnt some things from his time with Cook, there are some things which quite escaped him. One was what might be termed man-management – how to get the best out of people. It was a skill that the down-to-earth and approachable Cook had in spades. It was a quality which Bligh could never even recognise. Two examples demonstrate this: in one, Cook noticed that the ordinary sailors were reluctant to eat their sauerkraut, so he banned them from eating it while instead he had it served to the officers. The result: the men clamoured to be allowed to eat sauerkraut. Contrast this with Bligh, who sought to punish his men when they declined to eat the tough old beef, generally assumed to be horse-meat, acquired in Tenerife. The result: the meat had to be thrown overboard.

And then there was the obsession with staying fit to stay healthy. To Bligh, this meant dancing – compulsory dancing. You cannot imagine Cook flogging his men for not dancing – he would simply have demonstrated that he was allowing them to have fun. But as will be seen later, evening after evening Bligh insisted that the musician should play a tune while the men were required to dance. Somehow it never occurred to Bligh that any activity which is seen as compulsory can never truly be regarded as fun…

Bligh had returned to England in October 1780 after a voyage lasting over four years. To begin with there was no job for him in the Royal Navy. He briefly went back into service in February 1781, serving as Master on HMS *Belle Poule*, a fifth-rate ship of the line armed with thirty-six guns. On the *Belle Poule* he saw active duty during the Battle of Dogger Bank on 5 August 1781 – part of the conflict during the Fourth Anglo-Dutch

War; both sides suffered heavy casualties. The *Belle Poule* came across the Dutch ship *Holland*, by then severely damaged in the fighting and in the process of sinking. She was still flying her colours but the *Belle Poule* was able to secure the colours before the *Holland* sank, presenting them to the English commander, Vice Admiral Hyde Parker, as a spoil of war.

Hyde Parker was replaced as commadore of the fleet by Bligh's former patron (then Captain) Keith Stewart, in charge of HMS *Berwick.* Stewart was eager to make Bligh up to acting lieutenant and he received his commission on 17 September 1781. His appointment on HMS *Berwick* lasted three months before he was transferred, on 1 January 1782, to HMS *Princess Amelia*, a posting which lasted just two months. He then played a game of musical chairs, basically following Stewart as he moved from ship to ship. Between March 1782 and January1783 he was serving as sixth lieutenant on board HMS *Cambridge*, under Stewart's command. During that time he took part in the lifting of the Siege of Gibraltar. This involved some thirty-three ships under the command of Lord Howe, up against a combined fleet of some forty-six ships belonging to the French and Spanish navies. Rumour has it that there was a young cabin boy on board HMS *Cambridge* at the time of Bligh's posting who was to feature prominently in later events – a certain Fletcher Christian. This seems improbable, given the fact that Fletcher Christian attended school until the age of 16, but even if he 'bunked off' for a six-month trip to sea to check if a naval life was for him, it is far from clear that the two ever met. The ship had a complement of over 850 men and Bligh's posting lasted only a few months.

While the action was a success in lifting the blockade of Gibraltar, it was quickly followed by a serious down-turn in naval fortunes – peace was declared. Bligh was put on half-pay, along with many of his contemporaries, following the end of the American War of Independence. Suddenly, with the Treaty of Paris, no one wanted a large navy and lieutenants were two-a-penny.

But Bligh was fortunate – shortly after his return from the Pacific he had married Elizabeth Betham. Their wedding, on 4 February 1781, took place at St Peter's Church, Onchan, on the Isle of Man. Elizabeth, known to her husband as Betsey, was to prove to be Bligh's most loyal friend – some might say his only friend. They would have had in common with each other the fact that each had a father working for HM Customs & Excise, but in practice there was a considerable difference in wealth, education and class. Elizabeth Betham was very definitely a good catch for Bligh. She was well-educated, was of superior intellect and was far more sophisticated, more polished and more sociable than her new husband. She was fluent in French and Italian, was a good conversationalist, and had a lot of useful connections. These included family links with the Campbell family, and in particular with John Campbell, a man with a most distinguished naval career, who became a Vice Admiral and who ended up as Governor of Newfoundland.

William's new wife was happy to use all of these connections and friendships to promote her husband's interests and she remained a loyal and devoted supporter of William throughout their married life. A year after the marriage she had her portrait painted by John Webber, the official artist on Cook's final voyage, and this may well have been intended as a belated wedding present.

The Betham family were in a good position to assist Bligh in his chosen career. Elizabeth's father was Richard Betham, an esteemed scholar and a graduate of Glasgow University. He came from a distinguished and influential Scottish family and was a friend of John Hume and Adam Smith. As already mentioned, he held the post of Customs Officer at Douglas on the Isle of Man, and his daughter had probably first met William Bligh some years earlier when the young midshipman was operating out of Douglas while patrolling the Irish Sea on the sloop *Ranger*.

It was Elizabeth's uncle, Duncan Campbell, who was able to come to Bligh's rescue when Royal Navy jobs dried up. Not only did he own a fleet of vessels used in the slave trade and serving his plantations on Jamaica, he also subsequently bought the *Bethia* (named after the Betham family) later to become HMS *Bounty*. Here was an influential man who 'knew people in high places' and along with Sir Joseph Banks was to be a highly influential figure in Bligh's career.

Campbell was not having an easy time – his contract to transport criminals to America had ended with the Treaty of Paris and a new dumping-ground had to be found for the criminal detritus of a society which thought nothing of transporting minor miscreants to far-flung places. Campbell was an acquaintance of Joseph Banks, and the two helped develop the idea of using the newly discovered New South Wales as a suitable alternative to the American Colonies.

In the event, it was 13 May 1787 before the First Fleet of eleven convict ships destined for Botany Bay left England, arriving a year later. Meanwhile: what to do with all those criminals? The answer, in Campbell's mind, was to incarcerate them in rotting hulks, moored in the Thames. Parliament was keen to encourage a penal system which cost very little to run, and in 1776 passed the Criminal Law Act – generally known as the Hulk Act. The first floating prison ship was opened later that same year and there was money to be made out of the cargoes of human vice and misery.

In that year, 1776, Duncan Campbell was appointed the first superintendent of prison hulks stationed at Woolwich – a position he held for twenty years. Conditions were truly appalling, and certainly the superintendent did not want to have anything to do with life on board – he had deputies to do that. Disease was rife, especially typhus – known as 'hulk fever' – and dysentery. Records suggest that one in four of the interred convicts died onboard, and government supervision was almost non-existent. One of Campbell's responsibilities was to see that the felons were put to good use. They proved to be a cheap workforce, needed for dredging works to correct a drift in the muddy sediment at the bottom of the River Thames.

The *Stamford Mercury* reported in its edition of 8 January 1778: 'Most of the convicts at Newgate, under sentence of ballast heaving, were early this morning taken from that gaol, and put on board a lighter at Blackfriars-bridge, in order to be conveyed to the *Justitia* hulk, off Woolwich.'

But Campbell still had his sugar and rum interests to look after, based on his plantations at Saltspring in Jamaica. He had inherited the plantation from his brother-in-law and quickly diversified into hiring out slave labour to adjoining plantations, as well as rearing cattle. By the turn of the century he was recorded as owning 289 slaves.

The plantations needed reprovisioning from England and harvests needed to be transported back to London – and Campbell was in need of a reliable captain. And so it was that shortly after Bligh was laid off by the navy, Duncan Campbell offered him command of *Lynx*, a new ship he had purchased. On her, Bligh made several trips to the West Indies, and remained in the service of his wife's uncle on the *Cambrian* and the *Britannia* until 1787. There is no record that Bligh was involved in the actual transport of slaves from Africa to the Caribbean. Instead, he was simply reprovisioning and taking part in general trading in rum, sugar and molasses; the Lloyds Register of Shipping records at least ten such voyages. Through the prism of history we have to say that 'Duncan money was dirty money', and Duncan Campbell's influence was closely linked to the trade in human misery, whether in the form of slavery or the transport of felons. What the backing and support of

Campbell meant to Bligh is that by the time Banks was proposing the idea of introducing the breadfruit to the West Indies, there was no one around with more experience of the sailing conditions both in the Pacific and the Caribbean than a certain Lieutenant William Bligh. At that stage Banks had not even met Bligh, and arguably this was to Bligh's advantage. Two other candidates for the job of leading the breadfruit expedition were James Trevenen and George Vancouver, neither of whom were at all easy to get on with. By default, the unknown Bligh seemed to be someone Banks could rely on during the voyage of discovery, simply because he had a proven track record in the areas of the world where the voyage was to take place.

It was on *Britannia* that Bligh got to know Fletcher Christian, by then in his teens. Fletcher Christian was the seventh of ten children born to a well-to-do family which had fallen on hard times. Fletcher's father had died before the boy's fourth birthday and his mother had been forced to move to the Isle of Man to escape her creditors. The shortage of money meant that there was little choice but to send Fletcher to sea.

The teenager subsequently accompanied Bligh on at least two of his Caribbean voyages, first as an Ordinary Seaman and then as Second Mate. He appears to have got the job as a result of Betham family influence, since the Betham family had an indirect link with the Christian family. This came about after Christian's cousin had married into the Taubman family. The Taubman's, living at Castletown on the Isle of Man, were certainly close friends of the Betham's and were an important Isle of Man family, with Major John Taubman going on to hold the role of Speaker of the House of Keys.

The Isle of Man connection was strengthened by the fact that up until 1784 the Bligh family were living in Douglas and when their first child (Mary) was born she was christened at St Matthew's Church. Only then did the family move away to London, living in a house in Reardon Street, Wapping. The house has long-since been demolished, but was certainly convenient for Bligh because it was immediately alongside the perimeter wall of London's Western Dock. While there, Bligh was apparently sent a letter from Captain John Taubman suggesting that Bligh consider Christian Fletcher as a young crew member, stressing that the lad was eager to learn seamanship.

Bligh took the youngster under his wing and encouraged his interest in navigation. The two appear to have become friends and it is known that on at least one occasion Christian visited the Bligh home and met the family.

Others have hinted that Bligh's friendship with the young boy was not altogether innocent, with suggestions of a homosexual relationship which in some way contributed to their subsequent falling out. This has to be pure conjecture and it may simply be that Bligh enjoyed the kudos of seeing his young protégé follow in his own footsteps.

Father figure? No, for Bligh was only ten years his senior, but one rather suspects that William Bligh liked being followed around by a lad who looked up to him with starry eyes and who believed in him implicitly. It was only when Christian was older, and realised that his hero had feet of clay – and an extremely sharp and acerbic tongue – that the two fell out.

Chapter 3

Breadfruit

Detail from a portrait of Sir Joseph Banks, President of the Royal Society, in 1812.

William Bligh was not to know it, but his life was about to enter a stage when it would be totally dominated by *Artocarpus altilis*, better known as the breadfruit tree. It is a member of the same family of trees as the mulberry and jackfruit. The breadfruit had first been described a century earlier by William Dampier, an explorer with a keen interest in botany (and piracy!) after he encountered the plant on the island of Guam. Writing in his book *A New Voyage Round the World* about his first circumnavigation in 1688, Dampier introduced the word 'breadfruit' to the English language. He described it as follows:

> The breadfruit (as we call it) grows on a large tree, as big and high as our largest apple-trees. It hath a spreading head of branches and dark leaves. The fruit grows on the boughs like apples; it is as big as a penny loaf when wheat is at five shillings a bushel; it is of round shape and hath a thick tough rind.

He went on to say that the taste was sweet and pleasant when the fruit was ripe, i.e. when it was yellow and soft. He had noticed that the inhabitants of Guam used the fruit for bread, describing the method of preparing it as follows:

> They gather it, when full-grown, when it is green and hard; they bake it in an oven, which scorches the rind and makes it black; but they scrape off the outside black crust, and there remains a tender thin crust; and the inside is soft, tender and white like the crumb of a penny-loaf…. It must be eaten new; for, if it is kept above twenty-four hours, it grows harsh and choaky, but it is very pleasant before it is too stale.

'Very pleasant' was perhaps over-stating things. It has to be remembered that Dampier reached Guam after spending six weeks in the featureless, empty Pacific, having left Cape Corrientes in Mexico at the end of March 1686. That was six weeks with very limited rations, and a crew on the point of mutiny as a result of near starvation. Dampier and his men had covered over 6,000 miles on half-rations and his descriptions of Guam are understandably dominated by food. Dampier didn't just give 'breadfruit' to the English language – he was the first to describe the culinary virtues of plantains, describe bananas, and give us 'chopsticks', 'barbecues', 'avocados' and 'cashews'.

A similarly positive description of the breadfruit appeared in the journal of George Anson after he completed a circumnavigation of the globe in 1744. According to Anson, it was universally preferred by the ship's company to the (admittedly stale) bread supplies carried on board.

A slightly less enthusiastic description of the breadfruit plant appears in the journals of Captain Cook. To him, the flavour was insipid with a slight sweetness resembling 'that of the crumb of wheaten bread mixed with Jerusalem artichoke'. A more positive view was expressed by Joseph Banks, who accompanied Cook on his first Pacific voyage. He noted that Tahitians regarded the breadfruit as a staple part of their diet:

> Scarcely can it be said that they earn their bread with the sweat of their brow when their chiefest sustenance … is procured with no more trouble than of climbing a tree and pulling it down. Not that the trees grow here spontaneously but if a man should in the course of his life time plant ten such trees, which, if well done, might take the labour of an hour or thereabouts he would as completely fulfill his duty to his own as well as future generations.

To both Cook and Banks the breadfruit had a lot going for it: it was a heavy cropper, with a single tree able to produce up to 200 fruits every year; the trees were in fruit for eight months out of twelve; it was resistant to wind; it was easy to propagate and required little or no work to tend it. And those fruit were considered highly nutritious, with starch as its principal nutrient. It could be roasted, boiled, baked or fried, and it could be added to other ingredients such as banana and yam to make dishes which were known to be popular in Tahiti and other parts of the Pacific. Small wonder that botanists began to think that this particular superfood might have its uses in other parts of the globe.

The Tahitian breadfruit did not need to be grown from seed and could be propagated easily from root cuttings. In the words of Cook:

> I have inquired very carefully into their manner of cultivating the breadfruit tree at Otaheite; but was always answered that they never planted it. This indeed must be evident to everyone who will examine the places where the young trees come up. It will be always observed that they spring from the roots of the old ones which run along near the surface of the ground.

Cook had returned from his first Pacific voyage on board *Resolution* in 1771. And if he returned with his reputation enhanced, it was nothing compared with the elevation in fame and status of Joseph Banks. Over a few years he emerged as the unofficial chief scientific adviser to the government, and was appointed President of the Royal Society, a position which he held for forty-one years. His great ambition was to develop a national collection of plants from the entire world, centred on the Royal Gardens at Kew. These had been extended on the instructions of Augusta, Dowager Princess of Wales, following the death of her husband Frederick, the Prince of Wales, in 1751. Ten years later the architect William Chambers, co-founder of the Royal Academy, designed the Great Pagoda which still stands in the garden, and in 1781 Augusta's son, by then George III, acquired additional land which included a building then called the Dutch House, but now known as Kew Palace. Seedlings started to be sent to Kew from many distant parts and indeed there are still four trees in the garden which can 'trace their roots' back to 1762 when the royal gardens really got under way. And although he was not given a formal appointment to take charge of the gardens, Banks emerged as the most fervent supporter and spokesperson for what he saw as a collection of worldwide importance.

Banks was a product of an Age which saw Britain's tentacles spread across the globe and he shared these global ambitions. He saw the bigger picture – not for him a simple collection of plants, all classified within the new Linnaen system. He wanted to use those plants to extend Britain's power and influence and he devoted his energies to three main but interconnected areas – developing the cotton industry, establishing a self-sufficient penal colony in Australia, and finding ways of feeding the increasing slave population needed to farm the plantations in the Caribbean colonies.

Ever since he had visited Australia with Cook, naming Botany Bay because of its verdant flora, Banks had campaigned to use the newly charted land as a place to house miscreants. As already mentioned, these had been deported to the American colonies in the past, but the War of American Independence cut off that possibility. Originally, the Caribbean islands had been something of a dumping ground for petty criminals who would be transported in appalling conditions, forced to sign a ten-year bond which made them indentured servants (little better than slaves) – forbidden to marry, restricted in their movements, and forced to work long hours in harsh conditions. Then came the massive increase in the numbers of slaves captured across Africa and forcibly repatriated to the West Indies, especially to Jamaica and Barbados. The numbers are staggering – 450,000 slaves in 1770 had more than doubled by 1800. The tobacco-growing colonies such as Virginia and Maryland may have received the greatest number of slaves, but now that America was independent British merchants concentrated on the demand for slave labour in the Caribbean. And it was a double whammy – there were more and more mouths to feed, just at a time that the trade in foodstuffs between the American colonies and the Caribbean islands had come to an abrupt halt.

To compound matters, Banks had ambitions to develop the cotton-growing industry in the Caribbean. In Britain, as the mill towns across the Pennines expanded and Manchester mushroomed into 'Cottonopolis', there was an insatiable demand for raw cotton. Banks sought ways to find new strains of cotton plants which could be grown in the Caribbean, but picking and growing cotton was a labour-intensive business and Banks' plans would involve still more slaves, still more mouths to feed.

In practice, all these strands came together in 1787. In April that year, Banks dispatched a young Pole called Anton Hove to Gujerat in India, ostensibly to collect plants for Kew, but unofficially to collect cotton seeds. The First Fleet set sail for New South Wales the following month. It was a fleet made up of eleven ships, including six transport ships filled with convicts, making a complement of 1,400 people in total. Also, at the end of that year, Banks sent his protégé William Bligh on a mission to collect breadfruit plants from Tahiti and to transport them to the Caribbean. Initially it had been intended that the breadfruit venture would be combined with the New South Wales experiment, but Banks soon realised that the first colonists simply would not have the resources to equip, man and provision such an experimental voyage. Never before had an attempt been made to transplant flora across the world on such a large scale. This was not a few plantsmen collecting seeds and young plants and bringing them back to places such as Kew Gardens – this was a large-scale operation requiring a specially converted ship. So the decision was made to separate out Banks's pet projects.

Nowadays, Banks comes in for criticism because of his connection with the slave trade. In 2022 English Heritage announced that the reputation of Banks was being 'reassessed' because of his links to slavery. Following the Black Lives Matter protests, the organisation updated its online notes about the blue plaque memorial which records his birth at Soho Square in London. These notes now inform people that Banks was 'an enabler of slavery'. It added that Banks' transplantation of specimens across the globe had 'the ultimate aim of increasing the power and prosperity of the British Empire', adding that 'Banks was behind the global transplantation of many other botanic and live specimens across the globe, all with the ultimate aim of increasing the power and prosperity of the British Empire'. In the words of English Heritage, his 'attitude to other races was typical of Europeans of his era'.

But, if we are seeing Banks in context of what was or was not acceptable in the era in which he lived, it is worth bearing in mind that slavery was not *per se* illegal – nor was it to become so in Britain until 1833. The actual trade in slaves was abolished in Britain in 1807. And it was not just a case of legality – for many, it was not even seen as morally indefensible. The Church of England did not just turn a blind eye to slavery, it invested in it. It was the Society of Friends (the Quakers) who first emerged as the lone voice condemning slavery in all its forms. Quakers had no voice in Parliament because they were prohibited from standing as MPs, and their petitions went unheard until they managed to persuade a number of Anglican Ministers to join their campaign. The Society for Effecting the Abolition of the Slave Trade was formed as late as 22 May 1787 – and nine of the twelve founding members were Quakers.

Men such as Thomas Clarkson then spent years travelling the country, persuading people to sign petitions against slavery. Time and time again, Parliament, made up of landowners, many with strong financial interests in the Caribbean, voted against abolition. The point to make is that Banks was simply endorsing something which in the period in which he lived was considered acceptable. For economic reasons he was convinced that slavery would soon come to an end, but while it existed he was determined to make sure that there was enough food to keep the slaves alive. Yes, he enabled slavery, but that should not diminish his other achievements. Here was a man of considerable vision – his plans for introducing the Merino sheep to Australia from Spain ultimately led to the breed becoming the dominant strain across that continent. That was after Banks had managed to import two Merino rams and four ewes into Britain in 1787. Other purchases in 1792 led to the founding of the royal flock at Kew, and the Merino breed soon found its way out to Botany Bay and from there spread across Australia.

Another Banksian plan involved the introduction of the tea plant from China into British-controlled India. Banks was aware that importing tea from China was seriously depleting British reserves of silver – Chinese merchants wanted payment in cash. How much better it would be if the crop could be supplied from plants grown in India. In that sense, Banks and his ideas for transplanting breadfruit from one side of the world to another has to be seen as just one small part of his idea for Britain establishing itself at the centre of world affairs. It marked the birth of globalisation. That has, of course, caused as many problems as it has solved, and Banks was not to know the consequences of some of his extraordinary ideas. We can look back and condemn him for his imperialistic vision – but if so, we also have to accept that most of those ideas were undoubtedly well-intentioned.

He was not the first to link the transporting of breadfruit with the alleviation of food shortages on the plantations in the Caribbean. Hinton East, plantation owner and slave owner on Jamaica, had already raised the issue. Here was a man who was a member of the House of Assembly of Jamaica representing Kingston, He was also Judge Advocate General and Receiver General of Jamaica. More importantly, as a hobby he had created a private botanic garden at his home at Gordon Town on Jamaica. He stocked this garden with a number of exotic plants, including ones grown from seed sent out by Banks from the royal gardens at Kew. He expressed this view:

> The acquisition of the best type of breadfruit would be of infinite importance to the West India islands in affording a wholesome and pleasant food to our Negroes which would have great advantage over the Plantain Tree from whence our slaves derive a great part of their subsistence.

In his opinion, the tree could be raised 'with infinitely less labour and not be subject to be destroyed by every smart gale of wind'.

In April 1772 a plantation owner called Valentine Morris, later to become Governor of St Vincent, pressed Banks to draw up a plan to introduce the breadfruit plant. Three years later John Ellis, who was a friend of Banks and fellow-member of the Royal Society, published a pamphlet under the direction of the Society of West Merchants, recommending the introduction of both the breadfruit and the mangosteen. This was followed up in 1776 by the Society of Arts. They offered a prize to anyone successfully introducing the breadfruit plant and this was immediately matched by a similar offer from the Society of West Merchants 'but on a more ample manner than is provided by the Society of Arts and Manufacturers'.

The passing years had seen a number of proposals for sending ships to the Pacific to take plants to the West Indies via Cape Horn but nothing came of them. Any plans were mothballed when the American War of Independence broke out. More alarming for the Caribbean islanders, when American independence was secured, the British Government responded with the Navigation Acts. These had the effect of making illegal all trade between the islanders and the newly formed United States. It meant molasses could not be exported to America – and foodstuffs could not be imported.

It transpired that the French were the first to try and import breadfruit plants, following their success in introducing spices such as nutmeg and cloves to the island of Mauritius, then known as the Île de France. The involvement of the French was a spur to British action.

By January 1787 Banks had persuaded the government of William Pitt that the transplanting scheme was viable, and economically sound. Banks also used his influence with George III to ensure that the project met with royal approval. On 30 March 1787 Banks circulated a letter to Lord Hawkesbury, President of the Board of Trade and also to Lord Mulgrave – another member of the Board of Trade – and to Lord Sydney, Secretary of Home Affairs. The letter not only stressed that the transplanting should be a separate venture from the plan to move convicts to New South Wales but set out in considerable detail how, when and why the plant expedition should take place. The plan envisaged the purchase of a brig of around 200 tons. It would need to be converted into a floating plant nursery. It would need to have a crew of around thirty men. It would need to be provisioned and ready to sail by July at the latest, in order to avoid the worst of the storms in the area of Cape Horn.

Lord Sydney was clearly convinced by the argument, writing to the Lords Commissioners of the Admiralty on 15 May 1787:

> The Merchants and Planters interested in His Majesty's West India Possessions have represented that the introduction of the Breadfruit tree into the islands in those seas to constitute an article of food would be very essential benefit to the inhabitants and have humbly solicited that measures may be taken for procuring some trees of that description from the place of their present growth, to be transplanted to the said islands.

From that point on, matters moved swiftly. Banks was closely involved in the decision as to which ship should be acquired – after all, the navy did not have any particular expertise in growing, transplanting and looking after tender seedlings. Banks nominated David Nelson as his preferred choice of gardener to accompany the voyage. By way of background, Nelson had come to the attention of Banks while he was working as a gardener at Kew Royal Gardens. Banks had proposed him as on-board botanist on Cook's third and final voyage. Technically, he had gone as servant to William Bayly, the official astronomer, but in practice he had been tasked by Banks to locate and bring back to Kew as many different types of plant as he could find. When he returned, he worked for a further seven years at Kew before being offered the chance to take part in the great breadfruit experiment.

There remains the question: why Tahiti? After all, the breadfruit was already available rather closer to home – in Malaya, in the Philippines, in Indonesia. The choice of Tahiti may simply have arisen because originally the project was twinned with the plans to establish the settlement at Botany Bay – or more likely, it was part of an unofficial plan to strengthen ties between Britain and the Polynesian islands simply in order to thwart the French. France already had island links in the Indian Ocean – the Seychelles, Réunion and Mauritius – and were clearly intent on developing trade links further East. Nicolas Baudin, Louis Antoine de Bougainville, Jean-François de Surville and the Comte de Lapérouse would all lead expeditions to Polynesia.

Significantly, Nelson's earlier voyage under Captain Cook was shared with William Bligh, and Nelson was no doubt able to confirm to Banks that Bligh was 'a Cook man' – in other words, like Captain Cook, he was a fastidious and cautious man who could be trusted to carry out the undertaking with care and dedication. However, at that stage Bligh had not been appointed, and so it was that on a May morning in 1787, Banks turned up at Wapping docks, together with Nelson but minus Bligh, to consider the six ships which had been shortlisted.

Chapter 4

From *Bethia* to *Bounty*

Illustration of a ship-building operation – 1726.

The ship which was to become *Bounty* was born half a world away from where she was to end her days. Back in 1784, the Kingston upon Hull shipyard of Blaydes had received an order to build a snub-nosed vessel, 90ft 10in long, and a fraction over 24ft wide, and apparently destined for the local coastal trade – taking coal from the North-East down to the capital. None of the shipwrights cutting, shaping, pegging and caulking the timbers assembled at Number Two Drydocks on the banks of the River Humber could ever have imagined that this humble merchant ship was destined to become one of the most notorious Royal Navy ships in all history.

The yard was run by Benjamin Blayde, grandson of the founder who had started the yard in 1740. The yard had built up a good reputation constructing ships for the Royal Navy, but contracts with the navy ebbed and flowed with the risk or war. Ten years earlier it was all very different as the navy scrabbled to build frigates to ward off Spanish claims to the Falkland Islands. In 1774 the yard launched both HMS *Diamond* and HMS *Boreas*, but the contracts then dried up and Blaydes occupied their time constructing smaller, cheaper, ships. There had always been a demand for colliers, designed to fill the needs of the voracious city of London, where there was an ever-increasing demand for quantities of coal to heat the households and run the businesses of the city.

So it was that the *Bethia* was built. She had three masts, was full-rigged, and at 215 tons was relatively small for the job in hand. She was fitted with a flush deck – in other words, there was no superstructure housing cabins or steering platform. This was an early attempt at a radical design based upon scientific analysis – known as the 'cod mouth, mackerel tail' design. Boatbuilders had reckoned that if fish generally had a rounded front – the mouth – and an attenuated (i.e. narrowing) tail, then this was a design feature which ships should emulate. It reflected an observation on how ice cubes behaved in flowing water, that is to say, becoming rounded off at the front as the ice melts and narrowing at the rear. It was a design which became popular in the nineteenth century, even though it proved to be hopelessly inappropriate. As one wag has said, if you want to sail a 'cod mouth and mackerel tail' ship, you had best sail backwards!

Bethia had a flat bottom, and at a later date this was considered important for a vessel intended to sail in uncharted waters. A deep keel could be a risk if the ship had run aground on a hidden Pacific reef, causing the vessel to topple over. This flat bottom meant that on the one occasion when she later ran aground off Tahiti, she was quickly floated off again without damage or delay. As Bligh was to say on that occasion: 'to our great surprise we found that the ship was aground forwards. She had run on so easy, that we had not perceived it at the time.' In Bligh's words she was 'an excellent sea boat', and one which was 'roomy in accommodation and stowage'.

Construction of *Bethia* was completed in December 1784, and the figurehead was not, most unusually, a busty blonde displaying her ample charms, but a rather chaste figure of a woman in a full riding habit, wearing a cap. For a couple of years *Bethia* went to and fro, up and down the coast, until it became known that the Royal Navy were looking to acquire a specialist vessel for a most unusual task. At that point in time *Bethia* may well have been in the ownership of Duncan Campbell. As has been shown, his niece Elizabeth was by then married to William Bligh, and if so, it may well be the case that Uncle Duncan put forward William's name as possible captain of the ship. Duncan Campbell was clearly well connected and known to senior figures in the Admiralty and, most significantly, was acquainted with Joseph Banks. That connection meant that his firm were involved in all three of the first fleets taking convicts to Australia. As ever, it was not just a case of what you knew, but who you knew…

Bethia was one of six ships being considered by the Admiralty. The authorities had already decided that none of the 600 ships then belonging to the navy could be spared – or, if they could, were not suitable for being converted into a floating greenhouse. In May 1767 the Admiralty was approached by Lord Sydney, one of the Principal Secretaries of State, and on 9 May the navy approved the purchase of a suitable vessel not exceeding 250 tons. It seems clear that the navy was trying to do things as cheaply as possible – the whole project was not their idea, it was being forced on them by the King, aided and abetted by Joseph Banks. For that reason, the decision was made to use as small a vessel as possible. By entirely omitting any contingent of marines the Admiralty could get away with a vessel of 250 tons, but it was a decision which led directly to the success of the subsequent mutiny. It meant that just a small group of mutineers were able to take over the ship without significant opposition – and the mutiny could never have occurred if there had been two vessels, or if there had been even a handful of marines on board.

It is worth contrasting this with Cook's first voyage (with twelve marines on board the *Endeavour*); his second voyage (also a dozen marines, shared between HMS *Resolution* and HMS *Adventure*); and Cook's third voyage which had twenty marines, including an army lieutenant, on board HMS *Resolution* and HMS *Discovery*. Knowing of the unpredictable nature of the behaviour of the islanders, as evidenced by the attack resulting in the death of Cook, it really is remarkable that the decision was made not to have any troops whatsoever. It was a voyage to be undertaken on the cheap, meaning that the navy paid Bligh a meagre salary of £50 as a lieutenant, compared with a salary perhaps ten times as much if he had been awarded the status of post captain.

The other five ships being considered were the *Lynx* – ineligible at 300 tons but on offer at the price of £2,200; the *Shepherdess* at 270 tons; the

William Pitt lying at King Edward Stairs of 240 tons, available at £1,200; a new ship then being built at Newcastle intended to be 240 or 250 tons at a cost of £9 10s 0d per ton – and a latecomer called *Harriott*, a very much smaller ship of 140 tons newly built in Liverpool and destined to spend her life as a slaving ship. *Bethia* was being offered by owners Messrs Wellbank, Sharpe and Brown to the navy for £2,600, perhaps reflecting that she was only two-and-a-half years old. One suspects the owner recognised that the cod-mouth and mackerel-tail design meant the vessel was less capable of sailing to windward, and had decided that selling the vessel to the navy was the best way of cutting his losses. She wasn't particularly fast – nor was she particularly manoeuvrable. But those considerations were not important: what mattered was her ability to be converted into a floating greenhouse. *Bethia* was the smallest of the ships under serious consideration. Indeed, she was far smaller than earlier ships used in Pacific voyages. For instance, Cook's *Endeavour* displaced 368 tons, and *Resolution* 462 tons, against the *Bethia's* 215 tons. Nevertheless, the ship was inspected by Banks and Nelson and found to be suitable. If Bligh had been involved at that early stage surely he would have pressed for a larger vessel. *Bethia* barely had room for the men needed to sail her on such a lengthy voyage – let alone any room at all for armed marines to guard against insurrection or offer defence against hostile islanders.

The Navy Board confirmed the purchase at the price of £1,950 – £650 less than the asking price – on 26 May 1787 and the ship was taken from Wapping Old Stairs to Deptford to be fitted out for the voyage. At the request of Banks she was renamed and, as *HM Armed Vessel Bounty*, she was registered on the Royal Navy Ships List on 8 June 1787. On the recommendation of Banks, and using a prize put up by the Royal Society of Arts, Lieutenant Bligh was appointed as captain of the *Bounty* on 16 August, and only then became involved in supervising the way she was to be fitted out for her voyage. But if Bligh had hopes that the command would bring with it an elevation to the rank of commander he would be disappointed: *Bounty* was classed as a cutter, the smallest of naval warships, and cutters were placed in charge of a lieutenant, not a post captain. Furthermore, he would be the only non-commissioned officer on board.

The alterations were considerable; what would previously have been the captain's cabin was extended forward to cover roughly a third of the length of the ship. This was to be the main storage area for plants. An elaborate 'honeycomb' of timber squares, designed to hold pots, covered the floor, which had been lined with lead so that surplus water could be drained off and collected for subsequent use. A second deck was fitted within the cabin, to house more plants and a coal-fired heater was fitted so that the air in the cabin was kept warm when the ship encountered cold weather. It was known that the breadfruit tree was susceptible to frost damage, but the arrangement meant that some 620 plants could be tended in the main cabin on its long voyage. Other plants could be fitted on modified shelves attached by brackets to the inside of the ship's frame, while air ducts were installed so as to ensure a proper circulation of fresh air.

The decision was made to fix a copper sheath around the hull of the ship, as a deterrent to the wood-boring *teredos navalis*, better known as the naval shipworm. This use of copper sheathing was a fairly recent development – it had been tried before but it was found that the copper disintegrated in saltwater as a result of electrolysis, caused when iron used in the fixing nails reacted with the copper. Ferrous and non-ferrous metals don't mix. The lesson was duly learnt for the *Bounty*: copper and brass nails were used on all fittings below the waterline, instead of iron ones.

Arrangements were made to equip the ship with four short-carriage cannons, each capable of firing 4-pound cannon balls. Each cannon would have been around 6ft long, mounted on a wooden carriage and would have weighed some one thousand pounds. Four men would have been needed to fire it. Ten half-pounder swivel guns were fitted – enough to put the fear of hell into any war canoes approaching with hostile intent! Each swivel gun needed two men to operate it but they were highly effective anti-personnel weapons, easy to elevate and highly portable.

Together, all these improvements and alterations to the ship cost the Navy Board some £4,456 – more than double the amount spent on the acquisition cost. The changes also took time – time which Bligh knew to be desperately important.

It is clear from a letter which Lord Sydney wrote to Banks on 15 August 1787 that Banks was very much central to the scheme, writing:

> The Admiralty have, I understand, purchased a vessel for the purpose of conveying the Bread Fruit Tree and other useful productions from the South Sea Islands to His Majesty's West India possessions. She is to be commissioned in the course of a few days, to be called The Bounty and to be commanded by Lieutenant Bligh. As I am totally unacquainted with the nature

of the instructions which are proper to be given to Nelson and Brown, the two gardeners who are to collect the trees and plants and to be entrusted with their care and management during their continuance on board the ship, I shall think myself particularly obliged to you if you will prepare such instructions, as you may judge requisite for their guidance.

The letter outlined what was to happen to any plants collected by Bligh:

> Upon Lieut Bligh's return from the Society Islands [of which Tahiti forms part] he is to call at St Helena at which place may be left a small number of trees and plants; from thence he will be directed to proceed to St Vincents where the half of the cargo is to be deposited and the remainder is to be left at Jamaica.

Lord Sydney clearly had great confidence in Nelson, adding:

> The ship is to be fitted at Deptford and perhaps it may not be amiss that Mr Nelson shall superintend the equipment and suggest any alterations and improvements on the proposed plan which may occur to him for the greater security of the trees and plants which he is to take on board.

Bligh wasted little time in checking out his new vessel. As he was to write:

> I was appointed to command her [Bounty] on 16 August 1787 … In the cockpit were the cabins of the surgeon, gunner, botanist, and clerk, with a steward-room and storerooms. The between decks was divided in the following manner: the great cabin was appropriated for the preservation of the plants and extended as far forward as the after hatchway … I had a small cabin on one side to sleep in, adjoining to the great cabin, and a place near the middle of the ship to eat in. The bulk-head of this apartment was at the after-part of the main hatchway, and on each side of it were the berths of the mates and midshipmen; between these berths the arm-chest was placed. The cabin of the master, in which was always kept the key of the arms, was

> opposite to mine. This particular description of the interior parts of the ship is rendered necessary by the event of the expedition.
>
> The ship was masted according to the proportion of the navy; but on my application the masts were shortened, as I thought them too much for her, considering the nature of the voyage.

Writing about events the following month:

> On 3 September the ship came out of dock; but the carpenters and joiners remained on board much longer, as they had a great deal of work to finish.
>
> The next material alteration made in the fitting out was lessening the quantity of iron and other ballast. I gave directions that only nineteen tons of iron should be taken on board instead of the customary proportion which was forty-five tons. The stores and provisions I judged would be fully sufficient to answer the purpose of the remainder; for I am of opinion that many of the misfortunes which attend ships in heavy storms of wind are occasioned by too much dead weight in their bottoms.

It is interesting to see the description of the small boats taken on board *Bounty* – a 16ft long 'jolly boat', a 23ft launch and a 20ft clinker-built cutter. The larger launch was to figure subsequently in Bligh's marathon journey in the aftermath of the mutiny. The jolly boat had initially been selected by Fletcher Christian as the boat to be used for the castaways, but others interceded on behalf of Bligh, pointing out that not only was the boat too small for the job – it was only designed for ten men – but was also unseaworthy due to the poor state of the timbers. For Bligh, it was a fortuitous change of plan – the longer launch was newly built, probably by John Burr at a cost of £43. It was designed to hold thirteen men – in practice nineteen men were forced aboard after the mutiny. The launch had been intended for heavy work such as moving the anchors, transferring barrels of water and so on, and hence had a removable windlass and two davits. Designed to take six oars she also had the facility to have one if not two masts. In his subsequent journal Bligh refers to 'each mast' (i.e. more than one) when he describes the events of 10 May 1789: 'In the afternoon I fitted a pair of shrouds for each mast and contrived a canvass weather cloth round the boat and raised the quarters about nine inches by nailing on the seats of the stern sheets, which proved a great benefit for us.'

Stowing these boats on board *Bounty* cannot have been easy – lack of deck space and a lack of headroom under the sails meant that they may well have had to be stowed one inside the other – not a particularly stable arrangement.

Between 5 October and 4 November, the newly modified ship was taken to Spithead for final crew to be taken onboard, along with stores intended to be sufficient for a voyage of eighteen months. By the end of November, the ship was anchored at St Helens on the Isle of Wight, waiting for final orders and for suitable winds.

It must have been an infuriating delay for Bligh, anxious to get under way before winter. His anxiety may well have been exacerbated by the knowledge that his wife, already a mother of three daughters, was expecting again; she gave birth to twin girls, Frances and Jane, just five months after the ship set sail.

Bligh listed the ship's complement as being:

1. Lieut & Commander

2. Masters Mates

1. Gunners Mate
1. Master

2. Midshipmen

1. Carpenters Mate
1. Boatswain

1. Clerk

1. Sailmaker
1. Gunner

2. Qr. Masters

1. Armourer
1. Carpenter

1. Qr.Masr.Mate

1. Carpenters Crew
1. Surgeon

1. Boatswains Mate
1. Corporal
24 Able Seamen
Total. 45 One of which is a Widow's Man.

There was likewise a Botanist & his Assistant.

(A 'widow's man' was a fictitious seaman kept on the books of Royal Navy ships during the eighteenth and early nineteenth centuries in order to make payment to the families of any crew members who died. It was intended to prevent widows becoming destitute following the death of their seafaring husband, and helped make the Royal Navy a more attractive proposition for sailors, as opposed to working in the merchant navy).

The botanist was David Nelson and his assistant was William Brown. Brown had been born in Leicester, and had seen service as a midshipman and had been acting lieutenant on HMS *Resolution* in the early 1780s. At some stage he changed his career and had been working as a gardener at Kew. Doubtless his naval background would have been one reason why he was chosen for the expedition. He was later described by Bligh as being 'aged 27 years, five feet eight inches high, fair complexion, dark brown hair, strong made; a remarkable scar on one of his cheeks, which contracts the eye-lid, and runs down to his throat, occasioned by the King's Evil; is tatowed [tattooed]'. The King's Evil was otherwise known as scrofula – nowadays, mycobacterial cervical lymphadenitis – a form of tuberculosis affecting the lymph glands in the neck. For some centuries it had been thought that it could be cured by the monarch touching the victim, and many wealthier sufferers carried a gold touch-piece around their necks – in other words, a coin which had been pierced after it had been touched by the king, and then suspended on a ribbon.

The sailing Master was John Fryer. He was appointed by the Navy Board to serve on *Bounty* on 20 August 1787, having served as Master in the Royal Navy since 1781 when he was on HMS *Camel*. He had risen to Master of the Third Rate – a highly competent individual who, to begin with, met with Bligh's approbation: 'The master is a very good man, and gives me every satisfaction.'

Many of the crew members were chosen personally by Bligh. William Peckover, the gunner, and Joseph Coleman, the armourer, had been with Bligh when he was sailing master on HMS *Resolution* on Cook's final voyage. Christian, as we have seen, was well-known to Bligh and was well liked by him. There is a story, uncorroborated, that Bligh was accompanied by Christian on one of his trips to check out *Bounty* while she was being fitted out, and stopped for a pint at a tavern known as The Town of Ramsgate in Wapping. In the past, Bligh had mentored Christian and helped him become a highly-skilled navigator, and at a later date the sailmaker Lawrence Lebogue was to declare in his affidavit that:

> I knew Captain Bligh was a very great friend to Christian the Mutineer; he was always permitted to use the Captain's cabin, where I have seen the Captain teaching him navigation and drawing. He was permitted to use the Captain's liquor when he wanted it, and I have many times gone down at night to get him grog out of the Captain's case.

As will be seen, early on in the voyage, Bligh promoted Christian to the rank of acting lieutenant in March 1788, effectively making him second-in-command.

Also on board, as a result of pressure from Bligh's father-in-law, was the 15-year-old Peter Heywood. A Manxman and a distant relation of Christian, Heywood came from a naval family, with two uncles serving as admiral. He later went on to have an extremely distinguished naval career. Initially he enjoyed support from Bligh, but after the mutiny Bligh was convinced that Heywood had sided with Christian and had been conspiring against him. It certainly appears that Bligh wanted to surround himself with yes-men, and the young Heywood may have proved to be too independently minded.

He must not be confused with Thomas Hayward – an arrogant and lazy young man with a propensity for sleeping on duty, who was serving as midshipman. Hayward and John Hallett had both been taken on board at the request of Bligh's wife – John Hallett's sister was her closest friend. The pair of Hayward and Hallett were to prove to be unpopular with almost everyone on board – they were snobbish, they were indolent and when the mutiny took place Christian and others made it quite clear: they didn't want either of them to stay with them on *Bounty*.

The ship's complement was, to say the least, 'top heavy' with people who were not actually sailing the ship – there were just twenty-four able seamen. Given that Bligh subsequently introduced a system of three eight-hour watches (something he had borrowed from Captain Cook on his voyages) it meant that on any given watch there would be just eight sailors on duty. But as Bligh later wrote: 'I kept my few Men constantly at three Watches, even in the Worst of Weather, and I found them additionally alert on a call when their immediate Service was required.'

At the start of the voyage Bligh was 33; John Fryer, sailing master, was a year or two older, and the majority of those on board were under 30. Some of them were mere boys – Thomas Ellison (later, hanged), Peter Heywood (found guilty but pardoned) and John Hallett were all still 15 when they were mustered on board *Bounty*. Robert Tinkler was 17 and there were a handful of 21-year-olds on board, making it a remarkably juvenile and ill-experienced crew. It was perhaps inevitable that tensions would occur later in the voyage because of the lack of sufficient personnel, a situation exacerbated by the extremely limited amount of space on board. Think of it: a ship just over 90ft long – that's slightly less than the length of three London buses. And in it, forty-four men were to be cooped up for days, weeks and months on end, alongside hundreds and hundreds of breadfruit plants. It was not an auspicious start….

Chapter 5

The Voyage to Tahiti

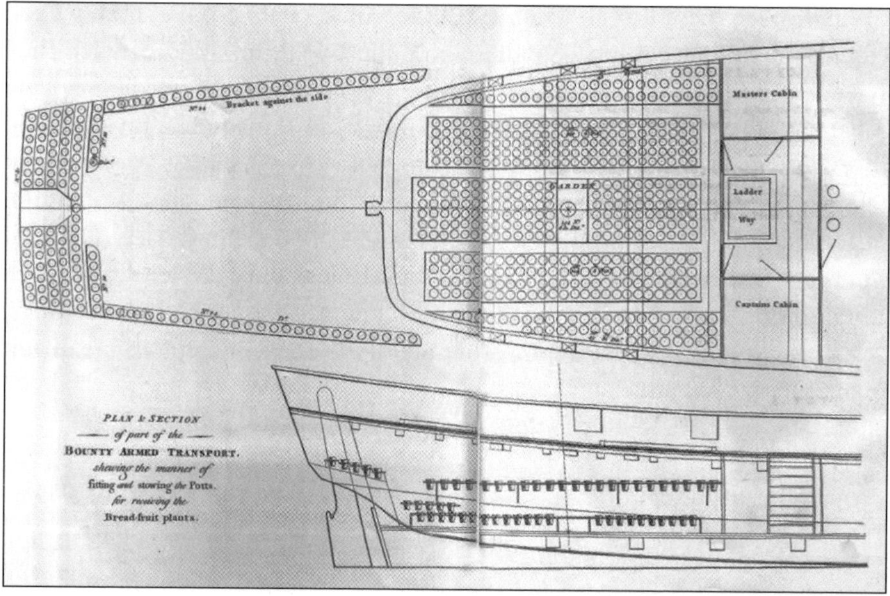

The plan and elevation of HMS *Bounty* showing the 'Garden' with its spaces for hundreds of plant containers.

Bounty may have come out of dock on 3 September 1787 but it was to be a delay of many weeks before she was ready to sail, as the carpenters swarmed over the ship completing the necessary alterations. At length Bligh received his final instructions from the Admiralty. The instructions commence with the usual preamble found in formal documents before getting down to the detail:

> By the Commissioners for Executing the Office of Lord High Admiral of Great Britain and Ireland, etc.

> Whereas the king, upon a representation from the merchants and planters interested in his Majesty's West India possessions that the introduction of the breadfruit tree into the islands of those seas, to constitute an article of food, would be of very essential benefit to the inhabitants, hath, in order to promote the interests of so respectable a body of his subjects (especially in an instance which promises general advantage) thought fit that measures should be taken for the procuring some of those trees, and conveying them to the said West India islands: And whereas the vessel under your command hath, in consequence thereof, been stored and victualled for that service, and fitted with proper conveniences and necessaries for the preservation of as many of the said trees as, from her size, can be taken on board her; and you have been directed to receive on board her the two gardeners named in the margin, David Nelson, and William Brown, who, from their knowledge of trees and plants, have been hired for the purpose of selecting such as shall appear to be of a proper species and size.

Then followed the gist of the instructions:

> You are, therefore, in pursuance of His Majesty's pleasure, signified to us by Lord Sydney, one of his principal secretaries of state, hereby required and directed to put to sea in the vessel you command, the first favourable opportunity of wind and weather, and proceed with her, as expeditiously as possible, round Cape Horn, to the Society Islands, situate in the Southern ocean, in the latitude of about eighteen degrees south, and longitude of about two hundred and ten degrees east from Greenwich, where, according to the accounts given by the late Captain Cook, and persons who accompanied him during his voyages, the breadfruit tree is to be found in the most luxuriant state.

The instructions dealt in some detail with the requirements for the first section of the second leg of the journey i.e. from Tahiti to the island of Java:

> Having arrived at the above-mentioned islands, and taken on board as many trees and plants as may be thought necessary

> (the better to enable you to do which, you have already been furnished with such articles of merchandise and trinkets as it is supposed will be wanted to satisfy the natives) you are to proceed from thence through Endeavour Straits (which separate New Holland from New Guinea) to Prince's Island in the Straits of Sunda, or, if it should happen to be more convenient, to pass on the eastern side of Java to some port on the north side of that island, where any breadfruit trees which may have been injured, or have died, may be replaced by mangosteens, duriens, jacks, nancas, lanfas, and other fine fruit trees of that quarter, as well as the rice plant which grows upon dry land; all of which species (or such of them as shall be judged most eligible) you are to purchase on the best terms you can from the inhabitants of that island with the ducats with which you have also been furnished for that purpose; taking care however, if the rice plants above-mentioned cannot be procured at Java, to touch at Prince's Island for them, where they are regularly cultivated.

In other words, it was recognised that some of the breadfruit seedlings might not survive the journey and if that were the case the vacant plant holders on board could be filled with replacements, such as mangosteen, the obnoxiously smelling durian, and various members of the jackfruit family. And although Bligh had been equipped with a collection of beads, baubles and nick-nacks with which to trade with the native inhabitants of Tahiti, he was also given a small supply of gold ducats with which to buy any extra plants from the Javanese islanders, who by then were well-acquainted with gold as a form of currency.

The instructions continued with detailed instructions about the route to be taken on the out-bound leg of the voyage (around the tip of South America) and how and where the plants were to be delivered on the return leg:

> From Prince's Island, or the Island of Java, you are to proceed round the Cape of Good Hope to the West Indies (calling on your way thither at any places which may be thought necessary) and deposit one half of such of the above-mentioned trees and plants as may be then alive at his majesty's botanical garden at St Vincent, for the benefit of the Windward Islands, and

> then go on to Jamaica: and, having delivered the remainder to Mr East, or such person or persons as may be authorised by the governor and council of that island to receive them, refreshed your people, and received on board such provisions and stores as may be necessary for the voyage, make the best of your way back to England; repairing to Spithead, and sending to our secretary an account of your arrival and proceedings.

The instructions, which were dated 20 November 1787, ended with a paragraph emphasising that Bligh and his crew were, above all else, to do their utmost to assist the two gardeners in collecting, looking after and transporting the plants:

> And whereas you will receive herewith a copy of the instructions which have been given to the above-mentioned gardeners for their guidance, as well as in procuring the said trees and plants, and the management of them after they shall be put on board, as for bringing to England a small sample of each species, and such others as may be prepared by the superintendent of the botanical garden at St Vincent's, and by the said Mr East, or others, for his majesty's garden at Kew; you are hereby required and directed to afford, and to give directions to your officers and company to afford, the said gardeners every possible aid and assistance, not only in the collecting of the said trees and plants at the places before mentioned, but for their preservation during their conveyance to the places of their destination.

In his journal, subsequently published as *A Voyage to the South Sea*, Bligh recorded that, on 9 October, the gunner's stores and guns were loaded on board, along with victuals to last eighteen months:

> we were supplied with sourkraut, portable soup, essence of malt, dried malt, and a proportion of barley and wheat in lieu of oatmeal. I was likewise furnished with a quantity of ironwork and trinkets to serve in our intercourse with the natives in the South Seas: and from the Board of Longitude I received a timekeeper, made by Mr Kendal.

The timepiece, a copy of the pioneering H4 marine chronometer designed by John Harrison as his submission piece for the Longitude Prize, was made by Larcum Kendall in 1771 and is generally known as K2. Whereas K1 had been found to be extremely accurate by James Cook on his second and third voyages, enabling him to measure longitude with considerable precision, Bligh found K2 to be slightly less reliable, losing between one and three seconds a day. Nevertheless, he was able to write that the watch 'performed remarkably well', and was 'the most superior watch … yet met with'. It would become famous as the chronometer taken to Pitcairn Island by the mutineers, finally being brought back to Britain in 1840 when it was given to the British Museum. It can nowadays be seen at the National Maritime Museum in Greenwich.

The orders to sail finally came through from Lord Hood on 24 November, but in the event it was yet another month before sailing conditions were favourable. The delayed departure date worried Bligh, especially as it meant that he would reach the tip of South America at the worst time of the year. He therefore wrote to the Admiralty asking for discretionary powers to alter his route if the Cape Horn passage was found to be impassable. On 18 December 1787 he received amended instructions:

> The season of the year being now so far advanced as to render it probable that your arrival with the vessel you command on the southern coast of America will be too late for your passing round Cape Horn without much difficulty and hazard, you are in that case at liberty (notwithstanding former orders) to proceed in her to Otaheite, round the Cape of Good Hope.

It was not until 23 December that *Bounty* finally sailed from Spithead 'with a fair wind' and headed down the English Channel. She was immediately lashed by gales and rough seas. As Bligh wrote:

> [On 26 December] blew a severe storm of wind from the eastward, which continued till the 29th, in the course of which we suffered greatly. One sea broke away the spare yards and spars out of the starboard main chains. Another heavy sea broke into the ship and stove all the boats. Several casks of beer that had been lashed upon deck were broke loose and washed overboard, and it was not without great difficulty and

> risk that we were able to secure the boats from being washed away entirely.

Hardly the most auspicious of starts! The ship hurried down to reprovision at Tenerife, reaching there on 7 January. A measure of the high esteem in which Fletcher Christian was held by Bligh is that the captain sent Christian to pay his respects to the island Governor. It was, however, an unhappy visit, and whereas Bligh was enthusiastic about the price and quality of the white wine, there was little else to be had. As he put it:

> Indian corn, potatoes, pumpkins, and onions, were all very scarce and double the price of what they are in summer. Beef also was difficult to be procured … The corn … is full five shillings per bushel; and biscuit at twenty-five shillings for the hundred pounds. Poultry was so scarce that a good fowl cost three shillings. This is therefore not a place for ships to expect refreshments at a reasonable price at this time of the year, wine excepted; but from March to November supplies are plentiful, particularly fruit, of which at this time we could procure none except a few dried figs and some bad oranges.

'Four quarters of miserable beef' were purchased, but the meat was subsequently thrown overboard because, according to James Morrison, the men were convinced it was from either an ass or a mule. When Morrison published his own rather different account of the *Bounty* voyage, he alleged that Bligh had been appropriating food intended for the journey. In particular, he recounts that Bligh deliberately created a furore, claiming that two cheeses had been stolen, using this to justify taking cheese off the menu. The cooper, supported by the clerk-cum-steward Mr Samuel, maintained that the casks in which the cheese had been kept were already opened before *Bounty* had set sail – allegedly on the orders of Bligh – and that two cheeses had been taken from the cask and delivered to the home of Captain Bligh.

According to Morrison, Bligh flew into a rage at the accusation and threatened the men (the cooper in particular) with a good flogging if any more was said about the incident. It is, however, an interesting anecdote in the light of the subsequent mutiny – the issue was not whether Bligh had stolen the cheese, but whether the men thought that he was unfairly holding back rations. As will be seen from accounts of many other mutinies in the later eighteenth century – some described in chapter 17– the quickest way to provoke a seaman's wrath was to hit him in the stomach, either by rationing his food in an arbitrary manner, or by limiting his supply of grog. These apparently minor squabbles about 'victuals' seem to have had a cumulative effect on ship-board morale, leading inexorably to a final showdown.

Later, as the ship approached the equator, Bligh apparently again lost his temper when the men seemed disinclined to eat pumpkin, which was starting to go off, yelling: 'You damned infernal scoundrels I'll make you eat grass or anything you can catch before I have done with you.'

Needless to say, Bligh's log made no mention of either incident. Most of the disagreements about food – and as the voyage progressed there were many of them – were due to the fact that the captain was combining his role with that of purser. On a larger, more appropriately manned vessel, there would have been a purser whose duties included monitoring and distributing food stocks. Having a separate purser would have deflected criticism from Bligh, whereas on *Bounty*, anything affecting the men's stomachs had a direct impact on their attitude towards Bligh. There was no one else to blame!

Off they sailed in the direction of Brazil, replenishing their limited supply of fresh water after some particularly heavy rainstorms, catching dolphins and snaring birds. On 3 March Bligh wrote: 'I gave to Mr Fletcher Christian, whom I had before directed to take charge of the third watch, a written order to act as lieutenant.' The promotion to acting lieutenant must have been a slap in the face for John Fryer, the ship's master and hence the immediate superior to Fletcher Christian. Fryer clearly despised Bligh and never changed his low opinion of him – which makes it all the more remarkable that when the mutiny occurred he stayed loyal to Bligh. Fryer emerges as a man of considerable ability and professionalism, and the suspicion must be that Bligh disliked him for those very qualities. Fryer alone could see through Bligh, his pettiness and his favouritism. Bligh may have had a low opinion of Fryer, but it is worth noting that Fryer went on to have a distinguished and honourable career. He reached the top of his profession in the Royal Navy in 1798 as master of the first rate, and remained in the navy until his retirement in 1812. Others thought highly of him and wrote letters of recommendation. One such was sent by Captain Thomas Foley of HMS *Britannia*, who wrote of Fryer:

> he conducted himself with sobriety, diligence, and obedience in the execution of his duty, and that in every respect he shewed himself to be a skilful Seaman and good Officer and that in the several difficult services there was to perform he gave his assistance with a zeal and ardour, that calls on me to recommend him in the strongest terms in the favour of the Navy Board, as one worth any Promotion they may have to bestow.

That has to be set against Bligh's later comments that Fryer was a troublemaker. Neither man had any respect for the other and Fryer's own account of the mutiny and the subsequent voyage in an open boat describes Bligh as being 'as Tyrannical in his temper in the Boat as in the Ship, and … his chief thought was his own comfort'. It is clear from his comments that Fryer was exasperated because Bligh always claimed credit for anything that went right – even if it was not his idea – and never accepted blame when things went awry – even if it was his fault. Perhaps for this reason, Fryer ended up in effect leading a rival faction, a man to whom the crew would look when they got fed up with Bligh and his constant complaints and bickering.

But all that was in the future, as Fryer swallowed his pride and carried on with his duties, despite seeing his subordinate promoted above him. By mid-March Bligh was writing that he 'found it necessary to punish Matthew Quintal, one of the seamen, with two dozen lashes for insolence and mutinous behaviour. Before this I had not had occasion to punish any person on board.'

In another version of the incident, Bligh added the words: 'Until this afternoon I had hoped I could have performed the voyage without punishment to any one, but I found it necessary to punish Matthew Quintal with 2 dozen lashes.' It is worth remembering that the offence normally carried a tariff of three dozen lashes, so this punishment was far from 'sadistic'. However, the fact that Bligh chose to make such a revision to his journal, expressing his wish to have avoided all corporal punishments, does seem a rather heavy-handed attempt to show himself in a good light and to head-off any accusation of brutality.

It was an invariable rule that all such punishments were recorded in the captain's log and researchers have shown that, contrary to what might be expected, Bligh administered the lash far less frequently than most of his contemporaries. The Royal Navy was a harsh employer, and insolent or mutinous behaviour would always be seen as meriting a good flogging. Bligh described Matthew Quintal as a 'seaman, aged 21 years, 5 feet 5 inches high, fair complexion, light brown hair, strong made, very much tatowed [sic] on the backside and several other places'.

In the longer term, the flogging did nothing to enamour Quintal towards Bligh. By all accounts Quintal was a brutal man and a constant troublemaker and he went on to become one of the mutineers, ending his days being killed by two of his fellow conspirators.

It leads on to the question of whether Bligh was over-zealous in dishing out corporal punishment. Far from it, if a comparison with others is to be believed. Captain Cook, universally regarded as a fair man, used flogging as a punishment far more than Bligh – and Cook was far more humane than most of his contemporaries. Cook, on board HMS *Resolution* between 1776 and 1779, ran up perhaps sixty separate flogging incidents (among a crew of 112). The offences varied from the most common ('neglect of duty – six or twelve lashes) to a dozen lashes for offences such as sleeping on his post as a sentry, or for insolence and contempt, or for drunkenness and insolence. Two dozen lashes were ordered by Cook for 'having connextions with women knowing himself to have the Venereal Disorder on him'. Viewed in that context, Bligh used the lash but rarely, and when he followed up his *Bounty* appointment by being put in charge of HMS *Providence* (see chapter 12) there were remarkably few floggings.

Bligh's problems really began when he reached the extreme tip of South America. As he was to write:

> The stormy weather continued with a great sea. The ship now began to complain and required to be pumped every hour; which was no more than we had reason to expect from such a continuance of gales of wind and high seas … With all this bad weather we had the additional mortification to find at the end of every day that we were losing ground; for notwithstanding our utmost exertions and keeping on the most advantageous tacks (which if the weather had been at all moderate would have sufficiently answered our purpose) yet the greater part of the time we were doing little better than drifting before the wind.

At that stage of the voyage the Great Cabin was still available for the use of the captain, there being no plants. He apparently agreed to allow the crew to share the cabin during the appalling weather – an action regarded as unusually kind and compassionate. Much has also been made of the fact that Bligh ordered hot porridge to be dished out to the crew for breakfast, but Morrison's version of the story suggests that the quantity of boiled wheat was so derisory that there was never enough to go round, with one gallon expected to be spread between forty-two men.

The crew were suffering in the appalling weather – ribs were broken, shoulders were dislocated, and eight of the men were on the sick list, mostly with 'rheumatic complaints'. To cap it all, the sheep and poultry on board succumbed to the cold. According to Bligh, when the last of the sheep died it weighed around fifty pounds and would make a very good Sunday lunch for them all. The crew apparently disagreed, considering the carcass to be inedible, and preferred to tuck into a meal of dried shark. It highlights an interesting distinction in perception: Bligh felt that he was compassionate and fair; his men often felt he came across as begrudging and ungenerous.

After thirty days of trying to batter his ship round the Cape, Bligh finally gave up and to the great joy of all on board, he turned to the east and made hell-for-leather for Africa, knowing that the westerlies would work in his favour. Before doing so, he called the men together and thanked them all for their efforts.

Those on board arrived generally in a healthy state when they landed and Bligh was rather pleased with himself: 'Perhaps a Voyage of five Months which I have now performed with out touching at any one place but at Tenarif, has never been accomplished with so few accidents, and such health among Seamen in a like continuance of bad Weather.'

His comments perhaps reveal a bit about how he viewed the common sailors:

> Seamen will seldom attend to themselves in any particular, and simply to give directions that they are to keep themselves clean and dry as circumstances will allow, is of little avail; they must be watched like Children, as the most recent danger has little effect to prevent them from the same fate.
>
> The Mode I have adopted has been a Strict adherence to the first grand point cleanliness in their persons and bedding, keeping them in dry Cloaths & by constant cleaning and drying

> the Ship with Fires. To this I attribute their having kept free of Colds so wonderfully as they have done.

The crew may have been less enthusiastic about the constant diatribes about cleanliness – nor were they keen on Bligh's insistence on exercise – or rather, on dancing. Bligh had written to Banks saying:

> Some time for relaxation and mirth is absolutely necessary and I have considered it so much so that after 4 o'clock the evening is laid aside for their amusement and dancing. I had great difficulty before I left England to get a man to play the violin and I preferred at last to take one two-thirds blind than come without one.

The blind fiddler was a 26-year-old Irishman called Michael Byrne, a man described later by Bligh as 'a scoundrel' and 'a great villain'. It is hard to see how much mirth was being generated by the dancing if the activity was compulsory – especially when two of the crew, William Brown the gardener and John Mills, gunner's mate, were punished for refusing to join in. Their punishment: their grog ration was withdrawn. Interestingly, all three of the men mentioned – Byrne, Brown and Mills – were to side with Christian when the famous mutiny took place.

The emphasis on 'joyless dancing' can be contrasted with the experience of the French explorer Louis Antoine de Bougainville, who had sailed to Tahiti just a few years earlier. Faced with appalling food shortages on board *La Boudeuse*, de Bougainville had resorted to reducing the rations to near-starvation levels. He even had to forbid the men from eating the leather used to wrap the sails, and yet he wrote in his journal:

> I must declare that not one suffered himself to be dejected, and that our patience under sufferings has been superior to the most critical situation. The officers set the example, and the seamen never ceased dancing in the evenings, as well in the time of scarcity, as in that of the greatest plenty. Nor has it been necessary to double their pay.

Bounty moored up in False Bay, near Cape Town and over a month was spent reprovisioning the ship and, in particular, recaulking all the timber because she was leaking like a sieve. Finally, on 1 July 1788, she set sail for Van Diemen's Land (now Tasmania) which she reached on 21 August after encountering westerly winds which Bligh described as 'very boisterous'. He was familiar with Adventure Bay, which he had visited with Cook during his previous voyage, and it offered a chance to reprovision and to collect wood and fresh water.

It was to be marked by an early display of discord – initially between Bligh and the ship's carpenter, William Purcell. The carpenter refused to carry out specific instructions about cutting wood for planks and claimed that Bligh had only followed him ashore in order to find fault. Bligh was in a difficult position: Purcell was a warrant officer and as such was immune from flogging. Bligh could lock him up in chains, but that would leave him short-handed for a potentially lengthy period. Purcell knew he had Bligh over a barrel and continued with his deliberate disobedience and insolence. As Bligh put it in his log:

> My Carpenter on my expressing my disapprobation of his Conduct with respect to orders he had received from me concerning the mode of working with the Wooding Party behaved in a most insolent and reprehensible manner, I therefore ordered him on board, there to assist in the general duty of the ship, as I could not bear the loss of an able working and healthy Man; otherwise I should have committed him to close confinement untill I could have tryed him: the prospect of which appears to be of so long a date made me determine to keep him at his duty.

Quite possibly the acrimony was more widespread, with James Morrison, boatswain's mate, later claiming that at Adventure Bay 'were sown seeds of eternal discord between Lieut. Bligh & the Carpenter, and it will be no more than true to say, with all the Officers in general'. In another version of the story, Morrison added: 'He [Bligh] confined the carpenter and found fault with the inattention of the rest to their duty, which produced continual disputes, everyone endeavouring to thwart the others in their duty.'

What is apparent is that Bligh was no great leader of men, no team-builder. Every sailor tried to keep his head down, did the minimum of work expected of him and blamed others if anything went wrong. The one thing that united the men was that they rejoiced in any small victory they could have at their captain's expense.

The animosity between Bligh and the obstinate carpenter was still going strong three months later when they reached Tahiti. As Bligh recounted on 5 December:

> In the afternoon I directed the Carpenter to cut a large stone that was brought off by one of the Natives, (Odiddee) requesting me to get it made fit for them to grind their Hatchets on, but to my astonishment he refused to comply in direct terms saying 'I will not cut the stone for it will spoil my Chissel, and tho there is law to take away my cloaths there is none to take away my Tools'. This Man having before shewn his mutinous and insolent behaviour: I was under the necessity to confine him to his Cabbin.

It has to be said: there would not be a carpenter alive who would want to see his best wood-working tools ruined by being used to cut, chisel or drill stone, and the episode shows a complete lack of appreciation by Bligh of the skills needed to be a ship's carpenter – and of the need of the carpenter to keep his tools sharp and undamaged.

From Tasmania, Bligh travelled to the south of New Zealand's South Island. An indication that all was not necessarily well was contained in Bligh's note of 9 October: the clerk John Samuel brought Bligh a message from Fryer, the master, saying that Fryer refused to sign off the monthly accounts unless and until the captain signed a certificate to the effect that Fryer had done nothing amiss during his time on board. Bligh was outraged at this. In his words:

> As I did not approve of his doing his duty conditionally I sent for him and told him the Consequence … I now ordered the Hands to be turned up. Read the Articles of War, with particular parts of the Instructions relative to the Matter, when this troublesome Man saw his error & before the whole Ships Company signed the Books.

James Morrison, in his version of events, described how the entire crew were summoned to hear Bligh order Fryer to sign the stock-taking accounts. Fryer's response was: 'I sign in obedience to your orders, but this may be cancelled hereafter.' There is nothing definitive to show what aspect of the accounts lay at the root of the problem, but one suggestion is that the captain had been syphoning off supplies and fiddling the accounts to hide the extent of his own theft. But if that were to be the case, it seems strange that the accusation never came to light in the subsequent court-martial proceedings, when men in fear of losing their life had no reason to hold back from making such an accusation. One suspects that Fryer thought that he 'had something on Bligh' which the captain did not want to be made public, but that Bligh called his bluff by assembling the entire ship's company and reading the Articles of War. Fryer backed down because he felt unable to substantiate whatever it was he thought Bligh had done. It was yet another example of Fryer and Bligh not getting on. Later, from Coupang, Fryer described an incident where Bligh had ordered him to supervise the work of the carpenter. Fryer responded to the effect that it was not his job to do this, causing the enraged captain to shout at him that he would have liked to have him locked up for his insolence. As Fryer stated: 'This is the sort of treatment the Officers in general have received from Mr Bligh in the course of the Voyage – which in my opinion has been the cause of all our difficult times.' He also recounted how, on the night before the mutiny, 'between 10 and 11 o'clock Mr Bligh came on Deck – as he alway[s] did to leave his orders for the night – we at that time was upon speaking terms – but I am sorry to say that was but seldom. [He said] 'there is breeze springing up'.

If nothing else, the confrontation shows that many of the men on board were already feeling 'got at' by Bligh, and it is highly possible that both Purcell and Fryer were responding to having been on the receiving end of constant and humiliating criticism. Why else would Fryer be asking for a 'letter of immunity'?

Another journal entry from that time recorded that one of the seamen, James Valentine, had died of 'an asthmatic complaint'. Poor Valentine – he had become unwell, causing him to be bled by Thomas Huggan, the ship's surgeon; the bleeding led to an infection, probably gangrene. He became delirious and died shortly afterwards, but Bligh was not informed of Valentine's condition until the very last moment. Bligh blamed Huggan, a perpetual drunk since the very start of the voyage. Indeed, Bligh had tried unsuccessfully to have Huggan removed from the crew list and at least had the foresight to insist that he was allowed to bring a surgeon's mate, Thomas Ledward, alongside Huggan. Ledward was subsequently made up to acting surgeon and turned out to be a quiet, conscientious man who remained loyal to Bligh to the end.

Chapter 6

Life on Tahiti

View of Tahiti drawn in 1777.

On 25 October 1788 *Bounty* was off the coast of Otaheite (Tahiti). As Bligh coyly put it

> As there was great probability that we should remain a considerable time at Otaheite, it could not be expected that the intercourse of my people with the natives should be of a very reserved nature: I therefore ordered that every person

> should be examined by the surgeon, and had the satisfaction to learn from his report that they were all perfectly free from any venereal complaint.

Despite such precautions, venereal disease was to infect a significant part of the native population over a period of just a few years. The English blamed the French under the command of Louis-Antoine de Bougainville, who had visited Tahiti in 1768, calling it 'the French Pox'. The French blamed the English, calling it '*le mal Anglais*', presumably believing that the disease had been brought to the islands eight months earlier in 1767 by the Englishman Samuel Wallis. Both Cook and Bligh were aware of the damage caused by bringing syphilis into the islands, and both captains maintained a policy of banning infected men from leaving the ship. However, many thousands of Tahitians were to die of newly introduced diseases – not just syphilis, but also tuberculosis, smallpox, whooping cough and measles; in the space of one hundred years after the arrival of Cook on his first voyage, the population had dropped from a perhaps somewhat exaggerated figure made by Cook of 204,000 people (Bligh thought that at the time of his visit it was nearer 100,000) to a mere 7,169 recorded in the census of 1865.

Bligh remained vigilant about the spread of venereal disease and later, just before leaving the islands, he again had the crew checked for symptoms. Four were found to be infected in early 1789, and within a fortnight the figure had risen to half a dozen. Meanwhile, Bligh noted with wry interest that it wasn't always a case of 'free love'. Bligh found that the islanders were not sleeping around with impunity after it was brought to his attention that a girl who had been sleeping with the coxswain gave another girl a beating for also having slept with him. In a separate case, a woman was discovered in bed with another islander by her husband. The lover was stabbed in the stomach by the husband but 'when each had taken their satisfaction the parties became reconciled and on as good terms as before'. However, Bligh was appalled at some of the sexual practices of the islanders, writing on 15 January 1789 that:

> It is strange that in so prolific a country as this, Men should be led into such sensual and beastly acts of gratification, but perhaps no place in the World are they so common or so extraordinary as in this Island. Even the mouths of the Women are not exempt from the pollution, and many other

as uncommon ways have they of gratifying their beastly inclinations.

So on the one hand we have the prudish Captain Bligh, appalled at the promiscuous behaviour and sexual practices of the island women, and on the other – forty men who had spent the last few months cooped up in a stinking ship and who could not believe their good fortune! One has to assume that by 'beastly acts' Bligh meant anal sex – and that 'mouths not being exempt from pollution' was a coy reference to oral sex. Bligh may have been appalled, but one rather suspects that his men were over the moon…

Because of the initial delay of several months in leaving England, exacerbated by the month lost in the futile attempt to round Cape Horn, Bligh had arrived at Tahiti many weeks later than anticipated – and at the wrong time of year to take root-cuttings from the breadfruit plant. The seedlings needed time to develop to a stage where they had their own root system, sufficient to enable them to survive the trip home. An anticipated stay of a few weeks stretched into five months.

Reading Bligh's account of his stay on Tahiti, written after the event, it is easy to get the impression that it was one long series of feasts, ceremonial introductions, displays of dancing and wrestling, and general socialising. Considerable numbers of gifts were handed out – small axes and other hand tools, looking glasses, necklaces and so on, in exchange for wild pigs, vegetables and other foodstuffs.

Bligh mentions the death of Huggan the surgeon on 9 December ('This unfortunate man drank very hard and was so averse to exercise that he never would be prevailed on to take half a dozen turns upon deck at a time in the course of the voyage'). He also remarks that the crew were getting on famously with the female islanders ('An intimacy between the natives and our people was already so general that there was scarce a man in the ship who had not his *tyo* or friend'). He also states that Nelson and Brown were hard at work preparing the young plants, first by taking root cuttings, then by potting them on and nurturing them under cover of a tent put up onshore, then moving them onto the ship when they were ready. Some withered and died necessitating replacements. Many simply remained dormant, leaving the gardeners no choice but to adopt a 'wait and see' attitude.

On 3 November a metal anchor fitting was stolen by one of the islanders and Bligh blamed Alexander Smith (otherwise known as John Adams) for not keeping an eye out to prevent the loss. In Bligh's words:

> I thought it would have a good effect to punish the boat-keeper [in the presence of the island chiefs] many of them happening to be then on board; and accordingly I ordered him a dozen lashes.

The punishment was certainly harsh – the anchor fitting was almost certainly stolen by an islander swimming underwater, unseen, and no amount of scrutiny by Smith could have detected it. The sense of injustice may well explain why Smith subsequently took an active part in the mutiny. He clearly loved island life and was one of the first crewman to receive a tattoo. Subsequently he set up home ashore with a girl he called Jenny, real name Teehuteatuaonoa.

Very occasionally other crew are mentioned but it is only by consulting the actual daily log, with remarks made at the time by Bligh, that you sense the undercurrent of friction. By Christmas Day 1788 Bligh was ready to leave his mooring in Matavai Bay, having brought 774 pots of young plants on board. He headed south west for a couple of miles to a new landing point at Toahroah Harbour – an excuse for more socialising. Petty thefts were a continuing problem, but Bligh generally blamed his own crew for being careless and untidy, rather than holding the islanders at fault for helping themselves to anything metal left lying around. So, when a meat cleaver was stolen from under the nose of the butcher Robert Lamb on 29 December, it was Lamb who was given twelve lashes. Lamb, a Londoner, turned out to be the only man flogged during the voyage who did not join the mutiny.

Worse was to come; on 6 January news was brought to Bligh at 4.30 in the morning that three men had gone missing – Charles Churchill, the ship's corporal; William Muspratt, tailor and cook's assistant; and Able Seaman John Millward. Of particular concern, they had absconded in one of the ship's small rowing boats and had also taken 'eight Stand of Arms and Ammunition'. Muspratt had been flogged nine days earlier for an unspecified 'neglect of duty'. Millward was later described by Bligh as being '22 years, 5 feet 5 inches high. Brown complexion. Dark hair, strong made. Tattooed under the pit of the stomach with a taoomy or breastplate of

Otaheite.' Churchill, a 30-year-old Mancunian, was also said to be heavily tattooed. He was to prove to be even more of a thorn in the side for Bligh, being one of the main instigators of the mutiny less than four months later.

Although the deserters had absconded in a rowing boat, they had abandoned it shortly afterwards and taken to a sailing canoe. The boat was retrieved and a number of islanders agreed to track down the missing trio. First, Bligh recorded his outrage at the neglect of the man who had fallen asleep during his watch, and who should have been able to stop the deserters if he had been alert. Bligh rages: 'Had the Mate of the Watch [Thomas Hayward] been awake no trouble of this kind would have happened. I have therefore dis-rated and turned him before the Mast.'

But Bligh's critical attitude towards his men in general is shown by the comments which followed:

> Such neglectfull and worthless petty Officers I believe never was in a ship as are in this. No Orders for a few hours together are obeyed by them, and their conduct in general is so bad, that no confidence or trust can be reposed in them. In short, they have drove me to every thing but Corporeal punishment and that must follow if they do not improve.

Bligh was a perfectionist, something of a micro-manager and he hated sloppiness. A couple of days later he exploded once more, after a spare set of sails were taken out of storage and were found to be mildewed to the extent that rot had set in. Earlier, on two separate occasions while on the island, Bligh had asked for the sails to be checked and had been told that everything was in order. As he wrote: 'Scarce any neglect of duty can equal the criminality of this.' He wrote in his journal that if only he had additional manpower he would have dispensed with the services of both the master and the boatswain. Bligh rather suspected that the sails had never been checked in the entire time since they left England – not just negligence on the part of these officers but a deception hidden by lies.

More bad news followed – the supplies of bread on board were thoroughly checked because of suspicions that it had become inedible. As Bligh put it: 'Completed overhauling the Bread and from the Master reporting to me that seventeen hundred and fifty four pounds were unfit for use, I ordered a Survey thereon and the whole quantity was condemned.'

Three weeks were to pass before bad weather relented, enabling the islanders acting on Bligh's instructions to track down the deserters. On 23 January in heavy rain and in the dark, Bligh led a party of men five miles to the house where the deserters were living. They gave up without resistance and the next day they got back on board by eight o'clock. The deserters were ordered into irons and prohibited from being given any alcohol. The next day Bligh ordered Charles Churchill to be punished with a dozen lashes, while Muspratt and Millward were each given two dozen. It must have been especially hard for Muspratt, whose punishment was repeated fourteen days later. Added to the flogging he received just prior to the desertion, it meant that he received a total of sixty lashes in less than six weeks, two thirds of them on skin which had barely had time to heal. Nevertheless, all three deserters were compelled to feel some sort of gratitude towards Bligh: desertion would normally have led to a court martial and an inevitable death penalty

By 25 January Bligh was more concerned about the state of his seedlings; they were, after all, the whole reason for the voyage. To his delight, many of the seedlings were so well established that their root systems had filled the containers and started to grow through the bottom of the pots. He was convinced that this meant that if only the ship had arrived earlier in the season their mission could have been completed in a single month on the island. Things were looking good: as Bligh wrote: 'Under these happy circumstances and the Plants easily cultivated, the success of the Voyage now only hinges on our passage home.' Three days later he was able to add: 'The Plants are going charmingly on and those we have only Potted within these three weeks are in as thriving a state as the others, owing to the season.'

He estimated that by now there were 1,015 plants on board – far more than originally provided for, a result achieved by converting the area previously set aside for chicken coops and livestock. No doubt Bligh was thinking of his patron Joseph Banks when he added that he had also collected: 'Vees, Ay-yahs, Plantains, Rattahs, Matte, Ettou and a few rare Botanical Plants'.

On 1 February Bligh recorded that he had flogged Isaac Martin. It was a punishment which must have rankled greatly with Martin, an able seaman, who had struck an islander who had been caught stealing an iron hoop. If he had done nothing, and permitted the theft of the hoop, he would have been flogged. As it was, he was flogged for trying to punish and deter such thefts – a real Catch 22 situation. Bligh had issued express orders that his men were not to attack or hit the islanders, and orders were orders.

The sentence was originally for twenty-four lashes, commuted to nineteen after the chief and his family pleaded for leniency.

February was spent caulking the ship's timbers, checking the rigging, and cleansing the ship of rats and cockroaches by means of scrubbing the woodwork with boiling water and smoking everything with tobacco. At that stage Bligh was planning to start his onward journey within the month and it was clearly important to get *Bounty* 'ship-shape' before the voyage to the Caribbean.

Various entries in the log cast light upon the activities on board during the final month on the island:

> [2 March] The Weather this 24 Hours being very bad and the night very dark, a Thief took the Advantage of us and stole from the Tent an empty water Cask and part of an Azimuth Compass. Also the Bedding out of Mr Peckover's Hammock while he had the look out … I now ordered the Thief into my Boat and took him on board and punished him with one hundred lashes severely given, and from thence into Irons. He bore it surprizingly and only asked me twice to forgive him altho' he expected he was to die. His Back became very much swelled but only the last stroke broke the Skin. I think proper to confine him as an Hostage for the good behaviour of others for the future.

> [7 March] Had given in written orders that the Mate of the Watch [Mr Stewart] was to be answerable for the Prisoners and to visit and see that they were safe in his watch, but I have such a neglectful set about me that I believe nothing but condign punishment can alter their conduct.

It was Bligh's contention that his men were so impudent as to deny having received verbal orders and that he was forced to go to the trouble of issuing orders in writing.

> [18 March] I now find we are subject to more petty thefts than we have hitherto, but it is to be expected when a ship is near the time of sailing. It amounts however to no other articles than such as are carelessly about. I cannot therefore blame the Indians for it, as I am perfectly certain that had the ship been

> lying in the River Thames, a hundred times as much would have been Stolen in the same time.
>
> [25 March] I issued to day written orders … for all the Cats to be taken out of the Ship likewise two Dogs, and that no one was to bring Curiosities into the Ship, but such as could be Stowed by the respective owners in their Chests. Likewise, that great care was to be taken that no Native secreted himself on board as I would allow no one to go to England.
>
> [4 April] My Stock on board consisted of as much fruit as I could Stow, 25 Hogs and 17 Goats. Water on board 47 Tons. Sick List: two Venereals.

Bligh later added in his journal:

> We left Otaheite with only two patients in the venereal list, which shows that the disease has not gained ground. The natives say that it is of little consequence, and we saw several instances of people that had been infected who, after absenting themselves for 15 or 20 days, made their appearance again without any visible symptom remaining of the disease. Their method of cure I am unacquainted with; but their customary diet and mode of living must contribute towards it. We saw a great many people however with scrofulous habits and bad sores: these they denied to be produced from any venereal cause; and our surgeon was of the same opinion.
>
> [Sunday 5 April] At 5 o'Clock … we bad farewell to Otaheite, where for 23 Weeks we were treated with the greatest kindness: fed with the best of Meat and finest Fruits in the World.

What comes across from the various incidents – thefts, disobedience, floggings – was that naval discipline had seriously broken down while the crew enjoyed island life. Undoubtedly, Bligh became more and more frustrated and angry at the lack of discipline and it is easy to imagine that he expressed his ire in language which became more and more vitriolic. He was always known for his 'intemperate' language – sometimes described as being 'fruity'. What is apparent is that he had an acid tongue, and thought nothing of humiliating and berating anyone who he felt was not living up to his high standards. It placed the recipient of the tirades in an impossible position – it was humiliating to be reprimanded in public and yet to have answered back in any way would have justified immediate punishment. So men such as Fletcher Chrisian just had to soak it up in silence.

It is safe to assume that Bligh's 'anxiety for the execution of his instructions' extended to the way he treated his men on Tahiti. Whether he was sarcastic, whether he belittled the men unfairly, whether he shouted profanities can only be guessed at – but what we can be certain of is that many of the crew would have had severe misgivings about being herded back on board *Bounty*, leaving behind a very pleasant lifestyle. Months spent ashore meant that many of them had simply 'gone native'. It was not their fault, nor Bligh's fault, that life on Tahiti had more allure than life on board ship…

Chapter 7

The Mutiny

Robert Dodd's picture entitled 'The mutineers turning Lt Bligh and some of the officers and crew adrift from His Majesty's Ship *Bounty*, 29 April 1789'.

For three weeks after leaving Tahiti *Bounty* sailed westward, visiting the two small islands of Huaheine, surrounded by a deep, crystal-clear lagoon. It is easy to imagine that those on board would not have been impressed with the magnificent bays and white-sand beaches – they would have preferred to have stayed behind on Tahiti. The men must have been preöccupied with thoughts of what lay ahead – and of what they had left behind. They travelled on to Whytootackee, which Bligh described as being 'one of the Friendly Islands'. Bligh noted a waterspout:

> It passed within ten yards of our stern, making a rustling noise but without our feeling the least effect from its being so near

> us. The rate at which it travelled I judged to be about ten miles per hour going towards the west in the direction of the wind.

From there *Bounty* headed for Annamooka, each island visit involving the same sequence: encountering native islanders, exchanging presents, bartering for supplies, and suffering repeated thefts of adzes and other metal goods before sailing on to the next island. Then on Monday, 27 April Bligh noted:

> The wind being northerly in the evening we steered to the westward to pass to the south of Tofoa. I gave directions for this course to be continued during the night. The master had the first watch, the gunner the middle watch, and Mr Christian the morning watch.

It was during that third watch, while Christian was in charge, that the mutiny took place. Bligh records:

> Just before sun-rising, while I was yet asleep, Mr Christian, with the master at arms, gunner's mate, and Thomas Burkitt, seaman, came into my cabin, and seizing me tied my hands with a cord behind my back, threatening me with instant death if I spoke or made the least noise: I however called as loud as I could in hopes of assistance; but they had already secured the officers who were not of their party by placing sentinels at their doors. There were three men at my cabin door besides the four within; Christian had only a cutlass in his hand, the others had muskets and bayonets. I was hauled out of bed and forced on deck in my shirt, suffering great pain from the tightness which with they had tied my hands. I demanded the reason of such violence but received no other answer than abuse for not holding my tongue. The master, the gunner, the surgeon, Mr Elphinstone, master's mate, and Nelson, were kept confined below; and the fore hatchway was guarded by sentinels. The boatswain and carpenter, and also the clerk, Mr Samuel, were allowed to come upon deck, where they saw me standing abaft the mizenmast with my hands tied behind my back under a guard with Christian at their head.

There followed a short period of 'negotiations', while Bligh, by now permitted to pull on trousers instead of being naked under his night-shirt, tried to reason with his captors and to persuade others to come to his assistance. Christian had seized a bayonet and held it to Bligh, who was then still tightly bound around the wrists, and made it quite clear that he would kill Bligh if he resisted. He forced his captain and eighteen men into the ship's longboat.

At one point Bligh allegedly told Christian, 'I'll give my bond never to think of this if you'll desist', and reminded Christian that in the past 'he had dandled my daughter on his knee'. Christian replied 'No, Captain Bligh, if you had any honour, things would not have come to this, and if you had any regard for your wife and family you should have thought of them before and not behaved so much like a villain.' When the bosun (William Cole) tried to intercede, Christian replied 'Tis too late. I have been in hell for this fortnight past and am determined to bear it no longer. And you know … that I have been used like a dog all the voyage.'

This passage is interesting because it suggests that Christian's 'agony' had occurred only since leaving Tahiti. He may have believed that he had been treated like a dog for the entire voyage, but it was the fact that he was 'homesick' for Tahiti (and, one suspects, for the comforts of his lover Maimiti) that caused him to be so distracted and in mental turmoil. One thing which should be borne in mind: Christian may well have been wondering whether Maimiti was pregnant. After all, they had probably been lovers for some months and Christian may well have been wracked with guilt at abandoning Maimiti and any child she might be carrying, particularly in view of his own experience as a very young child when his father died (see chapter 9).

Writing in his journal after the event, Bligh was at pains to explain that he could not reasonably have been expected to guard against the mutiny, writing that he did not have the luxury of a sentinel at his door while he slept, and pointing out that he always slept with his bedroom door open so that the officer of the watch could have access to him at all occasions. Bligh continued:

> Desertions have happened more or less from most of the ships that have been at the Society Islands; but it has always been in the commander's power to make the chiefs return their people: the knowledge therefore that it was unsafe to desert perhaps

> first led mine to consider with what ease so small a ship might be surprised, and that so favourable an opportunity would never offer to them again.

The fact that the mutiny was spontaneous, rather than carefully planned and organised for some days is reflected in Bligh's account:

> The secrecy of this mutiny is beyond all conception. Thirteen of the party who were with me had always lived forward among the seamen; yet neither they nor the messmates of Christian, Stewart, Haywood, and Young, had ever observed any circumstance that made them in the least suspect what was going on. To such a close-planned act of villainy, my mind being entirely free from any suspicion, it is not wonderful that I fell a sacrifice. Had their mutiny been occasioned by any grievances, either real or imaginary, I must have discovered symptoms of their discontent, which would have put me on my guard: but the case was far otherwise. Christian in particular I was on the most friendly terms with: that very day he was engaged to have dined with me, and the preceding night he excused himself from supping with me on pretence of being unwell; for which I felt concerned, having no suspicions of his integrity and honour.

What Bligh does not mention were any of the specific events which might have contributed to the mutiny. For that, it is necessary to look at the accounts of others, particularly as revealed in the subsequent court martial evidence. What is apparent from this is that Christian, perhaps over-sensitive, perhaps suffering real heartache at being separated from Maimiti, reacted badly to events. Six days before the mutiny Christian was heard to say to Bligh 'Sir, your abuse is so bad I cannot do my duty with any pleasure. I have been in hell for weeks with you.' At a later date another crew member remarked: 'Whatever fault was found, Mr Christian was sure to bear the brunt of the Captain's anger.'

Off the island of Anamooka on 24 April Bligh had words with Christian, calling him a 'cowardly rascal' for allowing fear of 'a set of naked savages' to interfere with his work of supervising the kegging of water. The captain became further enraged when an islander was able to dive and slip the grapnel, a small anchor, off its line. On another occasion he berated all his officers, calling them 'lubberly rascals' who, though armed, would have allowed themselves to be disarmed by 'five men with good sticks'.

Matters reached a head the day before the mutiny. According to Morrison, Bligh came up and was taking a turn upon the quarterdeck when he missed some of the coconuts that were piled up between the guns. He said that they were stolen and could not have disappeared without the knowledge of the officers, who were all summoned. They declared that they had not seen a man touch them, to which Bligh replied 'Then you must have taken them yourselves', and ordered Mr Elphinstone to go and fetch every coconut in the ship's aft.

Bligh then interrogated the officers. According to Morrison, Christian took great exception to being questioned, especially in front of others, saying: 'I hope you don't think me guilty of stealing.' Bligh apparently answered, 'Yes, you damned hound, I do – You must have stolen them from me or you could give a better account of them.'

He ended the confrontation with orders that rations for yams were to be cut in half, and that the serving of grog was to be cancelled, shouting out: 'God damn you, you scoundrels you are all thieves alike and combine with the men to rob me. I suppose you'll steal my yams next, but I'll sweat you for it you rascals. I'll make half of you jump overboard before you get through the Endeavor Straights.'

He then called Mr Samuel and said 'Stop these villains' grog, and give them but half pound of yams tomorrow, and if they steal then, I'll reduce them to a quarter.'

Afterwards, the officers had a discussion among themselves, convinced that the yams which they had acquired privately would be seized, so they set about secreting them away where they would not be found.

William Purcell reported that Christian was devastated by the incident and left Bligh with tears 'running fast from his eyes in big drops'. Why was there such a reaction from Christian when all of the officers were equally under suspicion? Was he expecting special treatment from Bligh? Had he in fact been salting away supplies? There is every likelihood that Christian may have already harboured plans to desert – not a mutiny involving taking over the ship, but escaping on a makeshift raft. Morrison, in his *Memorandum and particulars respecting the Bounty and her crew* writes:

> Finding himself much hurt by the ill-treatment he had received from Lieut Bligh, he [Christian] determined to quit

> the Ship; that very Night, he informed Messrs Cole, Purcell, Stewart and Hayward of his Resolution; and got some Nuts, Brads and other articles of trade which, together with a roasted pig, he put into a Bag, and prepared two staves for Rudder intending to take a large Plank which lay on the Starboard Hog-Stye. He intended to make this attempt, in the first watch, but finding the people in motion, he could not effect it, without being seen, he came up several times, but could get no opportunity favourable for his Design and at last went below & fell asleep, where he remained till the Quartermaster called him at 4 o'clock. He went up and relieved the Watch. Stewart then told him, he was glad he had not deserted, for the men's minds were in a Situation to attempt any thing. Much agitated in mind and finding Mr Hallet did not come up, and that Mr Hayward went to sleep, as soon as he was on Deck, he determined to seize upon the Ship; he informed Quintal of his intention, who went to Churchill and told him; it was soon agreed on and as soon put into execution.

In other words, Christian was sufficiently upset to be planning to desert and barely managed to get any sleep before being called to be on watch at four in the morning. In his tormented state he revealed his plans to two or three of the others, realised that he was not alone in not wanting to sail back to England, and more-or-less made the plan to mutiny on the spur of the moment.

Morrison went on to consider how such a small number of mutineers were successful:

> It will no doubt be wondered at, that a Ship with 44 Men on board, should be taken by so small a number as 10 or 11 which were the whole that ever appeared in arms; on that Day 10 muskets, 2 Cutlasses & 2 Pistols were all that appeared to have been in use when the Boat put off– But no resistance was made.
>
> It will here be asked why? It may be answered, that the Officers were not on such good terms with their Commander,

> as to risk their Lives in his service, and the Service of their Country was not at their Hearts.

Fryer, who was forced into the longboat when the mutiny took place but who never got on with Bligh, later wrote:

> It will very reasonably be asked – What could be the cause for such a revolt. in answer to which I can only say – that Christian was not particular[ly] attach to any woman at Otaheite. nor any of them except Mr Steward [Stewart] and James Morrison Boat'n Mate who were the only two that had there [their] particular Girls – [at least?] from what they said. I suppose that they did not like their captain – I was told since By Messrs Cole & Purcel that … the Night before we lost the Ship Christian was crying forward and tearing some letters to pieces in the Fore chains [and] said that he would not wish any Body to see his letters. Mr Cole told him to keep his heart up and not mind what had past – when Christian said to be count'd a thief was more than he could bear – but said if I was to take the [Bligh?] in my arms and jump overboard with him, it would be [a fine?] service or words to that effect.

It is noteworthy that Fryer did not think that Christian had any particular attachment to Maimiti. This would suggest that Christian had either taken up with the girl fairly recently, or had kept his feelings out of the public eye, possibly because he was also enjoying sex with other women. The fact remains that Christian went through a form of marriage ceremony with Maimiti shortly after he returned to Tahiti.

But the Fryer account does bear out that Bligh was for ever threatening the officers: 'many times in the Voyage has he told his Young Gentlemen that he would leave them at Jamaica – that they should not go home with him.' On other occasions he apparently said that he would make the men eat grass, or threaten them with reduced rations.

It was Fryer who interceded on Bligh's behalf when it came to the choice of boat to be provided for the castaways: 'I then said, what Boat are you going to put your Captn into? They told me the Jolly Boat – the Jolly Boat, I said, would not [do, since] the Bottom was almost eat out with worms. Damn his eyes they said, the Boat is good [enough] for him.'

Fryer persisted, and went to see Christian. According to Fryer, he said: 'For God sake give Mr Bligh a better Boat than the Jolly Boat [which?] Bottom is almost out and let him have a chance of getting onshore. He said no, that Boat was good enough.' In practice there was a change of heart and it was the longboat which was lowered and into which Bligh and the loyalists were placed.

Fryer also quotes this about the mutineers: 'frequently some of them said "shoot the Buggar" – meaning Capt Bligh – for I really believe that every thing was meant at him – they oft-times repeat'd "Now let the Buggar see if he can live on three quarter of a pound of yams."'

The unfair division of provisions may well have exacerbated the situation but it does not fully explain the mutiny; after all, the sailors had only been at sea a few weeks, and there were plenty of stores on board *Bounty* for the voyage ahead and none of the crew were exactly starving. Later, Peter Heywood claimed that he had not initially intended to be part of the mutiny and had simply understood that Bligh was to be seized and taken back to England as a prisoner, 'in order to try him by court-martial, for his long tyrannical and oppressive conduct to his people'. By the time he realised that the mutineers were actually taking over the ship, Heywood maintained that he stayed on board simply because he could see that the longboat was dangerously overladen and that those already on board were likely to be either drowned or killed by unfriendly islanders.

Later, giving evidence at the Court Martial, Heywood lay much of the blame for the success of the mutiny on the officers for failing to stand up to Christian, writing:

> The behaviour of the officers on this occasion was dastardly, beyond description. None of them ever made the least attempt to rescue the ship, which would have been effected had any attempt been made by one of them, as some of those who were under arms [i.e the mutineers who had armed themselves with pistols and muskets] did not know what they were about.'

He continued:

> Their passive obedience to Mr Christian's orders even surprised himself, and he said immediately after the boat was gone that something more than fear had possessed them to suffer themselves to be sent away in such a manner, without offering to make resistance.

No doubt, the gloom and despondency which must have been felt by all of those cast away in the longboat was more than matched by the euphoria which the mutineers must have felt as they realised that they had achieved all of their aims – without bloodshed. They were now free to return to utopia and live the dream. Only it wasn't a dream – it was to be a living nightmare.

Chapter 8

Bligh's Epic Voyage

Bligh's original logbook, held by the State Library, New South Wales.

When the mutiny took place, the *Bounty* was just three weeks into the voyage home and was some thirty nautical miles off the islands of Tonga.

The nineteen castaways had been given minimum supplies, calculated to last perhaps five days. In the event the men were to survive for seven whole weeks – in a boat open to the elements. It probably never crossed the minds of Christian and his supporters that Bligh might actually survive and make it back to England. No doubt this was why, as an afterthought, Christian had thrown four swords into the longboat – presumably so that Bligh and his men could defend themselves if they made it to landfall on Tonga. Well aware of the fate which had befallen Captain Cook, Bligh must have been in no doubt that he was being cast away to die.

Bligh started to write a journal and began by describing how he had been set upon while he was asleep in his cabin, his hands tied, and at gunpoint forced into the longboat. He also described that the others were allowed to collect specific items for their voyage: twine, canvas, a 28-gallon cask of water and the carpenter's tool chest. They were, however, expressly prohibited from retrieving any maps, sextant, or time keeper, and were barred from taking any books containing astronomical observations.

Bligh also had to leave behind all his sketches and survey reports. He described how 'a few pieces of pork' were thrown down to them, sixteen in all, each weighing two pounds. The rum amounted to twelve pints and the wine ran to six bottles. Bligh continued: 'After having undergone a great deal of ridicule and been kept some time to make sport for these unfeeling wretches, we were at length cast adrift in the open ocean.'

The men rowed towards landfall, realising that these provisions were never going to be enough to take them very far. Bligh had previously been on some of the 170 islands which make up Tonga. He even knew some of the leaders – but when they first reached landfall they encountered nobody.

Rough seas prevented them leaving their landing place, and the men survived for several days on a measure of grog and a small piece of bread.

At length the landing party managed to knock down twenty coconuts and take them back on board and on another expedition the men found a few plantains. These were brought back and shared out – together with a minute amount of the pork.

Bligh realised from the rough terrain and poor soil that they hadn't landed on one of the fertile, productive, islands. After a few days they came across islanders, who seemed friendly – and were prepared to exchange coconuts, plantains and breadfruit for a few buckles and beads. Gradually more and more islanders appeared, including some who recognised Bligh from his days with Captain Cook. Their initial affability turned to hostility. Bligh noted: 'the beach was now lined with the natives, and we heard nothing but the knocking of stones together, which they had in each hand. I knew very well this was the sign of an attack.'

Bligh told his men to expect the worst – but they were ill-armed to defend themselves. In particular, two of the four swords were still on board the boat, anchored offshore. A night-time escape seemed the best option, and as the sun set the men gathered their belongings and headed out into the surf.

The leaders of the group of islanders made it clear that they would be killed if they tried to leave the island, and suddenly some two hundred men, armed with stones, started their attack.

One of Bligh's men, John Norton, bravely ran to cast-off the stern rope but was caught, and stoned to death. As the islanders started to haul in the rope to bring the boat back to shore, Bligh had the presence of mind to cut through the rope with his knife and they desperately tried to row away.

The islanders set off in pursuit in their canoes, bombarding the escapers with large stones. Eventually, the attackers were distracted when Bligh threw some clothes overboard; the men stopped to collect them, and Bligh escaped.

The attack, combined with Bligh's recollection of what had happened to Captain Cook, made them realise that they were going to have to stay away from any islands which were inhabited.

Their heavily laden boat was barely seaworthy, with the sides just seven inches above sea level. The lack of protection meant that when the seas got rough, Bligh had little choice but to go with the waves, because trying to steer a predetermined course would inevitably have meant hitting waves side-on, causing the vessel to capsize. Seawater was constantly being taken on board so two men were engaged in baling out, constantly, day and night.

Having watched a colleague murdered in cold blood must have appalled all those on board, but in a sense it united the survivors. They begged Bligh to try and take them to the Dutch settlement on the island of Timor, then part of Indonesia – even though it was thousands of miles away and even though Bligh had no precise idea where the Dutch settlement was based. Unanimously, the men agreed to go on to reduced rations, amounting to one ounce of bread, and a quarter of a pint of water, per day. Bligh wrote:

> we bore away across a sea, where the navigation is but little known, in a small boat, twenty-three feet long from stem to stern, deep laden with eighteen men; without a chart, and nothing but my own recollection and general knowledge of the situation of places … to guide us.

They collected rainwater; they made a make-shift shelter with canvas; they tried to keep the bread dry in the carpenter's tool-box; and they prayed. They dreaded the nights because they were so cold, and yet Bligh was able to write that he thought that the wet, cold, weather was more merciful than an overbearing heat which would have killed them from heat-stroke and dehydration.

The rations had to be reduced still further as Bligh recalculated how much food they would need for the remaining journey. He wrote in his journal that each man was to be given roughly two thirds of an ounce of bread, and a quarter of a pint of water divided out at sunset, at 8 in the morning, and at midday. He was to write: 'To-day I gave about half an ounce of pork for dinner, which, though any moderate person would have considered but a mouthful, was divided into three or four.'

The bread was weighed against a piece of lead shot – which Bligh found in the bottom of the boat and which weighed roughly half an ounce. It proved to be an ideal balance for weighing out the portions of bread in an equal manner.

It is a testament to Bligh's remarkable skills of navigation that he was able even to consider what was to be a journey of over 3,600 nautical miles based entirely on his observations of winds, tides and currents, together with his rough memory of his previous visit to this area of the world. They followed a westerly course, past Fiji which they decided not to stop at, because of fears for their safety, and out into the empty, featureless sea.

Conditions were terrible, with gales and heavy rain keeping the men cold and soaked for days and nights on end. Even the teaspoonful of rum allocated most days can have done little to lift morale when facing near-certain death. They passed numerous small islands – but Bligh knew full well that without guns they wouldn't stand a chance against the native islanders and so they kept out at sea.

On 24 May Bligh made a journal entry that they had caught a bird, called a noddy. The bird is about the size of a pigeon, and it was duly killed, plucked and divided up into eighteen tiny pieces. In order to ensure a fair distribution of the pieces, which still included the beak and all the bones, one man turned his back on the others and had to answer the question put to him: 'who shall have this piece?' – a question repeated over and over, until all the portions had been allocated. In this way the 'treat' was allocated without favour, and it became a method of distribution used on a number of occasions when they were fortunate enough to catch either noddies or boobies, described by Bligh as being the size of a small duck. Later that day he wrote in his journal: 'Sun powerful. People faint'

By now all the men were suffering from constant stomach pains together with cramp from lack of exercise in their lower limbs. At the end of May they encountered the crashing waves which marked the edge of the Great Barrier Reef. It was one in the morning and hearing the thunderous noise of the waves must have been terrifying in the darkness. Bligh desperately changed course, travelling north, parallel to the Great Barrier Reef, until finally, he saw an opening, now termed the Bligh Boat Channel.

Crossing these breakers led them into calmer waters. Bligh and his men would have come ashore some 500 miles north of Cairns, half way up the Cape York peninsula, at an island which Bligh called Restoration Island – because he reached it on the anniversary of the restoration of the British monarchy on 29 May 1660. It was volcanic, and covered about 100 acres and appeared to be deserted. Bligh decided to make landfall and to send out search parties looking for fresh food. They returned in high spirits, having found oysters and fresh water.

Some of the men gorged themselves on berries which they found, despite the fear of poisoning, and became violently sick. Bligh noticed that one particular berry was eaten by the indigenous birds – and therefore reasoned that those berries were safe to eat. He was right.

One of the men, the gardener David Nelson, was struck down with heat stroke and nearly died. Bligh nursed Nelson, writing that in the evening they all ate oysters which they had found, 'except Nelson whom I fed with a few small pieces of bread soaked in half a glass of wine, and he continued to mend'.

After a few days collecting oysters and fresh water, the men could see that they had been spotted by native islanders; it was time to go and find another place to reprovision. But Bligh's journal makes no mention of the continuing tensions onboard. In effect, the men divided into two factions, one loyal to the master, John Fryer, and the other to Captain Bligh. Fryer's own notes, made subsequent to Bligh's printed journal, highlights one or two discrepancies and altercations. Of their time on Restoration Island Fryer writes of a row over how food such as oysters should be divided, and whether it should be 'every man for himself', or 'equal shares for everyone'. He writes:

> Cole and Peckover … said that Captn Bligh was in a sad passion, calling every Body the Name that he could think of [and] telling them – that If it had not been for him that they would not have been there. They said that he was very Right in what he told them. Poor Mr Nelson, whom I very seldom heard swear – said to me 'Yes, Damn his blood, it is his Oeconomy that brought us here.'

The men were relieved to find that Bligh spent most of the last day on Restoration Island sitting under a tree writing and correcting his 'narritive' – a preoccupation which pleased everyone ('He did nothing but make a great noise and write his remarks – which made every one happy about him').

Bligh had been able to make a fire by using a small magnifying glass, which he always had with him. He was to write: 'what was still more fortunate, among the few things which had been thrown into the boat and saved, was a piece of brimstone and a tinder-box, so that I secured fire for the future'.

They were able to cook in a copper pot which one of the men had fortuitously taken from the *Bounty* as he boarded the longboat. The men were getting increasingly fractious, especially over the distribution of food. On Sunday Island, at the end of May 1789, Bligh's authority was challenged by Purcell, the ship's carpenter. The comments made by Fryer at a later date, and transcribed by James R. Galloway on his *Fateful Voyage* website, but here slightly modernised to make them more understandable, describe the incident as follows:

> Mr Purcell had got to the Boat a little before me but when I was upon the Rock, with the oysters at my back, I heard a great noise in the boat [with] Captn Bligh calling some body a damn scoundrel. '[I] have brought you here when if I had not been with you – you would have all perish'd.'
>
> 'Yes sir' the carpenter said – 'if it had not been for you we should not have been here.'
>
> 'What's that you say sir?'
>
> 'I say, sir, if it had not been for you, we should not have been here.'
>
> 'You damn'd scoundrel, what do you mean?'
>
> 'I am not a scoundrel Sir,' the carpenter said. 'I am as good a man as you in that respect.'
>
> Captn Bligh snatched up a cutlass and went forward in the Boat and told the carpenter to take another, the carpenter said 'No Sir, you are my officer.'

> By this time I had got into the Boat – when I could not help laughing – to see Captn Bligh swaggering with a cutlass over the carpenter's head – when I said 'No fighting here – I put you both under an arrest.'
>
> Captn Bligh turn[ed] his conversation on me, 'By God Sir, if you offer'd to touch me I would cut you down.'
>
> 'I said, Sir this is a very wrong time to talk of fighting.'
>
> Captn Bligh said 'That man,' pointing at the carpenter – 'told me that he was as good a man as I am.' The carpenter made answer, 'When you call'd me a scoundrel – I told you that I was not, but as good a man as you in that respect and you said that you had brought us here I told you – that had it not been for you we should not have been here.'

Quite clearly, the men all blamed Bligh for getting them into their predicament – just as Bligh wanted to take credit for the fact that they were all still alive. The argument had arisen after Bligh ordered the carpenter to share out the oysters he had collected, and Purcell had refused, saying that the oysters belonged to the group that collected them and that this method of distribution had been agreed. After the row died down Fryer records:

> When I came back Captn Bligh call'd me to one side and said 'Mr Fryer I think that you behaved very improper.' I told him I was very sorry at the same time begged to know in what [way]. He said ,'In coming into the Boat and saying that you would put us under arrest.'
>
> I then said 'Sir you will give me leave to tell you how far I think you was wrong.'
>
> 'Me, wrong, Sir?'
>
> 'Yes Sir, you wrong. You put yourself on a footing [with] the carpenter when you took up a cutlass and told him to take another. If he had done so and cut you down – it is my opinion that he would have been Justifiable, in so doing.'

Fryer then told Captain Bligh that 'there were other methods in making people do as they were ordered without fighting them, but that he might rest assur'd that I would support him in that as far as was in my power'.

The incident gives some idea of the volatility of Bligh's temper, his inability to accept criticism and of his crew's frustration at having to tip-toe around him for fear of causing offence. To that extent, life in the longboat was no different to how it had been on board *Bounty*. It is also apparent that the suggestion that the carpenter was 'as good a man as Bligh' was like waving a red rag at a bull; Bligh saw himself as far superior to Purcell in every way and resented the impudence of the suggestion – so much so that Bligh's vindictive streak meant that he later singled out Purcell to be court martialled.

On a separate occasion, Bligh felt obliged to give one of the men, Robert Lamb, a good beating. As Lamb later admitted, he had gone off on his own looking for birds to bring back to the others, but instead caught nine noddies, which he killed and ate raw, without sharing with the others.

Up until that point Bligh had been able to record actual times in his journal, because the gunner had secretly kept his pocket watch when they boarded the longboat. But on 2 June the watch stopped, so that afterwards the only way that time could be measured was by reference to sunrise, high noon, and sunset. Bligh continued to sail a north westerly course, up the inside of the Barrier Reef, before entering the Torres Strait at the northern tip of Cape York peninsula. This was to lead him into the open ocean, heading westward in the direction of Timor.

The area of Torres Strait is a nightmare of reefs, islands and shallows. In places the main channel is only a few metres deep. It is now known that there are only two safe routes, one to the north and the other to the south of Prince of Wales Island, so Bligh must have had his wits about him as a navigator to have been able to pick his route safely through that lot – without a chart.

He chose the northern route, and the names Bligh gave some of the islands such as Wednesday Island and Friday Island showed his route. It became known as the Prince of Wales Channel and is still the main channel used by shipping today.

After leaving Wednesday Island, Bligh noted that: 'As an addition to our dinner of bread and water I served to each person six oysters.'

He also noted that they faced at least ten more days in the open ocean before they would be able to reach Timor, writing: 'Even in our present situation we were most deplorable objects; but the hopes of a speedy relief kept up our spirits. For my own part, incredible as it may appear, I felt neither extreme hunger nor thirst. My allowance contented me, knowing that I could have no more.'

Bligh was not exempt from the hunger and general malaise which enveloped the crew. Indeed, he seemed to pride himself in making sure that his own suffering was at least as great as the men who served him, writing:

> For my own part … the hopes of being able to accomplish the voyage, seemed to be my principal support; but the bosun very innocently told me, that he really thought I looked worse than any one in the boat. The simplicity with which he uttered such an opinion much diverted me.

Taken at face value those words are not the words of a monstrous tyrant, but the mark of a man who expected no special favours; he only expected the men to cope with what he himself was prepared to put up with. More cynical observers may feel that this was simply Bligh being self-congratulatory.

Days passed, with the same boring monotony – baling, trying to get dry, eking out the meagre supplies, keeping up morale. The men were deteriorating rapidly, and Bligh noted that two of the older men were on the point of death. He wrote that he gave each of them an extra two teaspoonfuls of wine, which he had carefully saved for just such an occasion.

Many of the crew were in a terrible state and on 10 June Bligh wrote:

> After a very comfortless night there was a visible alteration for the worse in many of the people. This gave me great apprehension. An extreme weakness, swelled legs, hollow and ghastly countenances, a more than common inclination to sleep, with an apparent debility of understanding, seemed to me the melancholy presages of an approaching dissolution.

Finally, on 12 June they reached part of the island of Timor and Bligh was able to write:

> It is not possible for me to describe the pleasure which the blessing of the sight of land diffused among us. It appeared scarce credible, that in an open boat, and so poorly provided,

> we should have been able to reach the coast of Timor in forty-one days after leaving Tonga, having in that time run, by our log, a distance of 3,618 miles.

Bligh still had no idea where the Dutch settlement was based but when the bosun and the gunner went ashore they returned with news that they had come across some friendly islanders. These gave the men a small quantity of dried turtle meat and some Indian corn. The men learnt that there was a settlement at Coupang, and Bligh persuaded one of the islanders to accompany them as a guide. Incredibly, the men had to find the strength to row the boat for much of the final leg of the journey, because the wind was against them.

Bligh awarded everyone a double portion of bread and a little wine, finally reaching Coupang on 14 June. To their amazement they came across an English sailor – and were quickly provided with food and brought to meet the Governor. As Bligh described it, they were like spectres: 'Our bodies were nothing but skin and bones, our limbs were full of sores, and we were cloathed in rags; in this condition, with the tears of joy and gratitude flowing down our cheeks, the people of Timor beheld us with a mixture of horror, surprise, and pity.'

Bligh was soon able to write that he had raised sufficient money from the locals to be able to purchase a small schooner; she was 34ft long, and he fitted her for sea, under the name of *His Majesty's Schooner the Resource*.

He then headed for the settlement of Batavia, now Jakarta, on the island of Java. Bligh set sail, but not before one of the men, David Nelson, the gardener who had previously been nursed back to health after getting sunstroke, had succumbed to what was described as 'an inflammatory illness' and died.

The survivors reached Batavia on 1 October – and Bligh was immediately struck down with a debilitating fever (quite possibly, malaria). A couple of the other survivors quickly died in the unhealthy, humid, climate.

Bligh was lucky; he recovered sufficiently after staying a few days in the interior to plan his departure. First, he wrote various letters, including one to his patron Joseph Banks in which he bemoaned the failure of the voyage:

> I even rejected carrying stock for my own use, & throwing away the Hencoops & every convenience I roofed a place over the Quarter Deck & filled it with Plants which I looked at with delight every day of my life.

> I can only conjecture that the Pirates (among whom is poor Nelson's assistant) have Ideally assured themselves of a more happy life among the Otaheiteans than they could possibly have in England, which joined to some female connections, has most likely been the leading cause of the whole busyness.
>
> If I Had been equipped with more Officers & Marines the piracy could never have happened.

Bligh left the island on a packet ship which departed Batavia, bound for the Cape, on 16 October. He was accompanied by two of his crew. Maybe it is unrealistic to think that he should have waited until there was room for all on board. That would have been far too noble for Bligh, far too egalitarian. He had done his bit for them. They were, however, promised a passage on the next ship, due to leave a fortnight later.

Bligh reached the Cape after two months, staying at Cape Town for the month of December – and his journal ends with the words: 'On 2 January, 1790, we sailed for Europe, and on 14 March, I was landed at Portsmouth by an Isle of Wight boat. THE END.'

Sadly, five more of Bligh's men died before they reached England – but in all, twelve of the nineteen who had originally been cast adrift survived the ordeal.

That ordeal has been described one of the most extraordinary maritime survival stories of all time, bracketed only with the achievement of Ernest Shackleton 125 years later in leading his men to safety after the destruction of the *Endurance* in the icy wasteland of Antarctica. At the very least it demonstrated that Bligh was no one-dimensional villain, just a compassionate leader who knew that without discipline the entire party had no chance of survival. He demonstrated strong leadership and confirmed his reputation as a brilliant seaman and navigator. He returned a hero, albeit only for a short time before his reputation was tarnished for ever by other accounts of the mutiny, which differed so greatly from his own.

On 22 October 1790 three vice admirals, six rear admirals, two naval captains and a man with the title of First Captain to the Commander in Chief, met up on board HMS *Royal William* at Spithead for a meeting chaired by the Honourable Samuel Barrington, Admiral of the Blue and Second Officer in Command of His Majesty's Ships and Vessels at Portsmouth and Spithead. Together they constituted the Court Martial called to 'inquire into the Cause and Circumstances of the Seizure of His Majesty's Armed Vessel the Bounty commanded by Lieutenant William Bligh which had been violently and forcibly taken from him on 28 April 1789'. The Court had in front of them a letter written by William Bligh when he reached Coupang, and dated 18 August 1789.

The letter explained:

> A little before Sun Rise Fletcher Christian who was Mate of the Ship, and Officer of the Watch, with the Ship's Corporal came into my Cabin while I was asleep and seizing me tied my hands with a Cord assisted by others, who were also in the Cabin, all armed with Musquets and Bayonets. I was now threated with instant Deth, if I spoke a Word. I however called for assistance and awakened every one, but the Officers who were in their Cabins were secured by Centinels at their Doors, so that no one could come to me. The Arms were all secured and I was forced on Deck in my Shirt with my hands tied and secured by a guard, abaft the Mizen Mast, during which the Mutineers expressed much joy that they would soon again see Otaheite.

The letter continued:

> I now demanded of Christian the Cause of such a violent Act, but no other answer was given but 'hold your Tongue Sir, or you are dead this Instant', and holding me by the Cord, which tied my hands, he as often threatened to stab me in the Breast with a Bayonet he held in his right hand. I however did my utmost to rally the disaffected villains, to a sense of their duty, but to no effect. The Boatswain was ordered to hoist the launch out and while I was kept under a guard with Christian at their head abaft the Mizen Mast, the Officers and Men, not concerned in the Mutiny were ordered into the Boat. This being done I was told by Christian, Sir your Officers and Men are now in the Boat and you must go with them and with the guard, they carried me across the deck with their Bayonets presented on every Side, when attempting to make another effort, one Villian said to the other, blow his Brains out. I was at last forced into the boat and we were then veered astern, in all nineteen souls.

Much of the remainder of the letter went on to describe the perils of the journey in the open boat after being cast adrift by the mutineers. Bligh listed the men loyal to him who were forced into the boat, as well as identifying the twenty-five men who stayed on board *Bounty*, specifically highlighting the names of the three men who had been detained on board against their consent. These three were Charles Norman and Thomas McIntosh, both of them described as being 'carpenter's mate', and Joseph Coleman, armourer. The letter also stressed that 'The Secrecy of the Mutiny was beyond all Conception, so that I cannot discover that any who was with me had the least knowledge of it, and the comparative lists will shew the strength of the Pirates.'

Bligh was then asked by the court if he had any complaint against any of the officers and he replied that he had no complaint except in respect of the carpenter (Purcell) who faced a court martial hearing of his own immediately after the main hearing finished. The officers were asked a few standard questions – did you know about the mutiny before it happened? Was there anything you could have done to thwart the mutiny? Where were the arms kept? Who had the keys to the arms cupboard?

It is interesting to note the testimony of Fryer, who was never a fan of Bligh but who spoke in his support. Bligh asked Fryer in court: 'Did you see me taken out of my cabin?' to which Fryer responded: 'I saw Lt Bligh going up at the Ladder with his hands tied behind him, and Fletcher Christian the Mate following him, holding the Cord he was tied with. He had a Cutlass in his hand.'

In answer to the question as to whether he had seen any other men carrying arms guarding the captain, Fryer asserted that he saw the Master at Arms Charles Churchill with three or four other people. He also stated:

> They took Captain Bligh on the deck abaft the Mizen Mast where they kept him in confinement. I got leave to go on deck to speak to him and after I came up I asked Mr Christian, who had then hold of Mr Bligh with a bayonet in his hand, what he could think of himself or what he was after, or words to that effect. He told me to hold my tongue, for he had been in hell for a week. After some little talk with Mr Bligh, Mr Christian ordered me to my Cabin again. I was kept confined to my Cabin till I was ordered into the boat.

Fryer confirmed that Bligh was the last man into the boat, adding: 'We were both at the gangway together, when they untied his hands in order to let him go into the boat.' No mention whatsoever was made of any earlier misconduct or complaint about Bligh's behaviour and hence the trial reports contain no criticism or comment likely to tarnish Bligh's reputation. It makes the subsequent destruction of his good reputation all the more remarkable.

The report of the court hearing ended with the words:

> The Court was cleared and was of opinion that the said armed vessel, the Bounty was violently and forceably taken from the said Lieutenant William Bligh by the said Fletcher Christian and certain other Mutineers, and did adjudge the said Lieutenant William Bligh, and such of the Officers and Ships Company as were returned to England and then present to be honourably acquitted.
>
> The Court was opened, Audience admitted and sentence passed accordingly.

The Court, made up of the same personnel, immediately went on to consider the case against William Purcell, starting off with the letter from William Bligh setting out his grievances against the carpenter. A number of incidents were described:

1. On 23 August 1788 in Adventure Bay New Holland, He while on Shore a-Wooding being found fault with by me, for having cut the Billets too long, told me with great contumacy and disrespect 'I suppose you are come on shore on purpose to find fault' and uttered other impertinent expressions.
2. On 23 October 1788 at Sea, when it was thought adviseable for every Person to take a half pint of Beverage made of the Elixir of Vitriol to prevent the Scurvy [i.e. a much-diluted solution of sulphuric acid!] he refused so to do which tended to create discontent and objections among the Crew, by saying 'I am well enough, and therefore I do not choose, nor won't take such stuff as this.'
3. On the 5th Dec'r 1788 in the afternoon on my ordering him to cut a Grinding stone for one of the Chiefs he directly disobey'd my orders and said 'I will not cut the stone, for it will spoil my Chissel, and tho there is Law to take away my cloaths, there is none to take away my Tools.' He repeated this in an insolent manner, and with a threatening aspect.

4. On the 31st May 1789 at Sunday Island on the Coast of New Holland, when under my Command in the Bounty's Launch he was insolent to a high degree and told me with a mutinous aspect that he was as good a Man as I was. I did not see where this would end, and therefore took hold of a Cutlass and told him to take hold of another and defend himself, when he began to make concessions.
5. On 19 June at Timor, I ordered some Chalk that was in the Carpenter's Tool Chest to be given out for the use of our friendly Governor Mr Van Este, there being very little or none at this place. This he very saucily refused, and told me I had no right to it, and behaved very refractory before I could get it.
6. That he has often besides the times already mentioned behaved with great impertinence, disrespectfull, and in such a general reprehensible manner, that early in the Voyage if it had been possible, I should have had him tryed by a Court Martial.

Vindictive and spiteful the charges may have been, but it led to an almost foregone conclusion. Three crew members gave evidence in support of Bligh's criticism, while making it clear that in all other respects Purcell was a capable and hard-working carpenter. The Court found the charges partly proved, and ordered Purcell to be reprimanded.

What happened afterwards to Purcell is not known, but he is rumoured to have ended up in a mental asylum, before dying in 1834. It is difficult to escape the conclusion that his main 'fault' was in being proud of being a skilled craftsman – and one who did not like being forced to imbibe sulphuric acid, however dilute it may have been…

You can almost sense Bligh's euphoria following the result of his court martial in 1790. Writing to his patron Joseph Banks on 24 October that year he said: 'I am happy to inform you that on Friday last I was most honorably acquitted respecting the loss of the Bounty – the sentence closed with – "You are hereby honorably acquitted".'

The letter went on to say:

> I came to Town on Saturday Night & yesterday morning I waited on Lord Chatham who assured me of promotion as soon as he had been with the King. I am to be introduced to his Majesty on Wednesday, who I hope will be graciously pleased to make me Post. I … beg of you Dear Sir to do your

> endeavors to secure me the rank of Post, for if this opportunity passes off, it may be lost forever.

To be made up to post captain was highly important – it meant a foot on a ladder which could lead, simply through passage of time, to promotion through the ranks right up to that of admiral. So, Bligh must have been cock-a-hoop to get the promotion, writing to Banks a few days later: 'it is with great pleasure I inform you that through your most friendly & kind exertions I am made Post. I trust that your usual partiality to me will accept these few lines as the gratefull thanks.'

Things were looking good for Bligh – he was the hero of the hour. The press was full of his heroic exploits and within seven weeks of his return there was even a pantomime put on, under the title of *The Pirates, or, the Calamities of Captain Bligh*. That same year, 1790, Bligh was able to publish his own account of the mutiny and his remarkable journey to Timor under the title of *A Narrative of the Mutiny on Board His Majesty's Ship Bounty*. It was followed up two years later by *A voyage to the South Sea* – or, to give it its full title: *A voyage to the South Sea, undertaken by command of His Majesty for the purpose of conveying the bread-fruit tree to the West Indies, in His Majesty's ship the Bounty, commanded by Lieutenant William Bligh, including an account of the mutiny on board the said ship, and the subsequent voyage of part of the crew, in the ship's boat, from Tofoa, one of the Friendly Islands, to Timor, a Dutch settlement in the East Indies. The whole illustrated with charts, etc*. It was stated as being published by permission of the Lords Commissioners of the Admiralty and by the time it came out, Bligh had already embarked on his second breadfruit voyage.

INTERLUDE

Rough Seas and a dangerous landing place, showing Botany Bay, Pitcairn, in 1825, when HMS *Blossom* visited, some thirty years after *Bounty* came ashore at the same place.

Chapter 9

Fletcher Christian – From Tahiti to Pitcairn

Engraved portrait (1812) claiming to represent Fletcher Christian.

Right: **Plate 1.** William Bligh painted at the age of 60 in 1814 by Alexander Huey.

Below left: **Plate 2.** Elizabeth Bligh (née Betham) painted in 1802.

Below right: **Plate 3.** Bligh in his uniform of a rear admiral painted in 1814.

Plate 4. A ship's carpenter by Thomas Rowlandson. William Purcell, carpenter on the Bounty, probably looked rather more morose!

Right: **Plate 5.** Rowlandson's *The ship's cook*. In practice, Thomas Hall, cook on board the Bounty, was never a unidexter....

Below: **Plate 6.** An interesting anachronism. The picture shows the Polynesian islander Omai, in the centre, with William Bligh standing in the longbboat. Although Bligh was with Omai when he was returned home to Tahiti by Cook on his Third Voyage, Omai had died some ten years before Bligh returned to the island to collect the breadfruit. Islanders are shown planting the young trees in wooden containers.

Plate 7. *A view of the Cape of Good Hope, Taken on the Spot, from on Board the 'Resolution', Capt Cooke*. Painted by William Hodges in 1772.

Plate 8. A scene in Tahiti, 1769.

Plate 9. Elizabeth Bligh painted in 1782.

Plate 10. William Bligh painted in 1791.

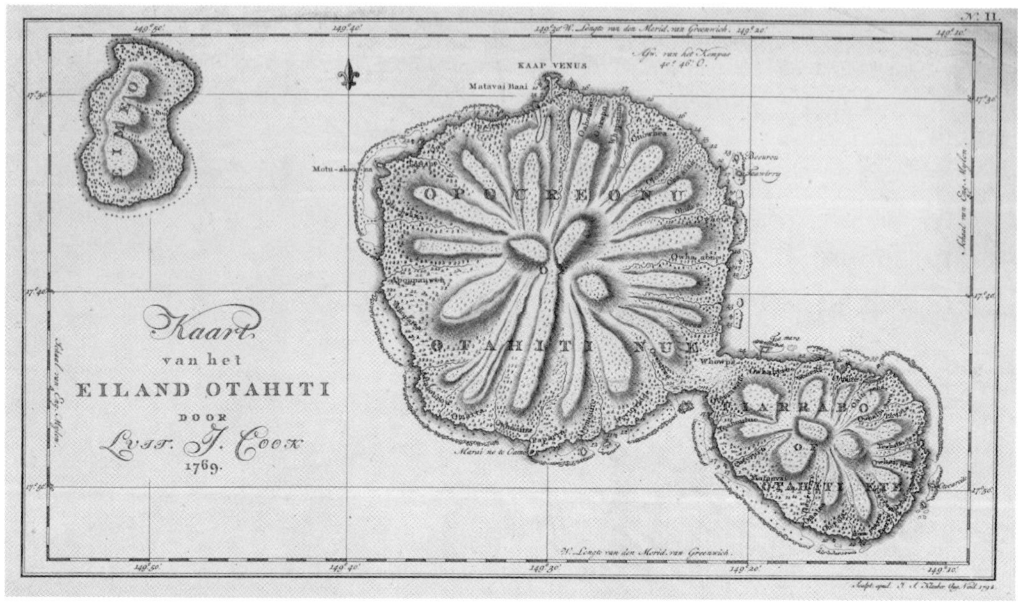

Plate 11. Chart of Tahiti drawn by James Cook in 1769.

Plate 12. Coconut trees, a cinnamon tree and a pinang tree in a tropical landscape.

Fletcher Christian. Aged 24 Years - feet In 5 - 9 High (Dark Swarthy Complexion

Complexion —— Dark & very swarthy

Hair —— Blackish or very dark brown

Make —— Strong

Marks —— Star tatowed on the left breast and tatowed on the backside. — His knees stands a little out, and may be called a little bow legged. He is subject to violent perspiration & particularly in His hands so that he soils any thing he handles.

George Stewart — Aged 23 — 5 In 7 High —

Complexion —— Good

Hair —— Dark

Make —— Slender & narrow chested & long Neck

Marks — Star on the left breast — one on the left Arm — tatowed on the backside — a heart with Darts on the left arm —— Small face & black eyes

Peter Haywood —— Aged 17 — 5 7

Complexion —— Fair

Hair —— light brown

Make —— well proportioned

Marks —— Very much tattowed and on the Right Leg is tattowed the Three legs of Man as that coin is. At this time he had not done growing — He speaks with the Manks or Isle of Man accent

Edward Young —— Aged 22. 5 8 High

Complexion —— Dark and a rather a bad look

Hair — Dark brown

Make —— Strong

Marks —— Lost several of his fore teeth & those that remain are all rotten. — A small mole on the left side of the throat and on the right arm is tatowed a heart & Dart through it with E.Y underneath and the date of the Year 1788 or 1789

Plate 13. A list of the mutineers as written out by William Bligh, in which he mentions Fletcher Christian's propensity to "violent perspiration".

Plate 14. Captain Peter Heywood, painted by John Simpson. For a convicted mutineer he did rather well for himself.

Plate 15. *The Great South Sea Caterpillar, transform'd into a Bath Butterfly* by James Gillray. It shows the head of Banks superimposed onto a butterfly arising out of the mud near the seashore. The 'Order of Bath' is pinned to his coat. Gillray is comparing Joseph Banks' rapid rise through the ranks of society to an insect which first 'crawl'd into notice from among the Weeds & Mud on the Banks of the South Sea; & being afterwards placed in a Warm Situation by the Royal Society…'

Plate 16. *'Germans Eating Sour-Kraut'* – a caricature by James Gillray. It wasn't just Germans who ate it – vast quantities of sauerkraut were taken on board ship by Bligh in the belief that it was a means of preventing scurvy. See pages 9–12.

Plate 17. Caricature entitled *The Delegates in Council or Beggars on Horseback*, showing the Nore mutineers, headed by Edward Parker (second from the right, wearing a hat and holding a blunderbuss) making their demands known to Admiral Bruckner (extreme left). Note the gaggle of six men under the tablecloth – identifiable as being opponents of the government and suggesting that leading politicians were behind the uprising, with Charles James Fox exclaiming 'We are at the bottom of it'.

Above: **Plate 18.** HMS *Hector* in Portsmouth Harbour. See chapter 11.

Left: **Plate 19.** Tiger cowrie or *Cypraea Tigris*. One of the many shells brought back by William Bligh as a way of keeping his beloved wife Betsey in touch with his distant travels. See chapter 13.

Plate 20. *Deux Tahitiennes* by Paul Gauguin, 1899. Perhaps more than anything else, it was the beauty and perceived promiscuity of the native Tahitian women which proved such a strong lure for Fletcher Christian and his fellow mutineers.

Plate 21. Portrait of William Bligh's married daughter Mary Putland, painted in 1803. See chapter 16.

Left: **Plate 22.** Silhouette of John Macarthur, nemesis of William Bligh, See chapter 16.

Above: **Plate 23.** Lt. Col. George Johnston painted in 1810.

Below: **Plate 24.** Government House, Sydney showing two guards and sentry box. See chapter 16.

Plate 25. Rowlandson's *Distress* gives some idea of the cramped conditions of survivors in a tiny boat in rough seas.

Plate 26. The tomb of William Bligh at Lambeth. Contrary to popular opinion, it isn't topped by a breadfruit!

Left: **Plate 27.** *The Botanic Macaroni* by M. Darly in 1772 representing Sir Jospeh Banks with magnifying glass and plant sketch in hand.

Below: **Plate 28.** *Sydney from the western side of the Cove* painted in around 1803 by GW Evans.

Plate 29. Portrait of Philip Gidley King (Bligh's predecessor as Governor of New South Wales) from around 1803. See chapter 16.

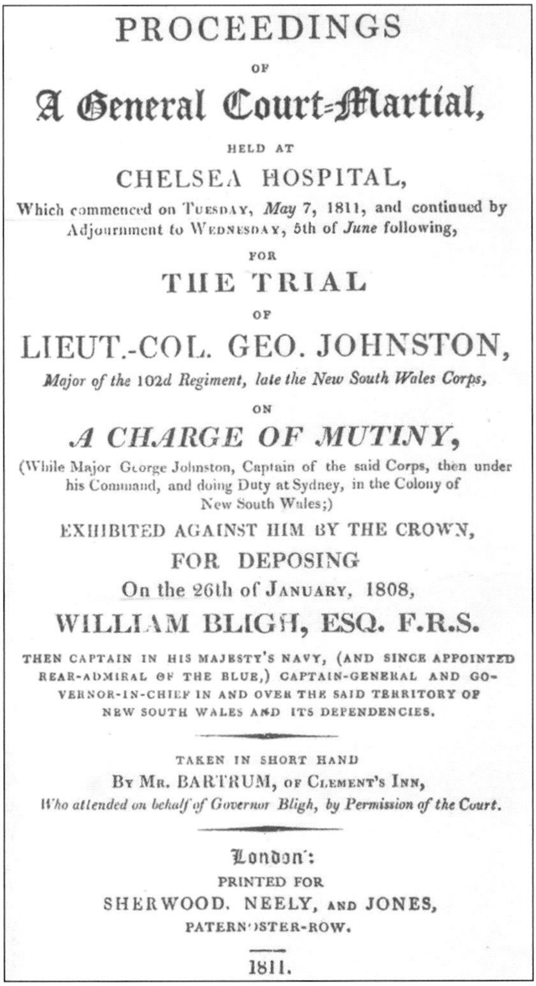

PROCEEDINGS

OF

A General Court-Martial,

HELD AT

CHELSEA HOSPITAL,

Which commenced on TUESDAY, *May* 7, 1811, and continued by Adjournment to WEDNESDAY, 5th of *June* following,

FOR

THE TRIAL

OF

LIEUT.-COL. GEO. JOHNSTON,

Major of the 102d *Regiment, late the New South Wales Corps,*

ON

A CHARGE OF MUTINY,

(While Major George Johnston, Captain of the said Corps, then under his Command, and doing Duty at Sydney, in the Colony of New South Wales;)

EXHIBITED AGAINST HIM BY THE CROWN,

FOR DEPOSING

On the 26th of JANUARY, 1808,

WILLIAM BLIGH, ESQ. F.R.S.

THEN CAPTAIN IN HIS MAJESTY'S NAVY, (AND SINCE APPOINTED REAR-ADMIRAL OF THE BLUE,) CAPTAIN-GENERAL AND GOVERNOR-IN-CHIEF IN AND OVER THE SAID TERRITORY OF NEW SOUTH WALES AND ITS DEPENDENCIES.

TAKEN IN SHORT HAND

BY MR. BARTRUM, OF CLEMENT'S INN,

Who attended on behalf of Governor Bligh, by Permission of the Court.

London:

PRINTED FOR

SHERWOOD, NEELY, AND JONES,

PATERNOSTER-ROW.

1811.

Plate 30. Proceedings of the Court Martial of Lt.-Col. George Johnston.

Plate 31. The London house where the Bligh family lived, at 100 Lambeth Road, Lambeth.

Plate 32. Film poster for the 1935 film *Mutiny on the Bounty*. (Public domain, per Wikipedia)

Up to this point, Fletcher Christian has merely been a passing figure in William Bligh's story, but it is worth looking at his own life. The first point to make is that he came from a well-off family. His father Charles was a senior judge on the Isle of Man known as a deemster – a position held by various family members. His family also had strong connections with an estate in Ireland. The surname 'Christian' was an Anglicisation of the Manx name McCrystyn. Charles was the son of John Christian, also a barrister, and one of his uncles was the High Sheriff of Cumberland. Their father, Ewan Christian, had apparently made sufficient money from gambling to be able to purchase a house called Ewanrigg at Dearham in Cumberland, together with the Lordship of the Manor. Writing in 1688 Mr Thomas Denton, the County Historian, said, 'Mr Ewan Christian hath built a good house out of the shell of an old tower,' which suggests it may originally have been an old look-out structure, known as a Pele tower. The walls of the tower were reputed to be over 5ft thick. Family money enabled the Christian family to embark on a total rebuild of the hall, converting it in 1753 into a spectacular stone-built house with views of the Solway Firth and the Scottish mountains beyond. The new building, built in the fashionable Palladian style, was impressive with eight good-sized bedrooms together with a large drawing room, a breakfast room and library.

This was where Christian's father Charles had been brought up – into a life of privilege and wealth. He went on to marry Ann Dixon at Brigham in Cumberland on 2 May 1751. She was from a prominent Cumberland family and the name 'Fletcher' was a tribute to Ann's maternal grandmother. Ann brought to the marriage a small but valuable property called Moorland Close, described as being 'a quadrangle pile of buildings … half castle, half farmstead'. They had a child, christened John, in 1752 and he eventually went on to be admitted to Lincoln's Inn in 1771 and hence was entitled to practice as a barrister. He was to prove to be the first of ten children born to Charles and Ann, but the next two died in infancy. There was to be a gap of six years before Ann gave birth to another son, Edward, who also went on to qualify as a barrister before becoming a Professor of Law at Cambridge University. In 1760 Ann gave birth to a daughter, Mary, who was to die at the age of 25 while living on the Isle of Man. A son, Charles, was born in July 1762 and he went on to qualify as a doctor and served as a surgeon in the Royal Navy.

At this point, it has to be said that the Christian family was both successful and well-connected, and when Fletcher Christian was born in

September1764 he might reasonably have been expected to follow his elder siblings into one of the professions, either legal or medical. But things were about to change. In 1766 Ann gave birth to a daughter, Frances, who lived for just a fortnight. Ann then gave birth to a son, Humphrey, who was baptised in December 1767. Ann must have been devastated when her husband died just three months later, on 11 March 1768, at the age of 38. Ann was now a widow with five young children on her hands, plus an elder son who, at that stage, was three years away from qualifying in his chosen profession.

By all accounts Ann was not good with handling finances and quickly ran up debts of £6,500 – a massive figure, equivalent nowadays to perhaps a million pounds. It may well have been the case that the extravagance of her elder children exacerbated the parlous state of her finances. During that time the 9-year-old Fletcher enrolled at Cockermouth Grammar School and he remained there until he was 16.

The creditors then pressed for payment. The family home at Moorland Close in Brigham was repossessed, and in 1779 Ann was forced to high-tail it to the Isle of Man to escape her creditors. Once there, English debts were unenforceable in what was a separate jurisdiction.

It cannot have been an easy childhood for Fletcher, losing his father before his fourth birthday; experiencing the family's descent into debt; witnessing his own prospects of a professional career disappear into the distance; and watching his mother forced to survive in 'genteel poverty' on a small annuity of £40 a year. It may well have given the young Fletcher Christian a somewhat jaundiced view about the importance of money. In turn, that may have influenced him when he subsequently encountered an idyllic life on Tahiti, where money and wealth were neither here nor there – no wonder that staying on a utopian Pacific island seemed a more attractive proposition than returning to a country where capitalism, consumerism and mercantile growth were all-important.

Fletcher accompanied his mother and younger siblings when they moved to the Isle of Man. He then joined the Royal Navy as a cabin boy 'of mature years' – he was 17, much older than most. Fletcher was promoted to midshipman on the HMS *Eurydice*, serving as acting lieutenant on a voyage back from the Indian city of Madras. He then left the Royal Navy and joined the merchant navy, serving under Bligh on board *Britannia* on a voyage to the West Indies. As already mentioned, this appointment probably resulted from the fact that Fletcher's family were friendly with the Betham's – Mrs Bligh's family – and the two families were neighbours in Douglas, on the Isle of Man.

One popular story is that in his late teens Fletcher was romantically linked with someone called Isabella Curwen, a rather good-looking girl who was heiress to her father's coal-mining fortune. By all accounts Isabella's immediate family felt that she could do better than marry Fletcher Christian, a young man with few prospects, and she came under pressure to ditch Fletcher and marry another, altogether more successful, cousin by the name of John Christian. The rejection left Fletcher devastated. If the story is true, it is another case of unrequited love to add to the misery of parental death and general insecurity which have to be considered when evaluating Fletcher Christian's later actions. It might also explain why, when Fletcher eventually married a girl called Maimiti on Tahiti, he generally called her Isabella, after his first love.

It would have been a lesson to Fletcher that his wealthier cousin John was able to secure the affections of Isabella, whereas he was not considered suitable 'marriage material' because of his lack of prospects. Quite possibly, this failed romance was what finally triggered the later mutiny – Christian had simply fallen in love when he reached Tahiti, and this was his chance to make a go of things, away from family pressures and expectations. In Tahiti his lack of wealth and high status counted for nothing.

On his second voyage under Bligh to the West Indies, Christian was made up to second mate and it is clear that he was a popular individual. His own attitude towards authority and discipline is perhaps revealed in a comment he apparently made to his brother Edward:

> It was very easy to make one's self beloved and respected aboard a ship; one had only to be always ready to obey one's superior officers, and to be kind to the common men, unless there was occasion for severity, and if you are, when there is a just occasion, they will not like you the worse for it.

Years later, after the court martial which followed the mutiny, other members of the crew, including Bligh loyalists, came out with comments about Christian such as: 'He was a gentleman; a brave man; and every officer and seaman on board the ship would have gone through fire and water to serve him.' That may be a slight exaggeration – after all, at least twenty people on the *Bounty* chose *not* to go through fire and water with him. But others commented: 'Every body under his command did their duty at a look from Mr Christian' – while another described Christian as perpetually good natured, adding: 'I never heard him say "Damn you", to any man on board the ship.'

To modern ears, 'Damn you' is a meaningless and even trivial expression, whereas in the eighteenth century it was a form of swearing which could shock and offend. Indeed, it was an expression which William Bligh used regularly – often with devastating effect.

It is apparent that, despite the disappointments of his earlier life, Christian was cheerful and popular, even if subsequent events show that he was no charismatic leader of men. What comes across is a man who had not appreciated that 'you cannot hunt with the hounds and run with the fox'. He was either an officer, required to give orders and see them carried out, or he was one of the crew and just did as he was told. The navy was not asking him to be popular, they were asking him to obey orders.

The problem with the mutiny was that it was badly thought out – no one had considered 'what happens next?' For many of the mutineers they thought no further than their next meal – and the next native girl they could take to bed. It was not the first time women had led sailors astray – when Captain Cook was planning to leave Tahiti in late 1769, two members of *Endeavour*'s crew decided to desert, having 'strongly attache'd themselves' to two girls, though Cook recovered them. But Christian didn't just desert, he had seized government property. Technically, this was not piracy but 'barratry', a crime defined as any unlawful act that injured the interests of the ship's owners. The crime invariably carried the death penalty. More to the point, every mutineer must have realised that whatever their distance from far-off London, there was no way that the Admiralty were going to sit back and say, 'What a shame, we have lost our ship'; instead, they would do their utmost to track down the fugitives and bring them to justice. For the rest of their lives they would be marked men.

Initially the mutineers thought that going straight to Tahiti was a bit too obvious: instead, they sailed for the island of Tubuai, some 350 miles to the south. There they found the native islanders hostile and unwilling to trade goods for food. More awkwardly, the islanders were not willing to share their women with the mutineers. Soon there were complaints that Christian and his closest cronies always got preferential treatment and, amid mounting tensions, the decision was made to sail for Tahiti and to try to get further supplies – both of food and of women. And so it was that after seven days of Tubuai friction, *Bounty* sailed for Tahiti, reaching the island on 6 June. Just ten days later, Christian married Maimiti.

The ship returned to Tubuai with pigs, chickens, goats and various foodstuffs and, most significantly, with nine Tahitian women and a young girl, along with eight Tahitian men and three boys. For the next two and half months, the mutineers struggled to build a community, despite open hostility from the locals. The men constructed an earth fort for protection, which they named Fort George, and at this stage it was apparent that Christian held the position of leader of the group. On one occasion, he returned to the ship from Fort George to find that two of the men, John Sumner and Matthew Quintal, had spent the night onshore. According to the account by Morrison, he called for them and asked how they came to be on shore without leave.

> Their reply was that 'the ship was moored and we are now our own masters'. Hearing this, Christian clapped a pistol (which he always kept in his pocket) to one of their heads and said: 'I'll let you know who is master' and ordered them both to be put in irons. This resolute behaviour convinced them that he was not to be played with, and when they were brought up the next day, they begged pardon and promised to behave better in the future, on which they were released.

The mutineers soon realised that they could never be self-sufficient when the other islanders refused to barter. Far better to abandon Tubuai, head back to Tahiti where they would be among friends, and then decide where to go next. They sailed *Bounty* back to Tahiti, arriving in the middle of September. Nineteen men on board, including all of the Bligh loyalists who had been unable to get into the longboat, wanted to stay on Tahiti. For the loyalists, it meant hoping that they would be rescued by the Royal Navy. For the mutineers, they hoped to be able to hide away and live out of sight of any pursuers. They were each set ashore after being given a musket and seventeen pounds of powder.

Some wanted to sail on to pastures new, where no one would find them, and so, on 21 September 1789, Christian, with eight of the mutineers, decided to search for an island which had been discovered some twenty-two years previously, named Pitcairn Island. The name honoured Robert Pitcairn, the young sailor who had first sighted it. He had been serving on board Captain Philip Carteret's ship HMS *Swallow* on its voyage of circumnavigation in 1767. Carteret had described the island as appearing:

> like a great rock rising out of the sea: it was not more than five miles in circumference, and seemed to be uninhabited; It was however, covered with trees, and we saw a small stream of fresh water running down one side of it. I would have landed upon it, but the surf, which at this season broke upon it with great violence, rendered it impossible.

Bligh had a copy of Carteret's book and it was included in the possessions which he was forced to abandon when the mutiny occurred. Christian, on reading the book, realised that this was an ideal place to search out, because in the days before a means of measuring longitude accurately had been discovered, the island had been misplaced on the naval maps. The latitude was known, and Christian correctly surmised that if he sailed along that latitude, zig-zagging east and west, he would eventually find his island paradise.

After months of searching, Christian rediscovered the island on 15 January 1790, some 188 nautical miles east of its recorded position. Christian must have been delighted at his find – it would certainly mean that the Royal Navy would be unlikely to be able to find them and, as events turned out, it was to be another eighteen years before the next ship called on the islands, when the American sealing ship *Topaz* visited in 1808.

But Christian and the nine mutineers were not the only people on board. Quite possibly as a result of being duped into thinking that they were being taken on a sight-seeing cruise around Matavai Bay, *Bounty* also had on board a dozen Tahitian women (including Christian's wife Maimiti), along with a young girl called Sarah who was accompanying her mother. There were also half a dozen men, a mixed group of Polynesians drawn from local islands. Many of these were unaware of Christian's real plan and they were simply kidnapped, taken prisoner in order to be of subsequent use to the mutineers.

The party heading for Pitcairn therefore consisted of the following:

The Europeans
Fletcher Christian
Ned Young
John Adams – originally known as Alexander Smith
Matthew Quintal
William Brown – known as Billy
Isaac Martin/Madden
John Mills/Main
John Williams – known as Jack
William McCoy – known as Bill

The Polynesian men

Menalee/Minarii	}
Nehou/Niuha	} from Tahiti
Te Moa	}
Tetahiti	}
Oher/Hu	} from Tubuai
Tarara	} from Raiatea

The Tahitian women
Maimiti ('Isabella') – married to Fletcher Christian and subsequently partner of Ned Young.

Teehuteatuaonoa ('Jenny') – partner of Isaac Martin.

Teraura ('Susanah') – consort of Ned Young.

Teio ('Mary') – consort of William McCoy and the fifth and final partner of John Adams.

Vahineatua/Bal'hadi ('Prudence') – partner of John Mills, and ultimately fourth consort of John Adams.

Obuarei/Puarai' – second of five consorts of John Adams.

Tevarua ('Sarah') – consort of Matthew Quintal

Teatuahitea ('Sarah') – consort of William Brown

Faahotu ('Fasto') – partner of John Williams.

Toofaiti/Hutia ('Nancy'), firstly, consort of Tarara, secondly, partner of Ned Young.

Mareva – shared between the two spare Tahitians.

Tinafornea – shared between the two Tubuains, and subsequently taken by John Adams.

Bounty landed on Pitcairn in mid-January 1790. Fearful of leaving any trace which might help the Royal Navy locate their whereabouts, and anxious to prevent anyone trying to escape, the settlers discussed torching *Bounty* after everything of value to the new settlers had been taken ashore. In the event, there was a lack of unanimity about literally 'burning their boat', until one of the men, Matthew Quintal, took matters into his own hands and set the ship ablaze. In fact, Quintal must have been just about the worst person with whom one could wish to be stranded on a remote island. He was a racist and a bully, forcing the islanders to work as slaves. When his companion William McCoy devised a way of distilling an alcoholic brew using the roots from one of the native plants, Quintal joined him in being permanently drunk.

To begin with, the burning of the boat must have given the new arrivals a sense of purpose: they had no choice but to try to make a success of what they had. They shared a common goal – clearing ground, planting crops, constructing shelters. But it quickly became apparent that the whole basis of their society was based on the idea of the supremacy of the Europeans – every mutineer had his Polynesian consort, whereas the six Polynesian men only had three to choose from. The Europeans were often too lazy to undertake manual labour, forcing the Tahitians to do all the hard work. There developed a seething resentment between the two groups – not helped when Fletcher Christian seemed to become more taciturn and weighed down by the enormity of his situation. He no longer tried to exert a role as leader, preferring to sit in solitude with his thoughts.

Many years later an article appeared in the *Sydney Gazette* of 17 July 1819 featuring an interview with Jenny (otherwise Teehuteatuaonoa) under the heading of *Account of the Mutineers of the Ship Bounty, and their Descendants at Pitcairn's Island*. She had originally been the partner of Adam Smith, but later switched to become the consort of Isaac Madden. The article quotes her as saying:

> The island is small; has but one mountain, which is not high but flat, and fit for cultivation. They put up temporary houses of the leaves of the tea, and afterwards more durable ones thatched with the palm, as at Tahiti. They found the bread fruit there, and all were busily engaged in planting yams, taro, plantains, and aute, of which they made cloth. They made small canoes, and caught many fish. They climbed the precipices of the mountain, and got birds and eggs in abundance.

She went on to explain:

> In the meantime many children were born. Christian had a daughter Mary; and two sons, Charley and Friday. John Main had two children, Betsy and John. Bill McCoy had Sam and Kate. Neddy Young had no children by his own wife; but by Tarara, the wife of the Raiatean, he had three sons, George, Robert, and William. Matt has had five children, Matt, Jenny, Arthur, Sarah, and a young one that died when seven days old. Adam Smith has Dinah, Eliza, Hannah, and George, by his wife. The Tahitians have left no children. Jack Williams's wife died of a scrophulous disease, which broke out in her neck. The Europeans took the three women belonging to the natives, Toofaiti, Mareva, and Tinafornea, and cast lots for them, and the lot falling upon Toofaiti, she was taken from Tarara, and given to Jack Williams. Tarara wept at parting with his wife, and was very angry. He studied revenge, but was discovered and Oher and him were shot.

From then on, things really got messy. In 1793, just three years after arriving at Pitcairn, matters reached a head on what became known as Massacre Day – 20 September. The Polynesian men, fed up with being treated as slaves and at having their women stolen by the Europeans, got hold of muskets and embarked on a plan to kill all the remaining Englishmen. They caught and decapitated Isaac Martin and John Mills, shot John Williams and William Brown dead, and are thought to have shot Christian while he was working in the fields. He was probably finished off with an axe blow.

Following this, three of the women took revenge, killing Te Moa and Nehou. The spate of killings then led Teraura, the wife of Ned Young, to behead Tetahiti while he slept.

That still left the brutish Matthew Quintal and his drinking buddy McCoy alive – they escaped the massacre by hiding in the hills. While in hiding they were joined by Menalee but a violent fight broke out in which the Tahitian was killed.

One story goes that the unpleasant and violent Quintal later bit the ear off his consort Tevarua in a drunken rage, because she had failed to catch enough fish. By the end of 1793, Tevarua is believed to have slipped and fallen to her death while collecting bird's eggs, but another version of the story is that she committed suicide by throwing herself off a cliff.

That left Quintal without a partner, and he simply decided that he would take Maimiti, Christian's widow, as his bed-mate. Maimiti – and her children – were horrified, but Quintal met his just deserts when Ned Young and John Adams decided to combine forces to murder him. He was invited round to Young's house, where they killed him with an axe.

As for McCoy, the effects of drinking his home-made hootch was all too apparent. He suffered from attacks of delirium tremens and supposedly, during one of those attacks, he tied a rock round his neck and jumped to his death off a cliff.

What all this carnage meant was that the island community, thriving with young children, was reduced to two adult males (Young and Adams) and a handful of women, headed by Maimiti. Edward Young died during an asthma attack in 1800 leaving John Adams as the sole surviving male. Fortunately for the tiny community, Young had been ill for long enough for Adams, barely able to read and write, to realize that the burden of male leadership was bound to pass to him. He also realised the importance of literacy and therefore took lessons from the ailing Edward Young. It meant that when Young died, Adams was able to turn to the Bible and give his 'flock' lessons based on the Scriptures. The rest of the community accepted Christianity, albeit alongside their island beliefs. And so they survived, with successive generations of children marrying and having more children, largely undisturbed by the outside world.

Adams had had a tough upbringing, in the London borough of Hackney, His father was a lighterman, but he died when John was 3 years old and he was brought up in the poorhouse, where he had the most rudimentary of educations. When he signed up for the *Bounty* he used the alias of

'Smith' – suggesting that he had previously been in trouble with the authorities.

Bligh had described Adams as 'being: '22 years, 5 feet 5 inches high. Brown complexion, brown hair, strong made, pitted with smallpox. Very much tattooed, scar on right foot.' His nickname of 'Reckless Jack' suggests an impulsive character who had learnt to be resilient on the tough streets of London. Was his subsequent conversion into a devoted Christian a smoke screen for his past villainy? Probably not, as evidenced by the behaviour of his charges on Pitcairn. If he had merely been paying lip-service, it is hard to see how he would have inspired such devotion from his followers. And after all, there was every reason why he should have given heartfelt thanks for being spared, after so much bloodshed, and when every single other mutineer had died within ten years of the mutiny.

It must have been a surprise to the captain of the American vessel *Topaz* when she called in at Pitcairn in early 1808, the first to visit the island since it was settled by the mutineers. The captain, Mayhew Folger, encountered a deeply religious community speaking in a mixture of English (spoken with a pronounced North-country accent) and Tahitian. So it was that *Topaz* eventually brought news to the world as to the fate of the *Bounty* mutineers – 'eventually', because it was not until October 1808 that Folger reached his destination of Valparaiso and was able to inform a Royal Navy representative. The news was passed on to the Admiralty on 14 May, 1809, but it was to be another year before the general public was told about the discovery. At that stage Bligh was still in New South Wales (see chapter 16).

Adams lived on, no doubt fearing that the Admiralty would send a further ship to capture him and bring him to face justice. In the event, the Admiralty did no such thing. Perhaps his devout Christian beliefs helped persuade the authorities that punishment was not appropriate. Six years after the *Topaz* visit, the British warships *Briton* and *Tagus* stopped at the island and the commanders allowed Adams to remain as patriarch presiding over a community of just over forty individuals. The community included seven of the original female settlers and nearly three dozen youngsters. Captain Philip Pipon of the *Tagus* had this to say about his meeting with Adams and of his impression of the islanders:

> When old Adams learned we had landed without arms and were not come to seize his person, [he] met us on the road and conducted us to his house; his wife accompanied him, a

> very old woman, blind with age. They were at first extremely alarmed lest our visit was intended against him, but as we observed to him we were not even aware of his being then living and that we had no intention of that nature…
>
> There is no debauchery here, no immoral conduct, and Adams informed me there is not one instance of any young woman having proved unchaste. The men appear equally moral and well behaved and from every information there has not appeared any inclination to seduction on the part of the young men as many of them assured me they wait patiently till they have acquired sufficient property to marry, and then if a proper choice is made Adams performs the marriage ceremony
>
> What delighted me most … was the manner with which John Adams had impressed on their minds the necessity of propriety of returning thanks to the Almighty for the many blessings they enjoy. They invariably say Grace before and after meals and frequently repeat their prayers.

Pipon was presumably told by Adams that he had nothing to do with the actual mutiny, hence his comment: '[Adams] was the only surviving Englishman that came away in the Bounty. He was not by his own account in the smallest degree concerned in the mutiny he being, at the time it happened, sick in bed.'

On another occasion Adams merely said that he was asleep, but in either case it is clearly incorrect: Adams was with Christian when the latter went to Coleman to demand the keys to the arms chest. And as Bligh himself later wrote when describing how he was arrested: 'Alexander Smith [i.e. Adams] … assisted under arms on the outside.' Adams was not one of the main leaders, but he certainly played an active part in the mutiny and was no doubt keen to play down his role at a time when it was far from certain that he would escape punishment.

Pipon also recorded conversations with old man Adams about Fletcher Christian:

> It appears that this unfortunate and ill-fated young man was never happy after the rash and inconsiderate step he had taken, but always sullen and morose … this moroseness however led him to many acts of cruelty and inhumanity which soon

> was the cause of his incurring the hatred and detestation of his companions here … and as we have every reason to suppose sensuality and a passion for the females of Otaheite chiefly instigated him to the rash step he had taken, so it is readily to be believed he would not live long on the island without a female companion, consequently after the demise of his wife he forcibly seized on one belonging to one of the Otaheitan men and took her to live with him; this exasperated them to a degree of madness. Open war was declared and every opportunity sought to take away his life and it was effected whilst digging in his own field. It is surprising he should not have been more upon his guard, for he was well aware of the hatred and enmity of all the blacks or Otaheite men. Thus terminated the miserable existence of this deluded young man, whose connexions in Westmorland were extremely respectable and who did not want talents and capacity to have become an ornament to his profession had he adopted another line of conduct.

In practice, this version of events transposes different people – it was not Christian's wife Maimiti who died. She outlived him and subsequently became the partner of Edward Young and bore him three children, Edward, Polly and Dorothea. It was the consort of John Williams who had died, but it was a joint decision by the European men that Williams should therefore be allowed to take a 'wife' away from the Tahitians. This was a decision repeated after Puarai died, and the Europeans decided that the widower, John Adams, should take as a wife Tinafanaea, the consort of the Tubuains, Titahiti and Oha. The sexual tensions and inequalities, more than anything else, were responsible for the subsequent disaster.

What impressed Pipon was how Europeanised and settled everything appeared:

> Their habitations are extremely neat, infinitely superior to what we saw at the Marquesas Islands. The little Village at Pitcairn forms a pretty Square. John Adams occupies the houses at the upper end & Thursday October Christian opposite him.
>
> The centre is a fine Lawn where the Poultry wander, but is fenced in so as to prevent the intrusion of Hogs &c. It was

> easily to be perceived that in this establishment, the labour & ingenuity of European hands had been exerted.

The settlement, still known as Adamstown, is famous nowadays for being one of the smallest capital cities in the world, with a population of less than fifty souls. Pipon added:

> The colony is now in a most flourishing state, having abundance of hogs, goats and Poultry. Of vegetables and fruit very fine yams plantains sweet potatoes turnips with breadfruit cocoa nuts bananas etc in that, as Adams expressed himself, they have every luxury to render life easy and comfortable.

When HMS *Tagus* and HMS *Briton* departed in 1815, reassuring Adams that the Admiralty were not going to come after him, life settled down on the island. It was to be another ten years before their next visitor arrived, a Captain Beechey on board HMS *Blossom*. His mission was to help resupply a land-based search for the Northwest Passage being led by John Franklin, at the same time as William Edward Parry was trying to chart the area by sea westward from Prince Regent Inlet. Beechey arrived at Pitcairn in December 1825 and was astonished to be met by young men eagerly rowing out in canoes to greet them. As Beechey described it:

> The activity of the young men outstripped that of old Adams, who was consequently almost the last to greet us. He was in his sixty-fifth year, and was unusually strong and active for his age, notwithstanding the inconvenience of considerable corpulency. He was dressed in a sailor's shirt and trousers and a low-crowned hat, which he instinctively held in his hand until desired to put it on. He still retained his sailor's gait, doffing his hat and smoothing down his bald forehead whenever he was addressed by the officers.

Beechey was intrigued by what the islanders were wearing:

> Their dress, made up of the presents which had been given them by the masters and seamen of merchant ships, was a perfect caricature. Some had on long black coats without

> any other article of dress except trousers, some shirts without coats, and others waistcoats without either; none had shoes or stockings, and only two possessed hats, neither of which seemed likely to hang long together.

Beechey obviously felt that after such a length of time since the mutiny, Adams had no particular axe to grind. The journal continues:

> it is satisfactory to show, that those who suffered by the sentence of the court-martial were convicted upon evidence which is now corroborated by the statement of an accomplice who has no motive for concealing the truth. The following account is compiled almost entirely from Adams' narrative….
>
> But to render the narrative more complete, I have added such additional facts as were derived from the inhabitants, who are perfectly acquainted with every incident connected with the transaction. In presenting it to the public, I vouch, only, for its being a correct statement of the abovementioned authorities.

Beechey referred to the events leading up to the mutiny, stating that:

> The officers, it must be admitted, had much more cause for dissatisfaction than the seamen, especially the master and Mr Christian. The latter was a protege of Lieutenant Bligh, and unfortunately was under some obligations to him of a pecuniary nature, of which Bligh frequently reminded him when any difference arose. Christian, excessively annoyed at the share of blame which repeatedly fell to his lot, in common with the rest of the officers, could ill endure the additional taunt of private obligations.

This was apparently a reference to the fact that in Cape Town, en route to Tahiti, Bligh had supposedly lent money to Christian. Given that sailors were traditionally paid at the end of the voyage, and not before, Christian would have had no means of repaying the debt before the voyage ended and it would have rankled if Bligh constantly made reference to the debt.

As for the events of the night leading up to the mutiny, Beechey states that the mutiny was not Christian's idea – he merely wanted to escape on a makeshift raft, taking with him a lead weight so that he could be sure of drowning himself if the raft failed to find land. In Beechey's words:

> A raft was soon constructed, various useful articles were got together, and he was on the point of launching it, when a young officer, who afterwards perished in the Pandora, to whom Christian communicated his intention, recommended him, rather than risk his life on so hazardous an expedition, to endeavour to take possession of the ship, which he thought would not be very difficult, as many of the ship's company were not well disposed towards the commander, and would all be very glad to return to Otaheite, and reside among their friends in that island. This daring proposition is even more extraordinary than the premeditated scheme of his companion, and, if true, certainly relieves Christian from part of the odium which has hitherto attached to him as the sole instigator of the mutiny.

This suggests that the mutinous idea was suggested by Stewart, who did indeed perish on the *Pandora*, but it may help explain why the plan was so poorly thought out. As for the involvement of Adams, Beechey went on to say:

> Adams was sleeping in his hammock, when Sumner, one of the seamen, came to him, and whispered that Christian was going to take the ship from her commander, and set him and the master on shore. On hearing this, Adams went upon deck, and found everything in great confusion; but not then liking to take any part in the transaction, he returned to his hammock, and remained there until he saw Christian at the arm-chest, distributing arms to all who came for them; and then seeing measures had proceeded so far, and apprehensive of being on the weaker side, he turned out again and went for a cutlass.

Beechey went on to confirm the narrative of the mutiny and of the subsequent trials and tribulations of the mutineers, pointing out that killing, and being killed, was 'the melancholy fate of seven of the leading mutineers, who escaped from justice only to add murder to their former crimes; for though some of them may not have actually imbrued their hands in the blood of their fellow-creatures, yet all were accessary to the deed.'

Beechey did not stay long on the island – long enough to conduct a marriage ceremony for Adams and Teio, his fifth and final partner. Adams died on the island in 1829 but not until he had given a number of conflicting accounts of the manner in which Fletcher Christian had died. One version suggested that he had committed suicide, another that he was shot, another that he was killed with an axe. Perhaps these differences helped encourage the story that these accounts were simply a cover for the truth: that Fletcher Christian had not in fact died, but had managed to effect an escape, cadging a lift on an unspecified vessel, ending up in Britain some years later. Various people, who had known him in his youth, attested to the fact that they had seen Christian in Plymouth, and in the North of England. Nothing has appeared to substantiate these rumours and they have to be seen as just about as credible as sightings of Adolf Hitler and Lord Lucan in the years after their disappearance in the Twentieth Century. Conspiracy theorists will always present such theories in the absence of anyone finding the skeletal remains of the deceased. Meanwhile, it has to be said that it is hard to see how someone as notorious as Fletcher Christian could possibly have made his way undetected across tens of thousands of miles of ocean without anyone realising who he was. Far more likely that he was killed in the orgy of murders which marked his poor leadership and the group's blatant racism and sexism. Those were the things which ultimately caused the Pitcairn experiment to fail so disastrously.

Chapter 10

Pandora – and Pandora's Box

The wreck of HMS *Pandora.*

News of the mutiny on HMS *Bounty* had preceded Bligh's return to England in March 1790. He was initially feted as a hero, and by August the Admiralty had made the decision to send a vessel to capture *Bounty* and to bring her rebellious crew back for trial. They chose HMS *Pandora* for the purpose. Launched in May 1779, *Pandora* was a Porcupine-class sixth-rate post ship; when she set sail in November 1790 she had a complement of 134 men – intended to be sufficient to man HMS *Bounty* once she had been captured. On board was Thomas Hayward, the man who had accompanied Bligh in his boat trip after the mutiny. Command of HMS *Pandora* had been given to Captain Edward Edwards, a man renowned for being a disciplinarian. He had previously been in charge of HMS *Narcissus* when a mutiny had broken out, following which eight of his crewmen were hanged. In the intervening eight years he had not received a single commission but it looks as though his experience exactly fitted the Admiralty's brief. His orders were clear: capture the mutineers and bring them back alive so that they could be brought to trial. The navy was not concerned with niceties such as how he was to treat the mutineers – he was to detain them and keep them alive, but above all bring them home so that an example could be made of them. To the Admiralty it was quite inconceivable that the men should be left alone, unpunished, in their Polynesian isolation. Nothing, but nothing, should distract Edwards from his mission, so there were no instructions to map unknown lands, no botanists onboard to collect and record flora, no missionaries to try to educate the natives….

Pandora reached Tahiti on 23 March 1791, travelling via Cape Horn. At that stage there were fourteen survivors of the mutiny living on the island, Charles Churchill having been murdered by Matthew Thompson – and Thompson, in turn, having been killed by islanders. As already mentioned, the other mutineers had followed Fletcher to a then unknown destination and the fourteen survivors on Tahiti had been living as beachcombers. Many of them had families with local women. It was known that some of the fourteen were not mutineers, but had simply been forced to stay onboard because of lack of space in the longboat. As it transpired, four of the survivors were not mutineers, but Captain Edwards was taking no chances – his aim was to seize all survivors and bring them home.

Several of the men surrendered immediately; others disappeared into the hills and had to be hunted down, and three men tried to use a somewhat unseaworthy vessel which they had built and named *Resolution*, to sail out to *Pandora*. The problem with *Resolution*, 30ft long, was that she had been constructed in difficult circumstances, with inadequate materials and tools. Specifically, there was a shortage of Tahitian wood with which to build her and even more significantly, there was no sail-cloth on the island and the woven matting used in lieu was simply not up to the job. However, Captain Edwards could see the value of an additional launch, even though she was described as 'crank and little seaworthy', and ordered repairs to be made to *Resolution*, renaming her *Matavy* and intending to use her as a ship's tender.

By 8 May 1791 *Pandora* was ready to set sail in search of Fletcher Christian and his followers. The fourteen men captured on Tahiti had been placed in a circular wooden cage specially constructed for that purpose on the main deck and named, not surprisingly, 'Pandora's Box'. The structure was described by James Morrison, one of the survivors:

> The Poop or Roundhouse being finish'd, we were Convey'd into it and put in Irons … This Place we Stiled Pandoras Box, the entrance being a Scuttle on the top of 18 or 20 inches Square, Secured by a bolt on the top thro' the Coamings, two Scuttles of nine inches square in the Bulk head for air with Iron Grates, and the Stern ports barr'd inside and out with Iron; the Centrys were placed on the top while the Midshipman walk'd across by the Bulk head. The length of this Box was 11 feet upon deck and 18 wide at the Bulk head, and here no person was suffered to speak to us but the Master at Arms, and His orders were not to speak to us on any score but that of our provisions.

Conditions were appalling. Morrison continued:

> The Heat of the place when it was calm was so intense that the Sweat frequently ran in Streams to the Scuppers, and produced Maggots in a short time; the Hammocks being dirty when we got them, we found stored with Vermin of another kind, which we had no Method of erradicating but by lying on the Plank; and tho our Freinds would have supplyd us with plenty of Cloth they were not permitted to do it, and our only remedy was to lay Naked, – these troublesome Neighbours and the two necessary tubbs [i.e. barrels used as toilets] which were Constantly kept in the place help'd to render our situation truely disagreeable.

Morrison explained that in the days prior to their leaving Tahiti, their families came out to the ship: 'During the time we staid, the Weomen with whom we had cohabited on the Island Came frequently under the Stern (bringing their Children of which there were six born, Four Girls & two Boys, & several of the Weomen big with Child).' He went on to explain that the women showed their grief by slashing their faces with sharp shell pieces 'till the Blood discolloured the water about them, their Female friends acting their part also and making bitter lamentations'.

Captain Edwards then spent three months zig-zagging around the south-west Pacific searching for HMS *Bounty*. All this time, the prisoners were kept shackled. Morrison later wrote:

> It being Customary for the Officer of the Watch to examine our Irons before he was releived, McIntosh happening to have a large Shackle had got one of his legs out in the Night, which was reported to the Captain and a general examination took place, when the leg Irons were reduced to fit close, and Mr Larkan the First Lieut. in trying the Handcuffs took the Method of setting his foot against our breasts and hauling the Handcuffs over our hands with all his Might, some of which took the Skin off with them, and all that could be haul'd off by this Means were reduced, and fitted so close, that there was no possibility of turning the Hand in them, and when our wrists began to swell he told us that 'they were not intended to fit like Gloves'.

George Hamilton, the surgeon on board *Pandora*, had a rather more rose-tinted view of conditions for the prisoners. He reported:

> A prison was built for their accommodation on the quarter deck, that they might be secure, and [kept] apart from our ship's company; and that it might have every advantage of a free circulation of air, which rendered it the most desirable place in the ship. Orders were likewise given that they should be victualled, in every respect in the same as the ship's company, both in meat, liquor, and all the extra indulgencies with which we were so liberally supplied, notwithstanding the established laws of the service, which restricts prisoners to two-thirds allowance: but Captain Edwards very humanely commiserated with their unhappy and inevitable length of confinement.

To begin with during the search, in uncharted waters, the captain chose to anchor up at night and to send *Matavy* ahead to scout out the route and to make sure that there were no shallows or hidden reefs. There was an agreed means of signalling between the two vessels and the intention was that at daybreak *Pandora* would sail to catch up with *Matavy*, reprovisioning the crew on a daily basis. However, on reaching Tutuila (nowadays the main island of American Samoa) in the last week of June 1791 the two vessels got separated. The nine men on board *Matavy* had no choice but to head off for the agreed rendezvous point of Anamooka, even though they had no charts, no proper provisions and hardly any fresh water. Their story is told by David Thomas Renouard, Midshipman on *Pandora* and transcribed by James R. Galloway on the *Fateful Voyage* website at Whalesite.org.

It is an interesting account, partly because the story happened as a direct consequence of the mutiny on the *Bounty*, and partly because it echoes Bligh's own voyage in an open boat. Renouard's journey was no less remarkable for having duplicated much of Bligh's journey, but it does show the extraordinary hardship faced by seamen exploring distant lands in the eighteenth century. Thirst and extreme hunger nearly finished off the nine crewmen as they frantically searched for their 'mother ship'.

Renouard recounts how *Matavy* came across hostile islanders who spent their time either threatening them or harassing them by stealing whatever they could lay their hands on. The crew were making do with just one gill (a quarter of a pint) of water per day and on reaching what they thought was Anamooka they waited in vain for *Pandora* to come into view. It was hardly their fault that they were waiting on the wrong island – Tofooa, where the natives were described as being amicable and 'the islands abounded in hogs, yams, bread fruit and sugar canes'. In reality they were moored up 'not many leagues to the East of Anamooka', in what were then called the Friendly Isles (now the island group of Tonga). They waited three weeks before abandoning all hope of ever seeing *Pandora* again and therefore embarked on an extraordinarily dangerous trip, heading for the Dutch settlements in what is now Indonesia. In Renouard's words:

> In our situation if a spirit of discontent or insubordination had manifested itself among our sailors, our case would have been desperate indeed, as it was by our united efforts only, that we could ever reasonably expect to surmount the difficulties we had to combat … As we had experienced great inconvenience and even some degree of danger from the clumsiness of our large sprit sails, we altered them, and rigged our little bark, after the manner of a schooner which answered infinitely better. Having taken in a sufficient proportion of yams to last on an average near 3 months, besides a number of Hogs and

> provender for them, with sundry other necessaries; we took leave of our copper colored friends, & set sail from the Friendly Islands on the 1st August 1791.

An estimated 3,000 miles of open ocean awaited them as they managed to avoid being drawn on to the Great Barrier Reef, then steered north of Cape York, through Torres Strait and into the hideously dangerous waters of Endeavour Strait, separating the northern coast of Australia from Prince of Wales Island. In Renouard's words:

> Our destruction seemed unavoidable; when in this moment of peril, that power, by which we had hitherto been so signally protected, rescued us from a watery grave; for the wind veering near a point in our favour we cleared the weathermost part of the reef, & found ourselves in smooth water, when we brought up for the night.
>
> So dangerous & intricate is the navigation of these straits, that we were buffeting about a whole week, before we had completely cleared them. Our passage was impeded by numerous shoals, sandy keys, and small islands, under shelter of which we generally brought up during the night.

After covering roughly one hundred miles a day, the small boat reached the island of Timor, but in doing so had overshot the settlement at Coupang. The crew carried on until they reached a Dutch settlement, which they called Cherebay, on the island of Java. Here the local Governor had already heard of the mutiny on *Bounty* and mistook the *Matavy* crew for the 'missing' nine mutineers (that is to say, Fletcher Christian and his followers who had disappeared into the vastness of the Pacific). As Renouard put it: 'The appearance of our vessel built entirely of Otaheitan wood, with other concurring circumstances, served to strengthen him in the opinion that we were in reality part of the Pirates who had seized on the Bounty.' Not only were the crew detained, but they also had to put up with the exceptionally dangerous climate of Java, so often fatal to Europeans. The crew were certainly not the first to discover that 'fever and flux' would decimate their number. Finally, they were escorted to the Dutch settlement at Saramang, providentially arriving there on 29 October 1791. 'Providential' because by an astonishing coincidence they arrived at the same time as the surviving members of the *Pandora* crew, now on board the Dutch East Indiaman *Rembang*. Not only could Captain Edwards vouch that they were not mutineers, but could give them a first-hand account of what had happened on *Pandora* after the vessels had become separated.

The crew learnt that after Captain Edwards had given up his search for Fletcher Christian and had headed for home, he had waited for a time when *Matavy* went missing, but then decided that his overriding responsibility was to ensure that the prisoners were taken back safely to Britain. According to the onboard surgeon, Captain Edwards:

> had lately adopted a most dangerous practice of running blindly on through the night. Until he made the coast of New Guinea, he had profited by the warning of Bougainville, the only navigator whose book he seems to have studied, and always lay to till daylight, but now, in the most dangerous sea in the world, he threw this obvious precaution to the wind.

In other words, without the *Matavy* to use as a path-finder, such was the eagerness of Edwards to get home that he decided to sail 'blind', round the clock. It was a decision he lived to regret.

It was dangerous for a ship cruising the area of the Great Barrier Reef, with jagged corals lurking below the waves, and the advice of de Bougainville – a great French navigator – was entirely sensible. To travel at night, with no means of seeing coral outcrops, was taking a huge risk, and on 29 August 1791 HMS *Pandora* ran aground and started to sink. A vivid description of events was written by the surgeon:

> Every possible effort was attempted to get her off by the sails; but that failing, they were furled, and the boats hoisted out with a view to carry out an anchor. Before that was accomplished, the carpenter reported she made eighteen inches water in five minutes; and in a quarter of an hour more, she had nine feet water in the hold.
>
> The hands were immediately turned to the pumps, and to bale at the different hatchways. Some of the prisoners were let out of irons, and turned to the pumps. At this dreadful crisis,

> it blew very violently; and she beat so hard upon the rocks, that we expected her, every minute, to go to pieces. It was an exceeding dark, stormy night; and the gloomy horrors of death presented us all round, being everywhere encompassed with rocks, shoals, and broken water. About ten, she beat over the reef; and we let go the anchor in fifteen fathom water [i.e. 90 feet of water].

In order to lighten the ship, Edwards ordered the guns to be thrown overboard. Hamilton continued:

> What hands could be spared from the pumps, were employed thrumbing a topsail to haul under her bottom, to endeavour to fodder her. To add to our distress, at this juncture one of the chain-pumps gave way; and she gained fast upon us. The scheme of the topsail was now laid aside, and every soul fell to baling and pumping. All the boats, excepting one, were obliged to keep a long distance off on account of the broken water, and the very high surf that was running near us. We baled between life and death; for had she gone down before day-light, every soul must have perished. She now took a heel, and some of the guns they were endeavouring to throw over board run down to leeward, which crushed one man to death; about the same time, a spare topmast came down from the booms, and killed another man.

Hamilton went on to explain that extreme fatigue set in as the exhausted men continued to operate the pumps:

> We had luckily between decks a cask of excellent strong ale, which we brewed at Anamooka. This was tapped, and served regularly to all hands, which was much preferable to spirits, as it gave them strength without intoxication. During this trying occasion, the men behaved with the utmost intrepidity and obedience, not a man flinching from his post. We continually cheered them at the pumps with the delusive hopes of its being soon day-light.

Just before dawn the officers met to discuss their options:

> it was their unanimous opinion, that nothing further could be done for the preservation of his Majesty's ship; and it was their next care to save the lives of the crew. To effect which, spars, booms, hen-coops, and every thing buoyant was cut loose, that when she went down, they might chance to get hold of something. The prisoners were ordered to be let out of irons. The water was now coming faster in at the gun-ports than the pumps could discharge; and to this minute the men never swerved from their duty. She now took a very heavy heel, so much that she lay quite down on one side.
>
> One of the officers now told the Captain, who was standing aft, that the anchor on our bow was under water; that she was then going; and, bidding him farewell, jumped over the quarter into the water. The Captain then followed his example, and jumped after him. At that instant she took her last heel; and, while everyone were scrambling to windward, she sunk in an instant. The crew had just time to leap over board, accompanying it with a most dreadful yell. The cries of the men drowning in the water was at first awful in the extreme; but as they sunk, and became faint, it died away by degrees. The boats, who were at some considerable distance in the drift of the tide, in about half an hour, or little better, picked up the remainder of our wretched crew.
>
> Morning now dawned, and the sun shone out. A sandy key, four miles off, and about thirty paces long, afforded us a resting place; and when all the boats arrived, we mustered our remains, and found that thirty-five men and four prisoners were drowned.

Four of the fourteen prisoners had indeed died – two of them still fettered (Richard Skinner in handcuffs and Henry Hillbrandt in leg irons). Human remains, identified as belonging to Hillbrandt, were discovered two centuries later, in a position which indicated that he had never escaped the confines of his prison. One other prisoner, James Morrison, was fortunate to have been freed from leg irons and had escaped drowning, despite having his hands tightly manacled. Two others (John Sumner and George Stewart) had been killed when a gangway fell on them.

That left ten surviving prisoners along with eighty-nine crew members, stranded on a tiny strip of sand, which they named Escape Cay. Here they stayed for two nights, gathering their strength and making preparations. Harrison takes up the story:

> A guard was placed over the prisoners. Providentially a small barrel of water, a cag [i.e. keg] of wine, some biscuit, and a few muskets and cartouch boxes, had been thrown into the boat. The heat of the sun, and the reflection from the sand, was now excruciating; and our stomachs being filled with saltwater, from the great length of time we were swimming before we were picked up, rendered our thirst most intolerable; and no water was allowed to be served out the first day. By a calculation which we made, by filling the compass boxes, and every utensil we had, we could admit an allowance of two small wine glasses of water a-day to each man for sixteen days.

Four small boats, described as a pinnace, a launch and two yauls, had been saved from the wreckage, some in a bad condition. Repairs were carried out using a saw and hammer salvaged from *Pandora*. A few other items were salvaged and put to good use including a lightning conductor made of copper, cut into fragments to make nails. A canvas strip was run round the top of each boat, fastened to wooden uprights, to try and stop seawater slopping over the sides. The four boats then set off on a journey very similar to Bligh's epic journey, following much the same route (up the York Peninsula, turning West through Torres Strait and across the Arafura Sea heading towards Coupang). The boats moved in convoy, attached by a piece of rope at night so as to ensure that they stayed together. The prisoners had been split up – two in the launch and in one of the yauls, three in each of the other two boats. The procession, desperately short of food and water, tried to land on several occasions but were met by hostile islanders and were forced to retreat. Eventually fresh water was found: a few oysters were located along with edible fruits and as Hamilton records: 'when every other thing was filled with water, the carpenter's boots were also filled. The water in them was first served out, on account of leakage.'

Moving out into the open sea, the flotilla was hit by violent squalls. On numerous occasions the tow-lines broke, making it impossible for the group to stay together but fortunately being able to reunite in daylight.

The men were suffering from sunstroke and dehydration, as well as from malnutrition. Finally, on 13 September 1791, the flotilla made landfall and was met by friendly islanders who took pity on their situation and provided them with pigs, fowls, milk and bread. Their spirits recovered, the men then made their way to Coupang and from there to Batavia, knowing that once there they could expect to be able to cadge a lift back to Europe.

Over the ensuing months this group were moved from the Dutch East Indies, across to the Cape of Good Hope on board the Dutch ship *Vreedemberg*, and then up through the Atlantic via Ascension Island. Along the way one of the prisoners jumped overboard and escaped and two others died of illness. Once the others arrived back at England on board HMS *Gorgon* they were taken on board HMS *Brunswick* at Portsmouth, awaiting trial for their crimes. Their story is told in chapter 11.

However, first to face a court martial was Captain Edwards and his officers. This was standard practice whenever a Royal Navy ship was lost and all of them were fully exonerated after a hearing in September 1792. For Edwards, then probably in his mid-fifties, he was never to receive another sea-going commission in the navy. Eventually, his long-service led to him being made up to vice-admiral in 1809, and finally as Admiral of the White. This was a time when the navy was divided into three squadrons, the most senior of which was the Red. Therefore, in title at least, as Admiral of the White he was Number Three in the navy pecking order. It may well have been the case that ill-health, brought on by the privations of his final voyage, dogged him until the end of his days. He died in 1815.

His reputation over the intervening years has been that of a cruel tyrant, but in fairness this is largely because his actions were rubbished by Peter Heywood, one of the mutineers, at his own trial. Much was made of the fact that Edwards made no distinction between mutineers and those who simply could not follow Bligh into the longboat. They were treated as guilty even though there had been no trial, and their incarceration in the Pandora's Box was cruel and inhumane. Critics point out that it was not Edwards who ordered the prisoners to be unlocked when *Pandora* went down – it was the armourer's mate, almost certainly acting on his own accord. And so it is that the reputation of Edwards, like Bligh, is forever tarnished. Neither of them were saints – but neither do they deserve to be cast as villains. Perhaps they both served their country as they both thought best.

Chapter 11

Courts Martial

Extract from the portrait by James Northcott of Admiral Lord Hood, who presided over the court martial of the mutineers.

It must have been a torrid time for the men taken by Captain Edwards from Tahiti – firstly treated to appalling conditions inside Pandora's Box, then the ordeal of the ship sinking and the hazardous journey in open boats to Coupang. Then they were incarcerated for seven weeks, first on land and then on board a Dutch East India ship heading for the Cape of Good Hope. On 5 April 1792 they set off for England on board HMS *Gorgon*, still in chains, arriving at Portsmouth on 19 June 1792. All along, they would have had the awful prospect of a court martial hanging over them – and the very real likelihood that they would be sentenced to death.

It must have been particularly worrying for the three men (Coleman, McIntosh and Norman) who had been left onboard the Bounty against their will. Before Bligh had cast off in the longboat the three had implored Bligh to put in a good word for them – but would he? At the time he reportedly stated: 'Never fear, lads, I'll do you justice if ever I reach England.' But their concerns would have been exacerbated when, on their return to Britain, they learnt that their captain was not even in the country, having embarked on his second breadfruit voyage, on board HMS *Providence*, a whole year earlier. As will be seen in Chapter 12, he did not return to England for another year and therefore their fate would depend largely on whether Bligh had remembered to exonerate them in the written report which he had lodged with the Admiralty before he left.

For all ten of the survivors it must have been a wretched time, full of fear and foreboding. All ten were transferred to HMS *Hector* awaiting trial. Confined below decks, they were probably unaware that it was one of the wettest summers on record, with rain day after day throughout July and August, and well into September. And so it was that on a grey damp morning on 12 September 1792 the ten prisoners, still shackled, were marched on board HMS *Duke* in Portsmouth harbour. HMS *Duke* was a second-rate ship of the line launched fifteen years earlier and, at 177ft long, was nearly twice the length of the *Bounty*. Even so, it must have made for a cramped encounter in the captain's great cabin where the court met, presided over by Lord Hood, Vice Admiral of the Blue and Commander in Chief of His Majesty's Ships and Vessels at Portsmouth and Spithead. In addition, the court was made up of eleven other men appointed by the Admiralty Board. They included naval worthies Sir John Thomas Duckworth, 1st Baronet; Sir Roger Curtis (later, Admiral Curtis); the distinguished Scottish sea captain Sir Andrew Snape Douglas; Captain John Nicholson Inglefield; and Richard Goodwin Keats, later to be knighted and made up to admiral. Also on the panel of judges was John Bazely, later to become admiral, and Captain Sir Andrew Snape Hamond, 1st Baronet, former Lieutenant Governor of Nova Scotia and later Comptroller of the Navy.

Another judge was Captain George Montagu, later knighted for his service, and who had been in charge of HMS *Hector* during the time that the prisoners were detained off Portsmouth. During that time Montagu had apparently got to know some of the prisoners very well, particularly Peter

Heywood, who he treated 'with the greatest humanity'. Almost certainly that was because Heywood came from a distinguished naval family and Montagu was a close friend of Commodore Thomas Pasley, (Heywood's uncle). Interestingly, another of the judges (Albermarle Bertie,) was related to Peter Heywood by marriage. Bertie, later 9th Earl of Lindsay, was a general with a distinguished military career, and with no particular link to the navy.

It was to be expected that these august personages would all be determined to see that the mutineers were punished – in as severe manner as possible, in order to act as a deterrent to other malcontents. There was no way that the men in chains could expect leniency. Two days earlier the same court had met, in the same room, and had acquitted Captain Edwards of the Pandora with the words:

> her loss was not in any respect owning to mismanagement or a want of proper attention to her safety, of the said Captain Edward Edwards his Officers and Ship's Company but that the said Captain Edward Edwards his Officers and Ship's Company did everything that was possible to be done for the preservation of His Majesty's said Ship Pandora, and for the good of His Majesty's Service and the said Captain Edward Edwards and the other Officers and Company of His Majesty's said Ship Pandora were honourably acquitted.

They were the good guys; now for the baddies. The trial was spread over seven days and all ten men faced the same charge: mutinously running away with the armed vessel *Bounty* and deserting from His Majesty's Service. More specifically, they were charged with violation of Article XIX of the Articles of War, which read: 'If any Person in or belonging to the Fleet shall make or endeavour to make any mutinous Assembly upon any Pretence whatsoever, every Person offending herein, and being convicted thereof by the Sentence of the Court-martial shall suffer Death.' There was no alternative sentence, no room for manoeuvre: you were either part of the mutinous assembly or you were not, and the only question to answer was whether passive inaction could be classed as 'taking part'. Throughout, the prosecution sought to establish that none of the prisoners had taken any steps to thwart the mutiny and that none of them had tried to get into the boat with Bligh.

The proceedings opened with the reading of Captain Bligh's letter from Coupang dated 18 August 1789, followed by written evidence from Captain Edwards as to the circumstances in which each of the men had come aboard *Pandora*. The clear implication was that evading capture was itself an indication of guilt.

The Admiralty's case was put forward by Deputy Judge Advocate Moses Greetham, a Portsmouth solicitor whose job it was to take the minutes of Courts Martial, offer opinions on the matter of civilian law and navy rules and regulations and to announce the outcome of the trial. He was a man with fingers in many pies – he was from a family of local property developers and with five daughters, all needing substantial dowries in order to obtain advantageous marriages, he also worked endlessly in various remunerative areas of the law. He was involved in a number of high-profile legal cases, had a financial interest in a Naval Agency Business in Piccadilly and dabbled in the stock-market. He was also involved as Judge Advocate in no fewer than 293 naval cases between 1784 and 1801. His work included what was described by his clerk as:

> a great deal of business relating to prizes, their condemnation, sale, proceeds, &c.; and on these occasions all the parties concerned met in a spacious room at the Crown Inn, where an elegant dinner, with wines in abundance, was invariably provided at the expense of the clients. These dinners occurred three or four times every week.

One wonders how he found time for his courts martial responsibilities, for which he was paid a princely £144 a year.

Once the background facts had been read to the court, Peter Heywood, one of only two of the accused to have any form of legal representation, asked the court that the matter should proceed by way of separate trials. One suspects that he was afraid of 'guilt by association'. After all, four of the accused (Burkett, Ellison and Millward and Muspratt) were pretty obviously active participants in the mutiny, having been observed by many to have been armed (either with a cutlass or a musket). Their only defence would be to blame others and hope to escape justice, so their evidence against Heywood might well be tainted.

The court wasted no time in dismissing Heywood's request: all ten accused would be dealt with at the same time. As Lord Hood proclaimed:

'The Bounty's Mutineers being charged with and were guilty of the same atrocious Crime, committed at the same time.'

First to give evidence to the court was John Fryer and he described how John Sumner and Matthew Quintal had burst into his cabin, waking him up and holding him down by leaning on his chest saying, 'You are a Prisoner', and when Fryer tried to object was told to hold his tongue or he would be a dead man, but that if he remained quiet no one would hurt him. Seeing Bligh being led up onto the deck in his night shirt, Fryer asked what was happening to the captain, only to be told by Sumner: 'Damn his Eyes, put him into the Boat, and let the Bugger see if he can live upon three fourths of a Pound of Yams a day.' He was then told to hold his tongue and that 'Mr Christian is Captain of the Ship and recollect that Mr Bligh has brought all this upon himself.'

Fryer then apparently tried to reason with the mutineers seeking to persuade them to lay down their arms. Their reply: 'O No, Sir, hold your tongue, it is too late now.'

Fryer recounted that he was told that Bligh was to be put into the small cutter – the one with a completely rotten hull. Fryer had said: 'Good God! the small Cutter's bottom is almost out, being very much eaten with the Worms', only to be met by the response: 'Damn his Eyes, the Boat is too good for him.' Fryer said that he hoped that they were not going to send Captain Bligh adrift by himself, and was told, 'No, his Clerk, Mr Samuel, Messrs. Hayward and Hallett, are going with him.'

Fryer said that he then asked to see Captain Bligh and to argue his case that the rebels should not force the captain into the small rotten cutter, and instead should give him a better boat so that at least he had a chance of reaching the shore. Bligh then told Fryer to 'knock Christian down' – an instruction given so audibly that it was heard by Christian. Fryer then stated: 'I whispered to Captain Bligh to keep his Spirits up, that if I staid on board I might be enabled Soon to follow him. Mr Bligh said, "By all means stay, Mr Fryer."'

At that point Fryer claimed that Christian put his bayonet to Fryer's chest saying 'Sir if you advance an Inch further, I will run you through.' Christian ordered his men to take Fryer down to his Cabin and once there Fryer tried to encourage others to fight back. In his evidence he stated:

> I said [to Morrison] in a low Voice, 'be on your Guard; there may be an opportunity of recovering ourselves.' His answer

> was 'Go down to your Cabin, Sir, it is too late.' I was then confined to my Cabin and a third Centinel put on, John Millward, who I thought seemed friendly. I winked at him and made a motion for him to knock the Man down that was next to him, which was John Sumner. Millward immediately cocked his Piece and dropt it pointed towards me, saying at the same time, 'Mr Fryer be quiet, no one will hurt you.'

Fryer persuaded his guards – the three 'centinels' – to allow him to go to the ship's cockpit, where Nelson, the botanist, and Peckover, the gunner, were being detained. A conversation followed in which Fryer urged the two men to wait on board and to see if they could jointly help recover control of the ship. The conversation was overheard by Henry Hillbrandt, the cooper, and he duly took word of it to Christian. Meanwhile Christian issued a drinks order, saying: 'Give every Man a dram out of Captain Bligh's Case, that is under Arms' – in other words, using the liquor taken from Captain Bligh's personal supply in order to encourage his armed supporters.

Fryer said he saw the issue of a dram of rum as an encouraging sign, reporting to the court 'Circumstance gave me great hopes that if I should stay on board, that they would get drunk and in a short time [we] might take the Ship.' It was not to be, but Christian did agree to the boat swap, which in turn meant that many more of the Bligh loyalists could be put on board. According to Fryer, Christian insisted – at bayonet point – that Fryer should take his place in the boat. Doubtless he realised that if Fryer remained on board, it would be a constant threat to his authority.

This would appear to have been the turning point in the entire episode of the mutiny – if Fryer had remained on board he would have been a focal point for resistance. Seeing him leave the ship crushed any thoughts which the more junior men may have had about trying to fight back.

Fryer reported that once the boat was full, he heard several of the mutineers say, 'Shoot the Bugger' (meaning Captain Bligh) and that Mr Cole, the Boatswain, said: 'We had better cast off, and take our Chance, for they would certainly do us a mischief if we staid much longer.' According to Fryer, Captain Bligh very readily agreed to cast the Boat off.

After this evidence was given, the prisoners were allowed a chance to put questions to Fryer. In the case of Peter Heywood, he handed in a paper for Judge Advocate Greetham to read aloud to the court. In it he wrote: 'I beg to defer asking any questions until I come up on my Defence – reserving to myself, however, the privilege of calling again any of those "Witnesses" who may be examined on the Part of the Prosecution.'

Next up was the statement by the bosun William Cole. He set out his recollection of events, and confirmed that Coleman, Norman and McIntosh had been detained on the *Bounty* against their will. Asked whether there were any other of the Prisoners detained against their Inclinations he answered: 'I believe Mr Heywood was, I thought all along he was intending to come away. I did not think anything else – he had no Arms and he assisted to get the Boat out and then went below.'

Cole also named the men who he had seen carrying weapons, particularly Millward and Muspratt, and dealt with questions put to him by the court and by the prisoners, and was then replaced on the stand by William Peckover, gunner on board *Bounty*. He testified that except for Coleman, Norman, McIntosh, and the blind fiddler Byrne, he 'had every reason to suppose' that the other six defendants supported the mutiny.

And so it continued, with each successive witness helping to build up a picture of 'who did what and when'. Purcell, the carpenter, testified that he saw Heywood with 'his hand on a cutlass', but added that Heywood dropped it as soon as he was challenged and that he seemed to be 'a person confused' – not even knowing that he had the weapon in his hand. Purcell was cross-examined at length about this incident, especially as it seemed improbable that the rebels would have knowingly allowed a person 'well disposed to the Captain' to get his hands on such a weapon.

When John Hallett, midshipman, was called he identified Ellison, Morrison and Burkett as being armed at the time of the incident and also confirmed that Coleman, Norman and McIntosh were all non-participants in the mutiny and were detained on board simply because there was no more room in the longboat. As for the blind Byrne, he was described as appearing 'pensive and sorrowful' throughout. Others referred to Byrne as sitting sobbing and very definitely taking no active part in proceedings.

Captain Edwards of the *Pandora*, along with two of his officers, then gave evidence as to the circumstances in which the various prisoners had come on board – some voluntarily, some having been captured.

At four o'clock on Friday 14 October the court adjourned until nine o'clock the following day, when each prisoner would be allowed to put forward his defence. In practice, after a brief cross-examination of the bosun by James Coleman, proceedings were again adjourned until the Monday morning, when Peter Heywood opened his defence.

Heywood's case was particularly interesting. He was, after all, just 16 years old at the time of the mutiny. As already mentioned, the fact that he was on board HMS *Bounty* was down to the fact that Bligh's father-in-law, Richard Betham, knew the Heywood family on the Isle of Man, knew that the family was in severe financial difficulties and had recommended the lad to Bligh. He was even invited to stay with Bligh's family in Deptford while *Bounty* was being modified and provisioned for the voyage to Tahiti. Bligh initially thought highly of the lad, writing to his uncle Colonel Holwell on 26 March 1790 to say that 'his conduct had always given me much pleasure and satisfaction'.

But the same letter continued:

> With much concern I inform you that your nephew, Peter Heywood, is among the mutineers. His ingratitude to me is of the blackest dye, for I was a father to him in every respect, and he never once had an angry word from me through the whole course of the voyage … I very much regret that so much baseness formed the character of a young man I had a real regard for, and it will give me much pleasure to hear that his friends can bear the loss of him without much concern.

In other words, Bligh faulted the lad for not rushing to his support and was happy to see him hanged, even though there was no evidence that Heywood had done anything more than stay frozen to the spot. But in Bligh's eyes, Heywood had betrayed his trust and should be counted as a ringleader just as much as Fletcher Christian. There is, however, one problem in suggesting that Bligh was misguided or vindictive – the fact that even at the time of the trial there were rumours that witnesses had been 'nobbled' by members of Heywood's family. Certainly Thomas Bond, Bligh's nephew, asserted in 1792 that 'Heywood's friends have bribed through thick and thin to save him', and there were specific rumours that William Cole had been bribed to testify that Heywood had been held against his will, unable to join the Bligh loyalists in the longboat. Intriguingly, many years later, John Adams was interviewed on Pitcairn Island (see chapter 9) and said that he recalled seeing Heywood on the gangway, not incarcerated below, and that 'he might have gone [in the longboat] if he pleased'.

Heywood's letter to his mother, sent from Batavia in November 1791, is interesting in setting out the lad's confusion at the time of the mutiny. He wrote:

> The morning the ship was taken, it being my watch below, happening to awake just after daylight, and looking out of my hammock, I saw a man sitting upon the arm-chest in the main hatchway, with a drawn cutlass in his hand, the reason of which I could not divine; so I got out of bed and inquired of him what was the cause of it. He told me that Mr Christian, assisted by some of the ship's company, had seized the captain and put him in confinement; had taken the command of the ship and meant to carry Bligh home a prisoner, in order to try him by court-martial, for his long tyrannical and oppressive conduct to his people. I was quite thunderstruck; and hurrying into my berth again, told one of my messmates, whom I awakened out of his sleep, what had happened. Then dressing myself, I went up the fore-hatchway, and saw what he had told me was but too true; and again, I asked some of the people, who were under arms, what was going to be done with the captain, who was then on the larboard side of the quarter-deck, with his hands tied behind his back, and Mr Christian alongside him with a pistol and drawn bayonet. I now heard a very different story, and that the captain was to be sent ashore to Tofoa in the launch, and that those who would not join Mr Christian might either accompany the captain, or would be taken in irons to Otaheite and left there. The relation of two stories so different, left me unable to judge which could be the true one; but seeing them hoisting the boats out, it seemed to prove the latter.
>
> In this trying situation, young and inexperienced as I was, and without an adviser (every person being as it were infatuated, and not knowing what to do), I remained for awhile a silent spectator of what was going on; and after revolving the matter in my mind, I determined to choose what I thought the lesser of two evils and stay by the ship; for I had no doubt that those who went on shore, in the launch, would be put to death by the savage natives, whereas the Otaheitans being a

> humane and generous race, one might have a hope of being kindly received, and remain there until the arrival of some ship, which seemed, to silly me, the most consistent with reason and rectitude.

At the Court Martial Heywood explained that he was asking his lawyer Francis Const to read out a written defence on his behalf and that 'owing to the long and severe Confinement he had suffered he was afraid he was not capable of delivering it with that force of Expression which it required'.

What followed was a rather long and emotional account, not likely to carry much weight before a court of hardened naval officers. Originally Peter's mother had wanted to employ two of the most prominent lawyers in the country to defend her son, but was talked out of this by another family member, Commodore Thomas Pasley (Peter's uncle). Pasley knew that the court was highly likely to take against any attempt to brow-beat them with fancy legal arguments, and instead suggested using Aaron Graham, a friend of his who was an experienced court martial judge; Francis Const was his assistant. Graham had a reputation for his integrity as a police magistrate in London. He had previously been a Purser in the Royal Navy and was considered unlikely to alienate the court.

In practice there was little that the defence could do, given that Heywood's youthfulness was never going to be accepted as an excuse. Bligh's condemnation of him, coupled with the mixed evidence from the other mutineers, meant that he was never likely to escape from the assertion that 'The man who stands Neuter is equally guilty with him who lifts his arms against his Captain.' He did however call a number of his colleagues as witness to his character and reputation. Fryer stated that he was 'Beloved by every body, to the best of my Recollection.' To Cole, he was 'Always, of very good character.' Asked by Heywood 'What was my Temper, disposition, and general Conduct on board the Ship?' Peckover responded: 'Of the most amiable, and deserving of everyone's Esteem.' To Purcell he was 'In every respect becoming the Character of a Gentleman, and such as merited the Esteem of every body.'

Heywood ended his defence by getting his lawyer to read out a statement stressing how he had rushed to give himself up as soon as *Pandora* appeared, how he had given a full account of his behaviour and how he had handed over his journal. He also claimed, somewhat ingenuously, that if Captain Bligh had only been able to attend the court then the captain would have spoken up for him, and that his absence and that of two other witnesses (Simpson and Tinkler) had made it harder to prove his innocence.

His defence was followed by Michael Byrne who asked for a short written statement to be read out. Basically, his point was that his bad eyesight meant that he was unable to carry out his intentions which were 'to quit His Majesty's Ship the 'Bounty' with the Officers and Men who went away'. He explained his tears at the time: 'the Sorrow I expressed at being detained was real and unfeigned'. Having called on Fryer to speak to his character ('I have nothing to alledge against him; he behaved himself in every respect as a very good Man.') he rested his defence.

Similarly brief written statements were lodged by Norman, McIntosh, and Coleman, with Norman having the additional benefit of a letter from Captain Bligh confirming his complete innocence. The letter, written by Bligh from No. 4 Broad Street, St Georges East, on 26 March 1790 read:

> Your unfortunate Brother, Charles Norman, was Carpenter's Mate with me and was kept in the Ship against his Will, and I have recommended him to Mercy – his friends may therefore be easy in their Minds on his account as it is most likely he will return by the first ship that comes from Otaheite.

McIntosh was also able to produce a letter from Bligh, dated October 1790 and addressed to his mother: 'Mrs Tosh. Your son who went by the Name of McIntosh is on board the Bounty in the South Sea – I was informed he remained on board contrary to his inclination, and therefore have recommended him to Mercy in case they should be taken.' While Coleman had no such letter, he was able to establish that he had tried to leave the ship with Bligh as shown by his conversation with Cole. Asked 'Armourer, what do you intend to do?' he had replied: 'To go with the Captain, go where he will', but was then stopped from getting into the longboat by Christian and forcibly detained on *Bounty*.

For those four men – Byrne and the three non-participants – there was a clear case of innocence and they were all duly acquitted. However, that in itself made it all the more important that the others should be found guilty. The navy needed a scapegoat, and the fact that Christian and his main conspirators had escaped justice altogether made it imperative that an example was set by the six remaining prisoners.

The case against Morrison was far from clear-cut. He claimed that the only reason he stayed on the ship was because he could see that the longboat was so overcrowded. They were 'a thousand leagues from the Friendly Isles', and in his words to the court:

> Judging by what I had seen of the Friendly Islanders but a few days before, that nothing Could be expected from them but to be plunder'd, or kill'd, and seeing no Choice but of one evil, I chose, as I thought, the least, to stay in the Ship, especially as I Considered it as Obeying Captain Bligh's Orders.

He also quoted Cole as having said 'God bless you, my boy, I will do you Justice if ever I reach England.'

Morrison also gave an interesting account of a possible attempt to regain control of HMS *Bounty*:

> I also inform'd Mr Thos. Hayward of My intention, and on his drop[p]ing a hint to me that he intended to knock Chas. Churchill down I told him I would second him, pointing at some of the Friendly Island Clubbs which were sticking in the Booms and telling him there were tools enough! I was heartily rejoiced to think that any Officer intended to make an Attempt, but was as suddenly damp'd to find that he went into the Boat without making the Attempt he had proposed, and now gave over all hopes, and resolved to bear my fate with as much fortitude as I was Able.

Morrison resolutely denied picking up arms to support the mutiny and denied that he had laughed or taken part in the jeering when others were led into the longboat and cast adrift.

In the case of the teenager Thomas Ellison, he described Christian as behaving 'like a madman', with his long hair hanging loose and with his shirt open. He stressed that he had every reason to be indebted to Captain Bligh saying:

> [He] took great pains with me and spoke too Mr Samule, his Clark, to teach me Writing and Arithmetick and I believe Would have taught me further had not this happend. I must

> have been very Ingreatfull if I had in any respect assisted in this Unhappy Affair agains my Commander and Benefactor.

In the case of Muspratt, he asked the court if it could acquit Norman and Byrne ahead of the other verdicts, so that he could call them as independent witnesses. The court refused this request, but noted that Muspratt claimed that this was contrary to the rules which would have applied in a normal criminal case. As far as Muspratt was concerned he was never part of the mutiny and only picked up a musket when he thought that Fryer was about to lead a counter-attack, intending to assist him. On finding that Fryer had abandoned the plan and got into the longboat, he, Muspratt, put down the musket. He maintained that if he had been able to call witnesses they would have backed up his claims.

For Thomas Burkett he ended his defence with the words: 'Alas! I have erred, I should have resisted, and died! – but error is the Lot of Mortals – forgiveness the noblest attribute of the Divinity – in full hopes and confidence of which, I resign my cause to the hands of this Honorable and impartial Court.' He had asked the court to consider that it was his efforts that meant that the longboat castaways were given a compass ('[it was] solely by my interception that the Boatswain was allowed to take the Compass in the Boat, without which, it would have been impossible for those who left the Ship ever to have reached Timor'), pointing out the irony that without the compass, without the extraordinary survival of Bligh and those loyal to him, he, Burkett, would never have been put on trial. Various witnesses described him as being 'a good man'; 'of good character'; 'a quiet and civil man'.

Millward, like Burkett, claimed that he only armed himself because he hoped to assist Fryer in retaking the ship. He had hoped to get into the longboat but heard Captain Bligh say 'For God's sake, my lads, don't overload the Boat; I will do you Justice if ever I reach England.' He also explained to the court that 'Christian's party were all around me watching every thing that was done.' However, Millward's problem was that no one could corroborate *his* claim about hoping to reclaim control of *Bounty*. He asked Cole: 'Did I not come down into the Cockpit and inform you of Mr Fryer's Intention of making an Attempt to retake the Ship At the time you were taking some Clothes out of your own Chest in your Cabin?' to which Cole replied: 'I don't remember anything of it at all.'

The court adjourned to consider its verdict, reassembling on Tuesday 18 September 1792. Its decision:

> Charges had been proved against the said Peter Heywood, James Morrison, Thomas Ellison, Thomas Burkitt, John Millward and William Muspratt, and did adjudge them and each of them to suffer Death by being hanged by the Neck … but the Court, in Consideration of various Circumstances, did humbly and most earnestly recommend the said Peter Heywood and James Morrison to His Majesty's Royal Mercy. The Court further agreed that the Charges had not been proved against the said Charles Norman, Joseph Coleman, Thomas McIntosh and Michael Byrn, and did adjudge them and each of them to be acquitted.

In response, Muspratt begged leave to inform the court that he much lamented not being allowed to call witnesses, and this appears to have carried some weight with the authorities, who granted him a stay of execution. Eventually Muspratt was given a royal pardon, but not until 11 February 1793. Heywood and Morrison did not have so long to wait and both received a pardon from King George III and were released on 26 October. Sentence was swiftly carried out on Ellison, Burkitt and Millward aboard HMS *Brunswick* in Portsmouth Harbour. A Captain Hamond watched the hanging and reported that:

> the criminals behaved with great penitence and decorum, acknowledged the justice of their sentence for the crime of which they had been found guilty, and exhorted their fellow-sailors to take warning by their untimely fate, and whatever might be their hardships, never to forget their obedience to their officers, as a duty they owed to their king and country.

The three prisoners were hanged by the yardarm on 29 October, 1792, at 11.26 in the morning. The bodies were left hanging in public view for two hours in the rain, before being cut down.

Post-script to the Trial

It was perhaps inevitable, in a trial in which neither of the main protagonists were present, that the result was somewhat unsatisfactory. The three men who were hanged were clearly not the central villains – they were never Fletcher Christian's main supporters, as evidenced by the fact that they chose not to accompany him to Pitcairn Island. Ellison was 17 at the time of the mutiny, Burkitt 26 and Millward 21. What is clear is that they were poorly educated and could not afford legal representation. Muspratt, on the other hand, did have a legal advisor, and of course was spared on a legal technicality. His subsequent movements are not recorded but he may well have continued a naval career and served on HMS *Bellerophon*. He is thought to have died towards the end of 1797 and there is a record of a grant of probate to his will being obtained by his brother Joseph Muspratt in January 1798. Messrs Norman, McIntosh, and Coleman all appear to have faded from public view, and nothing is known of the fate of Michael Byrne. It may well have been the case that Bligh's step-nephew Francis Bond found employment for Byrne, because Bligh wrote to Bond in August 1794 saying:

> As to the blind scoundrel, I can only beg of you to make the best of him, & get him flogged nobly whenever he deserves it, as he is certainly a very great Villain … Don't let him get on shore for I am sure he deserves no leave.

Good old Bligh, determined to have his revenge, right to the end!

The one person who really benefited from the trial was Peter Heywood. He had spent his time, after the verdict but before the royal pardon, on board HMS *Hector*, working on a dictionary of Tahitian words. When Captain Montagu summoned everyone onto the quarterdeck where he read out the royal proclamation, Heywood reportedly burst into floods of tears and issued a statement ending with the words, 'I receive with gratitude my Sovereign's mercy, for which my future life will be faithfully devoted to his service.' It has to be said: he kept his word. He enjoyed the patronage of Lord Hood, and was soon given a job as midshipman on HMS *Bellerophon*, the ship commanded by his uncle Thomas Pasley. Very shortly after that he was given a promotion and placed on the flagship HMS *Queen Charlotte*, an appointment which very clearly showed that William Bligh's star was no longer in the ascendancy and that his poor opinion of Heywood was not shared by the naval hierarchy. In 1795 he was made up to lieutenant, a quite remarkable promotion for a convicted mutineer! In 1803 he was made up to post captain, and in 1806 was appointed flag captain on HMS *Polyphemus*, spending several years carrying out detailed surveying operations in the area of the River Plate in Brazil. He retired from the navy after a distinguished career in 1816, married immediately and died fifteen years later. Had he not died it is generally accepted that through long service he would eventually have been made up to admiral.

But perhaps Heywood's greatest contribution to the Bligh story was the assistance he gave to Edward Christian (Fletcher's brother), assistance which led directly to a concerted campaign to vilify Bligh and to blacken his character forever. It all started off with a letter written by Heywood to Edward Christian on 5 November 1792, It read:

> I am sorry to say I have been informed you were inclined to judge too harshly of your truly unfortunate brother; and to think of him in such a manner as I am conscious, from the knowledge I had of his most worthy disposition, and character, (both public and private,) he merits not in the slightest degree: therefore I think it my duty to undeceive you, and to rekindle the flame of brotherly love (or pity now) towards him, which, I fear, the false reports of slander and vile suspicion may have nearly extinguished.
>
> Excuse my freedom, Sir:–If it would not be disagreeable to you, I will do myself the pleasure of waiting upon you; and endeavour to prove that your brother was not that vile wretch, void of all gratitude, which the world had the unkindness to think him; but, on the contrary, a most worthy character; ruined only by having the misfortune, (if it can be so called) of being a young man of strict honour, and adorned with every virtue; and beloved by all (except one, whose ill report is his greatest praise) who had the pleasure of his acquaintance.

The result was a meeting between the two men, followed by the publication of Edward Christian's *Appendix*. That in turn led to the flurry of counter-claims and corrections referred to in chapter 14, whipping up public opinion against Bligh and thereby helping to establish Christian as some sort of heroic figure.

PART TWO

William Bligh painted in 1775, at the age of 21.

Chapter 12

Second Breadfruit Voyage

Breadfruit tree growing in Papeete next to an ancient marae, or ceremonial meeting place.

When William Bligh landed back in England on14 March 1790 after his extraordinary voyage as a castaway, his wife had already received news of the mutiny because William had written from Coupang, en route to Batavia, on 19 August 1789: 'Know then, my own Dear Betsey, I have lost the Bounty.' The letter gave a brief account of events relating to the mutiny and the letter ended with instructions to 'Give my blessing to my Dear Harriet, my Dear Mary, my Dear Betsy & to my Dear little stranger & tell them I shall soon be home.' Well, by the time he got home, Harriet was 8, Mary was 7, Elizabeth was no longer the 1-year-old toddler he had left behind, but a 4-year-old who would not have known who her father was. And the dear little stranger? Actually twins, Jane and Frances, born at Lambeth on 11 May and baptised a month later at Tower Hamlets.

Bligh had little time to acquaint himself with his growing family as he was busy preparing reports for the Admiralty, writing letters and finalising the draft of his journal, which was published as the *Narrative of the Mutiny on the Bounty*. It became an instant best-seller and was followed by an expanded account, *A Voyage to the South Sea*, in 1792. In his narrative, set out in the Appendix, Bligh describes the voyage as being one of 'uninterrupted prosperity', and conveniently omitted mention of personal differences with the crew. In this respect the *Narrative* reflects numerous alterations made by Sir Joseph Banks, who told Bligh: 'We shall abridge considerably what you wrote … to satisfy the public and place you in such a point of view as they shall approve.'

Bligh was also preparing for his own court martial, which took place in October 1790 on board HMS *Royal William*, at that stage moored at Spithead, in the Solent, and presided over by Admiral Samuel Barrington. It was a complete formality and he was honourably acquitted – small wonder given that the only version known to the Admiralty was Bligh's own somewhat one-sided testimony. He was promoted to commander and then to post captain and as has been seen, his testimony also led to the carpenter, Purcell, being reprimanded for insubordination and misconduct at a separate court martial which took place on board HMS *Royal William* immediately after Bligh's acquittal.

It must all have been rather pleasing for William Bligh. He was quickly promoted to the rank of commander with effect from 14 November 1790, in charge of the brig *Falcon*. Exactly one month later he was posted captain of the 28-gun *Medea*.

In November 1790 the *Pandora* had set off on its quest to track down the mutineers, but by then it was known that the authorities were keen to resurrect the idea of introducing breadfruit to the West Indies – and Bligh was most anxious to be given the chance to 'finish the job'. In February 1791 the navy had purchased HMS *Providence*, then being built at Blackwall Yard dockyard on the River Thames. She had a crew of 134 and was classed as a sixth-rate frigate, with three decks, and was armed with a dozen carriage guns and fourteen swivel guns. Her tonnage was double that of *Bounty* and the navy had decided that henceforth any long-distance voyage of this nature should be accompanied by a second vessel, and that both should have a detachment of marines on board. Therefore, a second ship was chosen to sail alongside *Providence*, a much smaller brig known as HMS *Assistant*. She carried four 4-pounder guns and eight swivel guns and had a complement of twenty-seven men under the command of Nathaniel Portlock, a man Bligh knew well as both of them had accompanied Cook on his third and final voyage.

HMS *Providence* was copper-bottomed in preparation for the voyage. Extensive alterations were made for the storage of the breadfruit plants, including special arrangements to catch and recycle any run-off water which might result from the watering of the 825 plant pot holders on the aft-deck.

On 24 April 1791 Bligh had written to Sir Evan Nepean with his 'shopping list' of clothing, tools, ornaments and so on which he considered necessary to take with him on the voyage, intended as gifts to islanders. He estimated the value of the items as being £300 and the list is set out in full:

Three suits of cloaths for the King of Otaheite
Six cotton long gowns or dresses for the Queen and Chief Women
300 yards of printed cotton and two dozen pairs of Ribbon
Two dozen long gowns of an inferior quality
Fifteen dozen shirts
Eighteen dozen Coarse Men's Hats
Twenty gross of Toeys [i.e. just under three thousand knick-knacks]
Four gross [576] of knives with Wood Handles and Sheaths
Four gross of clasp knives
Three Hundredweight of six inch nails
Three cwt of three inch nails
1½ cwt two inch nails
Two cwt of one inch nails
Three gross hand saws
Three gross of files
Seven gross of Hatchets and Axes

Four gross of gimlets
Three gross of flat files
Ten dozen Rasps
Three gross of Looking Glasses
Four dozen Thick Hooks
24 dozen Dolphin Hooks
24 dozen of Albercore [large fish hooks]
Fifty pounds of White Beads
Thirty pounds of Red Beads
Fifty pounds of Blue Beads
Thirty dozen Drops for Ear-rings
One gross of stone Rings
Two gross of Scissors

It is an impressive list and gives an idea of the items which the islanders would prize in exchange for the breadfruit trees, food and other provisions. And when we consider that the women on Tahiti would sleep with a sailor for the price of a nail or two, those nine-and-a-half hundred weight of nails of assorted sizes must have given the mariners considerable buying power!

At the end of July Bligh had said farewell to his wife and young family. On 21 February that year his 40-year-old wife Betsey had given birth – to yet another daughter (their sixth). She was baptised Anne Campbell Bligh at St Mary's Lambeth in March 1791, but sadly later records refer to her as being 'mentally retarded', and probably prone to epileptic fits.

Before leaving, Bligh had his portrait painted by John Russell, an artist who had been made a Royal Academician three years earlier and who had also painted a portrait of Sir Joseph Banks. It seems likely that Banks introduced Bligh to the artist, and some years later Russell was to paint a rather flattering portrait of Betsey, in pastels, showing her as an attractive and vivacious woman. Indeed, both of the Blighs had a number of portraits painted in their lifetime – and perhaps that is not surprising given the amount of time the couple actually spent apart. At least Betsey had Bligh's portrait to remember him by during his long absences…

The small flotilla set off from Spithead on 3 August 1791 and headed down to Tenerife. On board *Providenc*e were two botanists, James Wiles and Christopher Smith, chosen as before by Sir Joseph Banks. They were to take charge of the horticultural aspects of the voyage as well as being directed to search out and bring back new varieties of plants, to enhance the collection at Kew Gardens. She also had on board Bligh's nephew, Francis Godolphin Bond, as first lieutenant. The son of William Bligh's elder step-sister Catherine, Bond went on to have a distinguished naval career, ending up as rear-admiral. It is clear that he found sailing with his uncle a most unpleasant affair, feeling constantly belittled and undermined and he vowed never to repeat the experience. At one stage he wrote in the log, for 28 November 1792, 'squally *within* board and without'. The fact that Bond underlined 'within' would suggest that this was a reference to Bligh's temper.

Bond's letter to his brother Thomas is worth setting out because it contains a detailed analysis of Bligh and his arrogance, his belligerence, and his inability to delegate properly. In the letter, sent from St Helena in December 1792, he writes:

> Yes, Tom, our relation had the credit of being a tyrant in his last expedition, where his misfortunes and good fortune have elevated him to a situation he is incapable of supporting with decent modesty. The very high opinion he has of himself makes him hold every one of our profession with contempt, perhaps envy. Nay, the Navy is but a sphere for fops and lubbers to swarm in, without one gem to vie in brilliancy with himself. I don't mean to depreciate his extensive knowledge as a seaman and nautical astronomer, but condemn that went [wont] of modesty in self-estimation. To be less prolix I will inform you that he has treated me (nay, all on board) with the insolence and arrogance of a Jacobs; and not withstanding his passion is partly to be attributed to a nervous fever, with which he has been attacked most of the voyage, the chief part of his conduct must have arisen from the fury of an ungovernable temper. Soon after leaving England I wished to receive instruction from this imperious master, until I found he publically exposed any deficiency on my part in the Nautical Art, &c. A series of this conduct determined me to trust to myself, which I hope will in some measure repay me for the trouble of this disagreeable voyage – in itself pleasant, but made otherwise by being worried at every opportunity. His maxims are of a nature that at once pronounce him an enemy to the lovers of Natural Philosophy; for to make use of his own

words, 'No person can do the duty of a First Lieut., who does more than write the days work in his publick journal!'

This is so inimical to the sentiments that I find the utmost difficulty in keeping on to tolerate terms with him. The general orders which have been given are to that purport. – I am constantly to keep on my legs from 8 o'th morning to 12 or noon, altho' I keep the usual watch. The officer of the morning watch attends to the cleaning of the decks; yet I am also to be present, not only to get it done, but be even mentally active on these and all other occasions. He expects me to be acquainted with every transaction on board, notwithstanding he himself will give the necessary orders to the Warrant Officers before I can put it in execution. Every dogma of power and consequence has been taken from the Lieutenants, to establish, as he thinks, his own reputation – what imbecility for a post Captn! The inferior warrants have had orders from the beginning of the expedition, not to issue the least article to a Lieut. without his orders; so that a cleat, fathom of log line, or indeed a hand swab, must have the Commander's sanction. One of the last and most beneficent commands was, that the carpenter's crew should not drive a nail for me without I would first ask his permission, – but my heart is filled with the proper material always to disdain this humiliation ... My messmates have remarked he never spoke of my possessing one virtue – tho' by the bye he has never dared to say I have none.

Every officer who has nautical information, a knowledge of natural history, a taste for drawing, or anything to constitute him proper for circumnavigating, becomes odious; for great as he is in his own good opinion, he must have entertained fears some of his ship's company meant to (submit) a spurious Narrative to the judgement and perusal of the publick ... The future will determine whether promotion will be the reward of this voyage. I still flatter myself it will, notwithstanding what I have said. Consistent with self-respect, I still remain tolerably passive; and if nothing takes place very contrary to my feelings, all may end will; but this will totally depend on circumstances, one of which is the secrecy requested of you concerning the tenor of this letter.

It is fair to assume that the qualities listed by Bond were the same qualities which so provoked Fletcher Christian during the previous voyage. Irritating, yes. Demoralising, yes. An appalling delegator, yes. But it still raises the question: why did Christian take it so much to heart? Why wasn't he able to swallow his pride and just keep his head down? For that, it is necessary to look at Christian himself, rather than Bligh (see chapter 9).

The second lieutenant on board *Providence* was James Guthrie. George Tobin acted as third lieutenant. He later published an account of the voyage, having kept an illustrated journal throughout, especially covering the times in Tahiti and Tasmania. The original journal, with illustrations, is now in the State Library of New South Wales. Bligh had been promoted to the rank of post captain at the start of the voyage but early on in the trip he was laid low with an illness, almost certainly a recurrence of malaria picked up while he was staying at Batavia. This was the 'nervous fever' referred to by Bond, and throughout the journey Bligh recorded the debilitating effect of constant headaches and an aversion to the strong sun. It is intriguing that Bligh handed over command during his incapacity not to his nephew Bond, the most senior officer, but to Captain Portlock. The latter moved on board *Providence* during the time he was in charge, reverting later on to the *Assistant* when the smaller ship really came into its own, charting the way through the shallows off the Australian coast and making sure that the route was safe for *Providence* to follow.

The ships called in at Tenerife for further provisions, and again at Porto Praya in the Cape Verde Islands. Bligh was seriously ill and took no pleasure in either island, writing:

> My illness seemed to increase on our anchoring at Porto Praya; a more miserable and burnt up and inhospitable place I never beheld; the shore is low and barren: the interior part mountainous, without a single spot of verdure to delight the eye or invite the stranger to land. The wind came in hot blasts from the shore, and I saw so little advantage to be gained by my stay here that I should have weighed instantly if the surgeon had not recommended me to send on shore to procure fruit … This was done … only a few oranges were obtained, and Mr Tobin found the place very sickly.

Crossing the Equator, the ships headed for Cape Town, arriving on 6 November 1791. Bligh was in very poor health, but apparently improved after a week resting in the cooler airs of Stellenbosch, then, as now, regarded as a wine growing centre. In Bligh's words, it was:

> a pretty village about 25 miles eastward of Cape Town … situated on a small plain watered by a charming river and shaded by luxuriant oaks in the neighbourhood of wild and inaccessible mountains. The adjacent hills give eligible situations for farms, and produce corn, grapes, peaches, apricots, almonds, and abundance of vegetables.

Bligh's 'distracted headache' coincided with his return to Cape Town, but he was able to record that the botanists on board had been busy exchanging plants – handing over nectarine bushes in exchange for some 240 assorted plants to be nurtured and propagated during the course of the voyage. The ships left the Cape at the end of the year, heading due East on a setting which would take them South of Australia, arriving off the southern coast of Tasmania (then known as Van Diemen's Land) on 8 February 1792.

It was Bligh's third visit to the area and he deliberately sought out venues he had previously visited, such as the place where wood had been gathered. Finding a message board recording Cook's visit, he added his own message: 'Near this tree Captain William Bligh planted seven fruit trees 1792: – Messrs. S. and W., botanists.'

The message was subsequently read by the French explorer and naturalist Labillardière, and he was shocked and dismayed by what he saw as 'the despotism which condemned men of science to initials and gave a sea captain a monopoly of fame'. He had a point, with Messrs Wiles and Smith reduced to mere cyphers, while Bligh boldly made off with all the credit. Various trees were planted at different places – nine oak seedlings in one place, seeds of a fir tree at another, as well as apricot and peach stones at another. During their journey to the Pacific the botanists had grown over 120 citrus fruit trees from seed, intending to introduce them wherever they stopped.

Bligh describes the fauna of the area, mentioning kangaroos, a platypus and the echidna. He also described the natives they encountered, giving details of their appearance, their canoes, their diet and so on. The two ships then headed for Tahiti, deliberately keeping away from the waters around New Zealand and ironically taking them on a course which passed close to Pitcairn Island where, unbeknown to them, Fletcher Christian was currently living. The ships reached Tahiti on 10 April and stayed exactly three months – time enough to select breadfruit cuttings to be potted on and placed onboard; time for Bligh to renew friendships with the local leaders; time for him to make further detailed observations as to the customs and beliefs of the islanders.

Bligh records how, as before, they were plagued by petty thieving. On one occasion in May he reported that one of the islanders was throwing stones – and insults – at his men. The man was apprehended, put in leg irons and after discussion with the local leader, was subjected to thirty-six lashes. As Bligh wrote: 'He received the punishment without wincing … it must be owing to the bodies of these people being constantly exposed that they are not susceptible … I ordered the prisoner again in irons.'

He also kept the botanists up to the mark: insisting they re-pot plants where they had forgotten to use broken sea shells at the bottom of each pot, to ensure proper drainage and to limit run-off; insisting that any potting-up should take place in the early morning so that the work was completed before the sun got too hot; making sure that the breadfruit collection was 'balanced' in the sense of containing examples of the various different types of breadfruit (there were at least eight) which they encountered.

In total, Wiles reckoned that they had 1,668 breadfruit plants on board, some planted together in tubs, some in individual pots. There were over three hundred other plants on board, including some thirty-two which were destined to be taken back to Sir Joseph Banks. Bligh describes the botanical hoard as being '25 vees [a sort of apple], 25 rattahs [a kind of chestnut], 25 ayeyahs [otherwise termed the 'Jambo of the East'], 12 orayahs [fine plantains], 9 peeahs [sago root], 6 mattees and 2 ettows ['the two last both produce a fine red dye'].

When the ships left Tahiti on 10 July there were two Tahitians on board, a royal prince called Mydiddee and a stowaway called, variously, Bobbo or Pappoo, but given the nickname of 'Jackets' by the English. He had previously lent a hand with bringing the plants on board and Bligh felt that the stowaway might be a useful assistant in Jamaica, so was allowed to stay. Bligh also had on board *Providence* thirteen men from the *Matilda*, shipwrecked near the island some five months previously, with another two men from the same wreck being carried onboard *Assistant*.

Bligh followed much the same route as he had already taken in the open boat, passing Fiji and Tonga on their way to New Guinea and then through the Torres Strait – this time taking detailed soundings and preparing accurate charts. It took seventeen nerve-wracking days to traverse the Strait, encountering poor weather, bad visibility and treacherous currents as the ships attempted to steer clear of hidden rocks, shallows and coral reefs.

On two occasions the ships were attacked by islanders in canoes and they felt obliged to respond with grape-shot and musket fire. Reaching Coupang, Bligh's malaria returned. In his words: 'During my stay here I had not a moment's intermission from a violent headache and touches of fever at times; from 8 in the morning till 5 in the afternoon I dare not expose myself to the heat of the sun.' Sickness also affected many of the crew – a reminder of the appalling pollution and unhygienic conditions in which the Europeans lived in this part of what is now Indonesia.

To Bligh's dismay the plants in 224 of the pots had died – probably because the water had been contaminated with salt, but also possibly indicating an inadequate arrangement to keep the plants circulating between the lower and upper deck. As a result, some plants may not have received regular sunlight. In Bligh's words:

> The botanists have been diligently employed to make up with what can be got here and with natives to assist have collected 92 pots of the best plants of this place. The plants taken up here are Mangoes, Jambelang Jambos, Balumbeng, Chermailah, Karambola, Lemon More-sang, Cosambee, Cattahpas, Breadfruit, Seereeboah, Penang or Beetle Nut, Dangreedah trees with which they perfume, Bughnah, and Kanangah. The Nanka or jack they could not get.

Bligh was in a difficult position: his whole mission revolved around something about which he had no personal knowledge and very little control – the successful transportation of dozens of young plants. There must have been times when he wondered whether this trip, like the one on *Bounty*, would end in unavoidable failure.

As Bligh sailed south-westward, sailing close to Madagascar and round the tip of the African continent, more plants started to die. On 11 December Bligh recorded plants in a total of 272 pots had been lost, over and above the 224 pots already identified. It meant that there were now just 830 plants left, held in some 655 containers. After a trip lasting ten weeks from Timor, the ships docked on St Helena. 'All needful refreshment' was taken on board, and the botanists were instructed to present the Governor with a number of fruit trees, intended to provide sustenance to the islanders on maturity. The Governor was delighted, remarking that seeing the ships 'had raised in them an inexpressible degree of wonder and delight to contemplate a floating garden transported in luxuriance from one extremity of the world to the other'. In turn, the island's botanist Henry Porteous presented Bligh with forty-six plants intended as a gift to the royal gardens at Kew. All were put on board *Providence*.

From St Helena the ships passed close to Ascension Island, crossed the Atlantic, and reached their primary destination of St Vincent on 23 January 1793. A hectic seven days were spent unloading part of the cargo of precious breadfruit – 333 saplings as well as over 200 other plants. In exchange they received several hundred pots and tubs containing plants destined for Kew, many of them collected on plant-finding expeditions in South America.

The ships then moved on to Jamaica, stopping off at four different points to distribute breadfruit plants across the island. It was at the botanic gardens at Bath, in the south-eastern part of the island, that Jamaica's botanist Dr Thomas Dancer met Wiles. He persuaded him to leave *Providence* and take up a far better-paid job as superintendent of a new botanic garden to be developed on the island. Wiles was joined by the Tahitian stowaway Pappoo, but the loyal helper was to die of disease before the year was out.

By 5 March 1793 the two ships had each completed their deliveries and met up at Port Royal, ready to sail for England. However, they had to wait for another three months, because Britain was at war with France, and Bligh was ordered to wait until he could take part in a protective convoy of eight other ships. By 3 June it was considered safe enough to depart, with some 1,283 plants bound for Kew, shared between the two ships. The return leg was uneventful and two years and four days after setting off, the ships moored at Deptford and two days later handed over the plants to representatives of the Royal Gardens. Banks was thrilled to bits, writing that the plants arrived 'in a state of Luxuriant vegetation, equal to what we see in our best-managed hot-houses and which I confess I thought impossible to attain on board a ship.'

Sadly, the arrival of *Providence* was marked by the death of Mydiddee, finally succumbing to one of the many Western diseases to which he had no natural immunity. Having recorded in his log the sad death of 'our Otaheitan friend', Bligh ended his report with the words:

> This voyage has terminated with success, without accident or a moment's separation of the two ships. It gives the first and only satisfactory accounts of the pass between New Guinea and New Holland, if I except some vague accounts of Torres in 1606; other interesting discoveries will be found in it.

For Bligh, his return marked a resounding success and a considerable vindication of his skills. Honours and gifts were showered on him: the Society for the Encouragement of Arts Manufactures and Commerce (later, the Royal Society of Arts) chipped in with a gold medal; the Governor at St Vincent presented him with silver worth a hundred guineas; the Jamaicans paid him a reward of a thousand guineas. As already seen, whereas his half-nephew Bond was extremely critical of Bligh's man-management skills, the fact remains that he achieved exactly what the Royal Navy expected of him: he did his duty. Even George Tobin, his third lieutenant on *Providence*, was forced to declare: 'in her commander I had to encounter the quickest sailor's eye, guided by a thorough knowledge of every branch of the profession needed on such a voyage'.

It is worth remembering that Bligh was suffering from severe headaches for much of the voyage, and clearly had been sent on this mission before he had recovered from his previous ordeal. It can be argued that of necessity, much of the leadership on the voyage actually came from Portlock, not Bligh. It is noteworthy that there were remarkably few floggings carried out on board either ship – and most of those occurred after the ships had reached the West Indies and the men were getting impatient to finish the voyage. Those disciplined with the lash were generally punished for 'the usual' crimes, including:

> 11 May 1792, James Coombe, marine, a dozen lashes for having carnal knowledge of the body of a young native woman when infected with venereal disease.
>
> 27 December 1792, John Carvey, seaman, eight lashes for insolence to a superior.
>
> John Latbie, the same punishment, for neglect of duty.
>
> 4 March 1792, Richard Upsdale and Richard Franklin, seamen, six lashes each for theft.

> 27 May 1793, the same Richard Upsdale, this time, twelve lashes for neglect of duty.
>
> 14 June 1793, George Thompson, twelve lashes for contempt and disobedience of orders.

Such a punishment record was by no means excessive and Bligh must have been horrified upon his return to find that the courts martial against the *Bounty* mutineers had destroyed his earlier reputation as a hero, and instead replaced it with the stain of being a brutal tyrant. It was a gross distortion and one from which Bligh never escaped. He may have been many things – a prickly ill-tempered, foul-mouthed perfectionist, but he was never cruel and did exactly what he thought was necessary to maintain discipline and order throughout the voyage. His men may not have liked him, but he wasn't there to be popular, he was there to make sure that the men did their job, so that in turn he could do what the navy had paid him to do – introduce the breadfruit tree to the slave plantations of the West Indies. The fact that along the way his crew felt that he cared more for his plants than for his crew, and apportioned limited water supplies accordingly, would not have worried Bligh in the slightest,

It was not his fault that the slaves declined to eat the fruit, because they preferred to eat plantains and yams. But taken in the long term, the fact remains that the breadfruit has, over the centuries, become a popular part of the Caribbean diet. The fruit feature in dozens of popular local dishes, not only in St Vincent and Jamaica, but on other islands where the trees are now commonplace. Islanders from Haiti to Barbados, from Puerto Rico to Trinidad and Tobago boil it to make soups, serve it in salads, use it roasted, fried or grilled, or even serve it up when ripe as a dessert.

Chapter 13

Mutiny at the Nore

Richard Parker, leader of the Nore mutineers.

When he anchored up on *Providence* on 7 August 1793 at Deptford, Bligh would not have been aware that his career in the navy was about to change direction: no longer an explorer, or a floating nursery-man, but a dedicated officer serving in a navy at war with the enemies of Britain; first, the Dutch, then the Danes, and always the French. But first, there was a period of time when he appeared to be 'surplus to requirements' as no new appointments were forthcoming.

It did, however, give him a chance to catch up with his beloved 'Betsey', by then aged 42. As with his other voyages he brought back with him shells from his travels – particularly from Tahiti, the East indies, Australia and from the Caribbean. These shells were accompanied by detailed notes prepared by William, presumably so that his wife could identify with where he had been. In time, Elizabeth built up a significant private collection of shells, contained in a specially-made mahogany cabinet consisting of forty drawers and lined with wood from Botany Bay. Eventually this collection was considered so important that after her death it was bought by the dealer John Mawer, who exhibited it in his shop in the Strand. Later, in 1822, he sold the collection at auction, prefacing the auction particulars with the words:

> To any voyager fond of this beautiful branch of Natural History, or to any collector resident on their shores, the South Seas offer a fine harvest; but the late Admiral Bligh had, from the situations in which his professional eminence placed him, the best opportunities of procuring whatever was most valuable and rare, from a field proverbially rich.

Several books were published in the 1820s, featuring the collection, including one by John Mawer himself. In 1821 he published *The Voyager's Companion, or Shell Collectors Pilot*. Nowadays it is considered to be the world's first shell-collecting guide and takes the form of a journey around the world, noting where rare and valuable shells could be located. It is a reminder of how popular conchology had become in the later Georgian and early Victorian period.

The family also decided to move house during this period, taking up residence at the newly built No. 3 Durham Place (now 100 Lambeth Road) Kennington, and it was to be their home for the rest of Elizabeth's life. It is still standing, an attractive Georgian terraced house marked by a blue plaque recording its famous resident.

In January 1795 Elizabeth became pregnant, for the second time with twins, but when the boys were born in 1795 they both died as day-old babies. The family therefore consisted of six daughters, then aged between 4 and 12 and it must have made for a bustling, hectic household.

In all, Bligh spent eighteen months kicking his heels before being made commander of the East Indiaman *Warley*, recently purchased by the Admiralty, renamed HMS *Calcutta* and armed with fifty guns. He took command in April 1795 and spent some months off the coast of Scotland before playing an important part in bringing an end to a mutiny on board HMS *Defiance*, then under the command of Captain Sir George Home.

Forget the mutiny on the *Bounty* – that was a mutiny which was, in a sense, a one-off. For the average sailor, abandoning the navy for a life in a tropical paradise was never going to be an option. But there were numerous mutinies on other ships, especially in the mid-1790s and they reflected a period of great change – and resentment – in the Royal Navy. For some it was a desire for more freedom, echoing the pressures for change in revolutionary America and France. For some it was a straight desire for better pay. Seamen's wages had not been reviewed for over a century, which did not matter when inflation was more-or-less static, but it really started to make its presence felt throughout the reign of George III. This is dealt with in more detail in chapter 17.

Coupled with this, sea voyages had become increasingly more 'anti-social'; absences from home started to become longer and longer as Britain started to stretch its reach around the globe. Men were likely to be away from their homes and families for several years at a time. There wasn't even the necessity of returning to Britain to careen and repair the ships – copper-bottoming of vessels meant that repairs necessitated by the depredations of marine life were fewer and further apart. Meanwhile, the construction of Royal Navy dry docks in places such as Bermuda and Antigua meant that ships could be refitted without the need for returning to Britain. It all made for longer voyages and longer gaps between home visits.

A number of these grievances came together in October 1795 on board *Defiance*. Captain Home was anchored off Leith when a night of disturbances and mayhem took place. The men were apparently outraged that orders had been given to water down the daily dose of grog (rum mixed with water) so that it was five parts water instead of the more usual 3:1 ratio. A number of men broke into the spirit room and liberated the rum casks, resulting in the captain placing eight leaders of the riot in leg-irons. At this point the rest of the crew, almost to a man, refused to carry out their duties. Faced with a mass mutiny the captain had to suffer a humiliating volte-face, especially as he had no marines on board to enforce discipline. The ringleaders were released, but having seen the power of their muscle and under the cry of 'Liberty', the men set out their four main demands: the replacement of the captain and first lieutenant with men of their choice; the reinstatement of the traditional rum ration; the introduction of better shore leave, and visits onboard from wives and girlfriends.

Defiance was part of Rear-Admiral Thomas Pringle's squadron, part of the North Sea Fleet commanded by Admiral Adam Duncan. On hearing of the mutiny, Pringle sent over the warship HMS *Jupiter* and his flagship HMS *Asia* to restore order. The mutineers, now reduced to fighting among themselves, refused to return to their duties and also refused to allow soldiers to come onboard. Pringle was unsure what to do, so played for time by writing a letter to the Admiralty and another to the local army commander-in-chief Lord Adam Gordon. Two ships stood by to guard *Defiance* – Captain Sir Charles Knowles on HMS *Edgar*, and Captain William Bligh on *Calcutta*. Nerves must have been fraught – would the men on *Edgar* and *Calcutta* really open fire on the colleagues on *Defiance* if ordered to do so, or might they too rebel?

Waiting for the dithering Pringle to make up his mind what to do cannot have helped, but in the end it was Bligh who came up with a working solution. He recommended placing two hundred soldiers on the deck of one of the ships, bringing it up alongside *Defiance*, enabling the soldiers to scramble on board. Their numbers would be sufficient to overcome the rebellious crew by force. Pringle again hesitated. Having accepted the proposal, he then changed the plan – just eighty soldiers would be given the task of subduing the mutiny. Bligh was put in charge as the soldiers were split into two groups, each advancing to a different side of the *Defiance*. Shots were fired at the approaching boarders, but Bligh steadfastly refused to discontinue the surprise assault. He led the charge on board, forcing his way onto the poop deck and quickly took control. The disaffected crewmen meekly surrendered and the eight men who had supposedly started the rioting were rearrested, along with another nine mutineers.

Nine men were sentenced to hang at the ensuing court martial on 4 February 1796, but when the punishment was due to be carried out on board the flagship HMS *Sandwich* a month later, four of those nine were reprieved at the last moment. The King's Pardon was denied the other five miscreants. The remaining prisoners were sentenced to receive between two hundred and three hundred lashes each. Two men were acquitted.

The incident showed that Bligh was rather more than the grumpy, sarcastic self-important man as portrayed by others after his earlier adventures. He was decisive and brave and, because he led by example, he was able to end the mutiny without serious bloodshed. From the Admiralty's viewpoint, the outcome was entirely satisfactory. Bligh had defused the situation, set a good example to others and was entitled to be given command of a larger vessel. On 7 January 1796 Bligh was appointed captain of HMS *Directo*r, with its sixty-four guns. She was a third-rate ship of the line, launched in 1784, but for much of the first year of his command Bligh was in poor health, probably not helped by the cold, wet and windy weather to be found in the North Sea. In particular Bligh took part in a blockade of the Dutch fleet at the Texel, an island off the North coast of Holland.

On 12 May 1797 a new mutiny broke out on ships anchored at the Nore (an anchorage at the point where the River Thames joins the North Sea). The mutineers took control of HMS *Sandwich* and were quickly joined by other ships anchored at the Nore, before moving towards London to set up a blockade of merchant shipping. This was potentially disastrous to Britain – trade in and out of London was vital. To make matters worse, Britain was at war with France and that war was largely conducted not on land but at sea. The insurrection severely restricted British attempts to keep the French fleet bottled in at Brest. The government also considered it possible that the mutineers were capable of treason and might actually hand the ships over to the French, or indeed travel to Ireland in order to promote an Irish uprising. All of these circumstances made it absolutely critical that the rebellion was nipped in the bud without delay.

The mutiny, about pay and conditions throughout the Royal Navy, quickly spread and soon reached the *Director*, which had returned just a few weeks earlier for a refit in the River Thames. There had been problems on board with insubordination and refusal to carry out instructions, as a result of which Bligh had had to order a number of floggings. Matters boiled over and the crew demanded the removal of Captain Bligh and three of his officers. Bligh went ashore, only to be asked to act as a confidential mediator between the Admiralty and the disaffected crews on a number of the ships.

On 26 May 1797 Bligh met with Admiral Duncan to discuss a strategy to end the mutiny, following which Bligh personally visited many of the ships, canvassing their views and trying to persuade them to give way on the Articles of Demand which had been presented to the Admiralty by the

Nore mutineers. These demands had been dismissed out of hand on 20 May. Officially their response was 'All that could reasonably be expected by the seamen and marines has already been granted them. Their Lordships cannot accede any further requests.'

The demands were:

Article 1: That every indulgence granted to the fleet at Portsmouth (Spithead) be granted to His Majesty's subjects serving in the Fleet at the Nore and places adjacent.

Article 2: That every man, upon a ship's coming into harbour (a certain number at a time so as not to injure the ship's duty) to go and see their friends and families; a convenient time to be allowed to each man.

Article 3: That all ships before they go to sea shall be paid all arrears of wages down to six months, according to the old rules.

Article 4: That no officer that has been turned down by any of His Majesty's ships shall be employed in the same ship again without consent of the ship's company.

Article 5: That when any of His Majesty's ships shall be paid, that may have been some time in commission, if there are any pressed men on board, that may not be in the regular course of payment, they shall receive two months advance to furnish them with necessaries.

Article 6: That an indemnification be made any men who have run and may now be in His Majesty's naval service and that they not be liable to be taken up as deserters.

Article 7: That a more equal distribution be made of prize money to the crews of His Majesty's ships and vessels of war.

Article 8: That the articles of war, as now enforced, require various alterations, several of which to be expunged therefrom; and if more moderate ones were held forth to seamen in general, it would be the means of taking off that terror and prejudice against His Majesty's service, on that account frequently imbibed by seamen from entering voluntarily into service.

None of these complaints were aimed at Bligh and there was no suggestion that his conduct was in any way responsible for a general dissatisfaction on his ship. The mutiny had fizzled out by 13 June, after the government cut off the mutineers' supplies of food and water and loyalist seamen had taken control of the rebel ships. A few concessions had been made, including better pay and the right to object to unpopular leaders, but the Admiralty were determined to punish the main organisers of the revolt. Bligh was still onshore and in his absence the first lieutenant on board *Director* was asked by the Admiralty to submit a list of the names of ten men who had been the ringleaders on the ship. It was generally assumed that these men would then be charged, as a deterrent to others, but that the remaining crew members would be pardoned. Bligh then discovered to his horror that the Admiralty intended to charge not just the ten but twenty-nine of his men for taking part in the mutiny. He regarded this as a breach of good faith, given the promises made to the men, and he fought tooth and nail to get pardons for his crew. In the end he succeeded, and it reflects well on his character that he was prepared to stand up and fight for his men. It is also noteworthy that in return for his loyalty the men were loyal to him. One of the terms of the settlement of the dispute was that the mutineers on the various ships were permitted to submit a list of one hundred names of men they did not wish to serve under. Bligh's name was not on that list. It certainly suggests that Bligh was not an unpopular tyrant – even though by then Bligh had learnt that his generally accepted nickname throughout the fleet was 'that Bounty bastard'.

The upshot of the mutiny was that thirty men were hanged, including Richard Parker who was regarded as the ringleader and who had been elected as 'President of the Delegates of the Fleet'. He met his fate on the yardarm of HMS *Sandwich*, the vessel on which the mutiny had started. Another twenty-nine men were imprisoned, nine were flogged and a number of others were sentenced to be transported to New South Wales.

It is hard to see how any blame attaches to Bligh – yet the Nore Mutiny is generally added to the list of events involving insurrection for which Bligh is held responsible. He was simply caught up in events and in practice did a remarkable job in bringing the revolt to a satisfactory conclusion.

Chapter 14

Reputational Damage – Claim and Counterclaim

By Authority of the LORDS COMMISSIONERS of the ADMIRALTY.

This Day was publiſhed,

In Quarto, illuſtrated with Charts, Price Seven Shillings.

LIEUTENANT WILLIAM BLIGH's NARRATIVE of the MUTINY by which he was deprived of the Command of HIS MAJESTY's SHIP BOUNTY; and his ſubſequent Voyage in the Ship's Boat from TOFOA, one of the Friendly Iſlands to TIMOR, a Dutch Settlement in the Eaſt-Indies.

Printed for George Nicol, Bookſeller to his Majeſty, Pall-Mall.

Newspaper cutting announcing the publication of Bligh's first book, in 1790.

Going back to the year 1793, when Bligh completed his second breadfruit mission, he must have been feeling pretty pleased with himself. He would have learnt that while he was away the mutineers had been court-martialled and that three men had been hanged – and although he would have been miffed to learn that Haywood had been pardoned, he had no reason to believe that his own reputation had been sullied by the trial. And then the proverbial really hit the fan: Haywood's letter to Edward Christian, set out in full at the end of Chapter 11, had led to extensive research and the questioning of all relevant parties by Edward Christian. In particular, Edward had obtained the detailed minutes of the trial prepared by Stephen Barney, the lawyer representing William Muspratt. The result: the 1794 publication of *Minutes of the Proceedings of the Court Martial held at Portsmouth 12 August, 1792. On Ten Persons charged with Mutiny on Board His Majesty's Ship the* Bounty. *With an Appendix, Containing a full Account of the real Causes and Circumstances of that unhappy Transaction, the most material of which have hitherto been withheld from the Public.*

The story gained great publicity, prompting a letter to *The Times* on 16 July, 1794 from Edward Harwood, the man who had been surgeon on HMS *Providence*. In it he complained that 'The obvious tendency … is to palliate the conduct of Fletcher Christian, his brother, and ultimately to asperse the character of Captain Bligh.' It continued:

> This publication, Mr Editor, is disgraced by gross misrepresentations, and low malevolence, of which innumerable instances could be adduced … the shafts of envy are ever levelled against conspicuous merit, but they recoil with redoubled force on the impotent adversary. Captain Bligh's general conduct during the late expedition, which was crowned with the most ample success, his affability to his officers, and humane attention to his men, gained him their high esteem and admiration, and must eventually dissipate any unfavourable opinion, hastily adopted in his absence. I trust that this imbecile and highly illiberal attack, directed by the brother of the Arch-mutineer, will be received by the world with that indignation and contempt it so justly deserves.

But the genie was soon out of the bottle and the State Library of New South Wales holds a newspaper cutting, apparently taken from the *Cumberland Packet* and picked up by other newspapers. It reads:

> THE late most interesting trial at Portsmouth, of the unfortunate mutineers of the Bounty, has produced such an investigation of the subject, that the world will be astonished at the information, which will be shortly communicated by a gentleman who attended the trial as an advocate; the public will then be enabled to correct the erroneous opinions, which, from a certain false narrative they have long entertained, and to distinguish between the audacious and hardened depravity of the heart which no suffering can soften, and the desperation

> of an ingenuous mind torn and agonized by unprovoked and incessant abuse and disgrace.
>
> Though there may be certain actions, which even the torture and extremity of provocation cannot justify, yet a sudden act of phrenzy, so circumstanced, is far removed in reason and mercy from the soul deliberate contempt of every religious and virtuous sentiment and obligation, excited by selfish and base gratifications. – For the honour of this county we are happy to assure our readers, that one of its natives, FLETCHER CHRISTIAN, is not that detestable and horrid monster of wickedness, which with extreme and perhaps unexampled injustice and barbarity to him and his relations he has long been represented, but a character for whom every feeling heart must now sincerely grieve and lament.

The newspaper report ended by saying that

> Mackintosh, one of the seamen, added with an honest simplicity, – 'Oh! he was a gentleman, and a brave man, and every officer and sailor on board the ship, would have gone through fire and water to have served him.' The mystery of this melancholy transaction will soon be unravelled, and then the shame and infamy of it will be distributed in the just proportions, in which they are, and have been, deserved.

The Appendix made sensational reading. One passage read:

> Captain Bligh used to call his officers 'scoundrels, damned rascals, hounds, hell-hounds, beasts and infamous wretches' and that he frequently threatened them that when they reached Endeavour Straits 'he would kill one half of the people, make the officers jump overboard and would make them eat grass like cows'.

The Appendix went on to say that Captain Bligh was accustomed to abuse Christian much more frequently and roughly than the rest of the officers, or, as one of the persons expressed it, 'whatever fault was found, Mr Christian was sure to bear the brunt of the Captain's anger'. It also claimed that the captain 'frequently shook his fist in Christian's face'. However, it said that the event which really pushed Christian over the edge was the episode with the missing coconuts. Christian had been called over by Bligh, who allegedly accosted him with the words 'Damn your blood, you have stolen my coconuts', to which Christian replied: 'I was dry. I thought it of no consequence.' This elicited the response that he was a lying scoundrel and that he had stolen not one coconut but half the pile. This apparently left Christian very hurt and agitated, saying 'Why do you treat me thus, Captain Bligh?' To this, Bligh 'shook his fist in Christian's face and called him a thief and other abusive names'.

Later that afternoon, at around four o'clock, there was another altercation between the pair, resulting in Christian being reduced to floods of tears. Purcell, the carpenter referred to seeing him with 'tears running fast from his eyes in big drops'. Purcell, of course, was no ally of Bligh and was accustomed to receiving a tongue-lashing from him, and remarked 'Do I not receive as bad as you?' Christian's reply was interesting:

> You have something [ie a warrant] to protect you and can speak again, but if I should speak to him as you do he would probably break me, turn me before the mast and perhaps flog me, and if he did it would be the death of both of us for I am sure that I would take him in my arms and jump overboard with him.

The point was that as a warrant officer, Purcell knew that he could not be flogged, whereas Christian had no such protection. Were he to be flogged, in front of his men, he would have found it totally humiliating – hence the reference to a preference for committing murder/suicide.

The Appendix gives various examples of where Bligh had deliberately humiliated Christian, especially in the company of the islanders on Tahiti where rank and status were incredibly important. To the Tahitian chiefs, Christian was a 'tyo' or friend. But Bligh disabused them of this, calling Christian a 'towtow' or servant. 'These circumstances, although comparatively trifling, are such as to be distinctly remembered; but they prove that there could be little harmony where such painful sensations were so frequently and unnecessarily excited.'

Christian also expressed the opinion that going through the Endeavour Straits was going to be 'hell' and was heard to say, tearfully, that 'I would rather die ten thousand deaths than bear this treatment. I always do my duty as an officer and as a man ought to do, yet I receive this scandalous usage.' All agreed that they had never previously seen Christian in tears ('No, he was no milksop'). The Appendix continues with an account of Christian's plan – not to lead a mutiny, but to escape on a makeshift raft. He handed out his Tahitian souvenirs to his colleagues and tore up various letters and threw them overboard. He asked for nails from the carpenter so that he could fashion a makeshift raft out of a wooden platform. In doing so he said that he realised that he would never be able to reach Tahiti, but hoped that he might be rescued by friendly islanders in their canoes. For sustenance, he had stashed away a secret pile of food. This would explain the circumstances in which Tinkler 'a young boy, one of Christian's mess mates' was hungry in the evening and apparently went below to get a piece of pork and 'found it packed up with some breadfruit in a dirty clothes bag in Christian's cot'.

This story of the makeshift raft would certainly account for the idea that right up until his four o'clock watch, Christian had no conception of taking over the *Bounty*. During the time he was on watch, Christian was accompanied by two lads of 15, Hallett and Hayward, both of whom were fast asleep, and there is no record of who else Christian might have spoken to. Even as late as five o'clock, when Bligh was woken from his slumbers and marched on deck, there may only have been a plan to cast Bligh ashore with three of the crew, using the small, rotten, cutter. The three would have been Hallett, Samuel and Heywood, and it was only when Christian could see that half the men on board wanted to leave the ship with Bligh that he selected the longboat and allowed as many as could fit in the boat to scramble on board.

The Appendix goes on to say that although Christian was the first to propose the mutiny and had suggested turning the captain on shore at Tofoa he:

> declared afterwards in the ship, he never should have thought of it, if it had not been suggested to his mind by an expression of Mr Stewart, who, knowing of his intention of leaving the ship upon the raft, told him: 'When you go, Christian, we are ripe for anything.'

Ironically, Stewart was not part of Christian's watch and was asleep in his bunk when the mutiny occurred – so even if he planted the seed of an idea, he was not the person confided in by Christian. He did, however, rejoice at Bligh's comeuppance, reportedly clapping and dancing with glee at his captain's discomfort ('in the Otaheite manner') and saying that it was the happiest day of his life. Later, Stewart was one of the unfortunate men drowned on board *Pandora*.

The Appendix is interesting in suggesting that although Christian was partial to female company he did not, prior to the mutiny, have a specific attraction to any one woman in particular. This is contrary to the statement by Lawrence Lebogue to the effect that he remembered Christian 'had a girl, who was always with him'. It is known from the logbook entries that Christian had been to see the surgeon to be treated for a venereal disease, so he may well have been 'casting his favours'. The Appendix gives us this explanation:

> Although Christian was on shore … yet the officers who were with Christian … declare that he never had a female favourite at Otaheite, nor any attachment or particular connexion among the women. It is true that some had what they call 'their girls', or women with whom they constantly lived all the time they were upon the island, but this was not the case with Christian.

If that is correct it makes it all the more surprising that Christian took Maimiti as his bride almost as soon as he reached Tahiti after the mutiny, taking her with him to Pitcairn. It would certainly suggest that it was more a case of being in love with the lifestyle, the sexual freedom, and the freedom from toil – rather than genuinely being in love with Maimiti. For Christian, rejected in love several years earlier, then confined in a stinking ship with only men for company, it must have been heaven on earth to have a sexual partner who satisfied his every desire! And she could cook. And she was an expert in making fine white tapa cloth out of bark, useful for clothing. And, well, she was a natural in the role which she later adopted – as matriarch of a community which thrived on Pitcairn despite all the odds.

The Appendix ends with words which will no doubt find favour with twenty-first century ideas about workers' rights and about oppression and bullying: 'the crime itself in this instance may afford an awful lesson to the navy and to mankind, that there is a degree of pressure, beyond which the best formed and principled mind must either break or recoil.' It ended with bemoaning that:

> a young man is condemned to perpetual infamy, who, if he had served on board any other ship, or had perhaps been absent from the Bounty a single day, or one ill-fated hour, might still have been an honour to his country, and a glory and comfort to his friends.

It was not long before others leapt to Christian's defence. This was, after all, just after the French Revolution and here was a poster-boy for Man's fight against tyranny and oppression. It was also portrayed as a story of the power of love – even if perhaps it was more about lust, rejection and revenge.

Published in 1794, the Appendix provoked an immediate response from Bligh, with his *An Answer to Certain Assertions contained in the Appendix to a Pamphlet entitled Minutes of the Proceedings on the Court Martial….* Edward Christian had tried to show his brother as a romantic, hard-done-by young man, bullied beyond endurance by the domineering Captain Bligh. The captain responded with his *Answer to Certain Assertions*, in which he portrays himself as an affable and humane captain. He had the support of Edward Harwood, surgeon on board HMS *Providence*, who, as already mentioned, wrote a letter to *The Times* giving his support to Bligh, ending with the words: 'I trust that this imbecile and highly illiberal attack, directed by the brother of the Arch-mutineer, will be received by the world with that indignation and contempt it so justly deserves'.

Bligh backed this up with the testimony of a number of his former crewmen who denied statements attributed to them by Edward Christian: Lawrence Lebogue, John Smith, Joseph Coleman and John Hallet all made affidavits to that effect. Influential friends such as Edward Lamb wrote a letter in support (*Letter from Mr Edward Lamb Commander of The Adventure, in the Jamaica Trade to Captain William Bligh*). Bligh's contention was that Christian had been suffering from some kind of mental illness. The following year Edward Christian responded with *A Short Reply to Capt. William Bligh's Answer*, in which he cast doubt upon the testimonials of those who had supported Bligh in his *Answer to Certain Assertions*. In particular he raged at Lebogue's statement ('I am obliged to declare that the [affidavit] which is made by Lawrence Lebogue, is the most wicked and perjured affidavit that ever was sworn before a magistrate, or published to the world')

Pamphlets and books by various interested parties followed in succeeding decades. Perhaps the most thorough review of all the available documents was made by Sir John Barrow, Secretary at the Admiralty, in 1831 with his book *The Eventful History of the Mutiny and Piratical Seizure of HMS Bounty*. In it, he concluded:

> no conspiracy nor pre-concerted measures had any existence, but that it was suddenly conceived by a hot-headed young man, in a state of great excitement of mind, amounting to a temporary aberration of intellect, caused by the frequent abusive and insulting language of his commanding officer. Waking out of a short half hour's disturbed sleep, to take the command of the deck – finding the two mates of the watch, Hayward and Hallet, asleep (for which they ought to have been dismissed the service instead of being, as they were, promoted) – the opportunity tempting, and the ship completely in his power, with a momentary impulse he darted down the fore-hatchway, got possession of the keys of the arm-chest, and made the hazardous experiment of arming such of the men as he thought he could trust, and effected his purpose.

The same book gave credibility to reports of the alleged sightings of Fletcher Christian back in Britain, which has already been touched on at the end of Chapter 9.

> About the years 1808 and 1809, a very general opinion was prevalent in the neighbourhood of the lakes of Cumberland and Westmoreland, that Christian was in that part of the country, and made frequent private visits to an aunt who was living there. Being the near relative of Mr Christian Curwen, long member of Parliament for Carlisle, and himself a native, he was well known in the neighbourhood.

Barrow added Peter Heywood's comment that he was convinced he had seen Christian walking down a street in Plymouth, adding fuel to the claims of the conspiracy theorists.

Another important book putting forward the pro-Christian view was written by Peter Heywood's step-daughter in 1870. As Lady Diana Joliffe Belcher she published *The Mutineers of the Bounty and Their Descendants in Pitcairn and Norfolk Islands*. She had the advantage of access to family papers and also to the diaries of James Morrison, and a review of the book in 1871 stated that 'This gives additional proof – if such indeed were needed – of the tyrannical bearing of Captain Bligh.'

And so it continued for much of the Victorian era, with each book adding another layer of tarnish on top of previous tarnished layers. The sparkling reputation of Bligh circa 1790 was utterly destroyed – all it needed was for Hollywood to come along in the next century and invent a totally twisted version of Bligh and we are left with the somewhat cardboard and one-dimensional 'Bad Guy' to set against the noble and heroic Christian.

Chapter 15

Naval Success: Camperdown and Copenhagen

'The Battle off Camperdown fought on 11 October 1797'

After playing his part in subduing the Nore mutiny, Bligh had been given the task of surveying the shifting sands along the River Humber. He was then ordered to join Admiral Duncan as part of the force blockading the Dutch fleet off the Texel. Since 1795, Holland had been overrun by the French and forced to become a puppet state, with the formidable Dutch navy being used to bolster French interests. To counter this, the British North Sea Fleet had been given the task of keeping the Dutch bottled up in port. This involved a tedious game of cat and mouse, not helped by distractions such as the Nore mutiny. It was not until early October 1797 that Admiral Duncan decided to slip back to Yarmouth for fresh supplies on HMS *Venerable*, along with a number of other vessels. He left instructions for a lookout to disguise his absence by making fictitious signals, fooling the Dutch under the command of Jan de Winter into thinking that the ship was communicating with invisible vessels just beyond the horizon. This ruse may have worked for a day or two, but de Winter then led his ships out on a raiding trip. The British lookout ordered a lugger to sail back to Yarmouth to inform Admiral Duncan, who immediately left harbour and raced across the Channel, arriving eighteen miles off the Dutch coast opposite the village of Kamperduin ('Camperdown').

He found the Dutch fleet already assembled in line of battle and conventional naval tactics would have been for the English fleet to form a parallel line, so that both fleets could pummel each other with broadside after broadside until one side prevailed. But Duncan did not have the time, or possibly the inclination, to wait while everyone got into position and instead split his squadron in two. One attacked the vanguard while the other, which included Bligh on the *Director*, attacked the rear.

Under prevailing arrangements on board, the naval day ran from midday to midday so although the battle is recorded to have taken place on 11 October, it was actually 12 October when the fighting commenced. Hampered by poor visibility and by haphazard signalling, the ships in each of the two sections were pretty well left to make their own decisions as to where and when to attack the enemy. The *Director* immediately engaged with the *Haarlem* and the *Alkmaar*, and in the ensuing melee the Dutch line disintegrated. Duncan, in particular, showed great courage on board his flagship *Venerable*, sailing straight across the Dutch line immediately behind de Winter's flagship *Vrijheid*, taking the battle to the next ship in line, the *Staaten Generaal*, before ending up in the centre of the battle, surrounded on all sides.

At the height of the battle a cannon shot shattered the *Venerable*'s mast on which the admiral's colours were flying. Normally, striking the colours would be a sign of surrender – but a sailor by the name of Jack Crawford saved the day by climbing the main mast and literally 'nailing the colour to the mast' as the battle raged around him. By mid-afternoon Duncan was able to observe that ten enemy ships had been captured, following a ferocious battle between the evenly numbered forces, each with thirteen warships. The one ship which was not captured or destroyed was de Winter's *Vrijheid*, and it looked as though the Dutch admiral was intending to fight the British single-handedly. In the event, Bligh, on *Director*, gave chase to *Vrijheid*, and in a savage exchange of cannon shot brought down all three masts on the Dutch flagship. Not only could *Vrijheid* not escape, but the masts fell in such a way as to obstruct the guns on the starboard side. Bligh drew his ship up within yards of the stricken vessel and called upon de Winter to surrender. He was having none of it and tried to raise a signal for other Dutch ships to come to his aid. Seeing this, Bligh came alongside and boarded the stricken ship, only to discover that de Winter was engaged with his carpenter in trying to fix a small boat so that he could join another vessel and resume command. Bligh informed de Winter that he was a prisoner of war and took him on board HMS *Venerable* so that a formal surrender could take place – de Winter being an admiral, he could hardly be expected to surrender to a mere captain. In the event, de Winter offered his sword to Admiral Duncan, as a traditional sign of surrender, but this offer was declined by Duncan. He announced that he would far prefer to shake the hand of his brave adversary. And so it was that later that evening, the two admirals sat down after supper for a game of whist; de Winter reportedly lost, exclaiming that it really was too bad to lose twice in the same day and to the same man…

Great heroism and courage was shown on both sides, but it was a total rout of the Dutch fleet. Many of the captured ships were beyond salvaging – as also were several of the British warships, which limped back to port and were found to be beyond repair. On board *Director* just five men had been wounded, whereas on *Vrijheid* almost half of the entire complement on board were either killed or wounded, along with every single officer apart from de Winter.

National rejoicing took place in Britain and the government was delighted to see that the morale and fighting spirit of the British sailors had not been eroded by the events off the Nore just a few months earlier. Admiral Duncan was created Viscount Duncan of Camperdown and Baron Duncan of Lundie. One of his admirals was granted a baronetcy; two of the captains were knighted and a jubilant King George III travelled to welcome home the victorious fleet. He even pardoned 180 of the Nore mutineers who were being held in a rotting hulk in the River Medway.

However, despite his role in capturing not just de Winter himself but also his colours and his flagship, Bligh received no special commendation. He wasn't even mentioned by Admiral Duncan in his report, possibly because the action in which *Vrijheid* was captured was unseen by anyone else in the fleet. A small consolation: he did get to go to St Paul's Cathedral on 23 December when the King led a thanksgiving procession. At the ceremony Admiral Duncan carried de Winter's flag from *Vrijheid*, with all the English captains following in line. And Bligh got the Naval Gold Medal 1795 – just as all the other captains were given. The particular one given to Bligh was sold at auction in Australia in 2011 for $235,440, far more than its estimate. It is a reminder of the continuing fascination with Bligh and his life story. His image, in miniature, was also included on a highly patriotic 'thanksgiving memento' painted by John Smart and subsequently engraved by George Noble.

Bligh emerged from the episode as a brave and skilful battle-hardened captain, respected by his crew. All of them would eventually share in the value of the prize money attributable to the captured Dutch ships, even though, as mentioned, many of them were of little value because they were no longer seaworthy.

After the tumult of battle things quietened down for Bligh. He remained with *Director* on half pay until 1800 and during that time carried out a great deal of hydrographic work for the navy. In particular he surveyed the mouth of the River Liffey and the port of Dublin – notorious for inaccurate charts, shifting sands and unmarked shipwrecks. The work took Bligh three months, from October to December 1800 at which point he was able to present the Admiralty with a detailed chart together with recommendations for work to be carried out to improve port access. These included designing the North Bull Wall at the mouth of the River Liffey. When constructed, the barrier helped direct the river flow through a more narrowly focused channel, thereby getting rid of the sandbar which was posing a danger to shipping. Bligh recommended the construction of a number of harbour walls in Dublin Bay, creating a refuge harbour. The idea for a refuge harbour was to receive a huge impetus after two British troop ships were driven ashore in a storm in November 1807 with the loss of over four hundred lives. This disaster led to the construction of a new naval base between 1816 and 1820. Initially known as Kingstown on account of a royal visit, it was eventually named Dún Laoghaire.

Further survey work was carried out at Holyhead and at Fowey, Dungeness and Flushing. Then, on 13 January 1801, Bligh received a new appointment, as captain of HMS *Glatton*, a former East Indiaman which had been purchased by the navy in 1795. Unique for her time, she was equipped solely with carronades – short-barrelled guns made at the Carron iron-foundry in Stirlingshire. With twenty-eight 68-pounder carronades on her lower deck and another twenty-eight 32-pounder carronades on the upper deck, she packed a huge punch, especially in close-quarter combat. Bringing the carronades to bear on the enemy was never easy because the ship's gun ports were too small to allow for the gun barrels to be moved from side-to-side. In other words, the ship had to be positioned so that the carronades could fire broadside, often at a distance of less than a hundred yards. To get that close, the ship would inevitably be exposed for a considerable period of time to the much greater range of the enemy's longer guns. Conversely, once she was at close quarters her guns could fire much heavier shot than the longer guns. It all meant that the fourth-rate *Glatton* could let rip with a heavier broadside than the first-rate *Victory*, launched in 1765 and armed with 104 guns. The carronades were much lighter and more stubby than the traditional long barrelled guns, used far less gunpowder and needed fewer men to operate.

Bligh hardly had time to acquaint himself with the ship, its crew and its new-fangled carronades before he was sent into action. It was at a time when a fleet under the command of Sir Hyde Parker was about to depart for the Baltic. The second-in-command of the fleet was Vice-Admiral Horatio Nelson and the fleet was hoping to 'persuade' Denmark to withdraw from an alliance involving France and Russia. Diplomatic persuasion having failed, force was seen as the only answer.

HMS *Glatton* joined the fleet as it sailed from Yarmouth and took up position facing the Danish capital. Parker realised that the shallow water meant that the larger ships in the fleet were never going to be able to manoeuvre without risk of running aground, so he ordered Nelson, with a dozen ships having a shallower draft, to carry out the attack while he watched the battle from the north. Nelson changed ships, preferring the shallower HMS *Elephant* to the somewhat larger HMS *St George*. Almost immediately three of Nelson's ships, HMS *Agamemnon*, HMS *Russell* and HMS *Bellona* ran aground. They were not only sitting ducks, stuck on a sand bar, but impeded Parker's view of the naval engagement which followed.

Things had started badly for the British and then appeared to get worse. At one stage an enemy ship approached HMS *Elephant*, intending to attack, but Bligh deliberately sailed into the line of fire and caught most of the enemy's broadside. *Glatton* was damaged but the *Elephant* was unharmed.

Believing the battle had reached a stalemate, Parker raised the signal to retreat. Nelson famously disregarded the signal, announcing that 'I have the right to be blind sometimes', and then, holding his telescope to his blind eye, said 'I really do not see the signal!'

Nelson acknowledged receipt of the signal but continued to fly the number '16' (i.e. his 'close action' signal) from the mast-head. Bligh, sailing alongside *Elephant*, was one of the few captains in a position to see both the signal from Parker, and Nelson's response. One other officer saw the two conflicting signals, Captain Riou on HMS *Amazon*. Riou was in charge of the frigate squadron and felt that he had no choice but to obey the senior officer. He ordered the ships under his command to turn round and retreat. As *Amazon* turned away her vulnerable stern was exposed to the Danish shore batteries and in the resulting fusillade Riou and a number of his crew were killed. It was a huge loss to the navy – Nelson described Riou as 'irreplaceable'. He was a man well known to Bligh as they had served together on Cook's final voyage, on board *Resolution*. Riou was also present in Cape Town in 1789 when Bligh landed there after his remarkable voyage to Timor following the *Bounty* mutiny.

Unlike Riou, Bligh chose to disregard Parker's order and followed Nelson's example by continuing to fly the signal '16' for attack. Had he not done so, and had turned to retreat, there is every likelihood that the rest of the fleet would have followed his example. As it was, the tide of battle turned in Nelson's favour and victory quickly followed. At the end of hostilities two Danish ships had been sunk, one had exploded, and twelve had been captured. Casualties were heavy on both sides, with an estimated 1,600 to 1,800 Danes either killed, captured or wounded. British figures suggest the navy suffered 963 killed or wounded.

Bligh's own account of the battle was concise:

> At 10:26 the action began. At noon the action continuing very hot, ourselves much cut up – our opponent the Danish Commodore struck to us but his seconds ahead and astern still kept up a strong fire. At 11:24 our fore topmast was shot away, seven of our upper deck guns disabled by the enemy.
>
> The action continuing very hot at 2:45 it may be said to have ended. Our losses 17 killed, 34 wounded. Mast very dangerously wounded. Rigging and sails shot to pieces. Seven upper deck guns, and two lower disabled by the enemy's shot.

> Our number of men on board, including officers were 309 so that we had 1/6 of the whole killed and disabled. All the ships and vessels to the southward of the Crown Battery struck and except one or two, was destroyed or taken. We fought at a cables length distant from our opponents.

After the battle Nelson called Bligh onboard HMS *Elephant*, and in front of the other officers, thanked him for his courageous support. Bligh then returned to Britain so that *Glatton* could undergo extensive repairs, leaving Bligh to be transferred to a number of short-term appointments. So it was that after just one month in charge of *Glatton*, and just ten days after the Battle of Copenhagen, he was appointed captain of the seventy-four gun HMS *Monarch*. Less than a month later the ship was laid off at the Nore and Bligh was transferred to HMS *Irresistible*, a posting which lasted just over a year and which terminated on 28 May 1802. *Irresistible* was the flagship of Rear-Admiral Bartholomew Samuel Rowley, and under Bligh's command operated in the Channel until July 1801. Subsequently, the ship operated under the flag of Vice-Admiral Christopher Parker off the Dutch coast. Peace brought with it more mundane duties, and in 1803 Bligh started work surveying the entrance to the Schelde river.

On 2 May 1804, Bligh was given the command of HMS *Warrior*. It was during this period that he fell out with one of his officers, who claimed that a leg injury made him medically unfit for duty. Bligh disagreed and in the shouting match which followed Lieutenant John Frazier was arrested for refusing duty. Two courts martial followed, one involving Frazier and the other Bligh. The court met on 25 and 26 February 1805 on board HMS *San Josef*, moored at Torbay, and conducted under the auspices of Vice-Admiral Sir Charles Cotton. Frazier was acquitted and the court moved on to look at his complaint against Bligh. Frazier alleged that Bligh:

> Did publicly on the quarter deck on His Majesty's Ship Warrior grossly insult and ill treat me being in the execution of my office by calling me rascal, scoundrel and shaking his fist in my face … and behaved himself towards me and other commissioned, warrant and petty officers in the ship in a tyrannical and oppressive and un-officer-like behaviour contrary to the rules and discipline of the Navy.

One of the men giving evidence against Bligh was George Mortimer, who served under Bligh on HMS *Warrior* as Captain of the Marines, and testified that Bligh 'was frequently very violent and passionate and that his conduct was tyrannical and un-officer-like'. Bligh's defence to the charge of excessive behaviour and of using bad language is interesting:

> I candidly and without reserve avow that I am not a tame and indifferent observer of the manner in which officers placed under my orders conduct themselves in the performance of their several duties. A signal or any communication from a commanding officer has ever been to me an indication for exertion and alacrity to carry into effect the purport thereof and peradventure I may occasionally have appeared to some of those officers as unnecessarily anxious for its execution by exhibiting an action or gesture peculiar to myself to such.

The case against Bligh was in part proved: he was reprimanded for his tyrannical behaviour and advised to moderate his language. He was, however, permitted to resume command of *Warrior*, but in practice left the ship just three months later.

Chapter 16

New South Wales and the Rum Rebellion

The arrest of Governor Bligh, by an unknown artist.

From the end of April 1805 Captain Bligh had been put on half-pay, no doubt still smarting from being reprimanded and facing the prospect of kicking his heels with boredom and getting under his wife's feet. But it would have been with mixed feelings that he heard that his name was being put forward for a totally shore-based appointment – as Governor of the far-off penal colony of New South Wales. The colony had not even been in existence for twenty years – and it was an extremely tough environment, hardly suited to a married man with six daughters in trail. However, his name had touted for the job by his old supporter Sir Joseph Banks, who wrote a letter in the light of the governorship of Philip Gidley King coming to an end. In the letter, dated 15 March 1805, he had been asked:

> [I]f I knew a man proper to be sent out in his stead – one who has integrity unimpeached, a mind capable of providing its own resources in difficulties without leening [sic] on others for advice, firm in discipline, civil in deportment and not subject to whimper and whine when severity of discipline is wanted … I immediately answered … I know of no one but Captain Bligh who will suit.

The salary on offer for the governorship was, at £2000 p.a., double the rate paid to King, which surely gave a hint as to the poisoned chalice which the appointment entailed. It would mean a significant increase in pay for Bligh, as well as kudos and status. A key consideration was that Bligh's wife had no intention of giving up a life of respectability and calm in order to travel to the other side of the world, to live in a sort of exile in Government House, without 'polite society' and surrounded by a community of convicted felons and armed soldiers. She would no doubt have heard of the dire shortages suffered by the early settlers, because she would have heard about conditions from her uncle, Duncan Campbell. He had been actively involved in all three of the early fleets to take convicts out to the nascent colony and would doubtless have told her that this was no place for a lady used to sophisticated refinement.

William Bligh would have known that all the earlier governors had encountered great problems in asserting their authority, especially in standing up to the corrupt and devious demands of the military, operating as the New South Wales Corps ('NSW Corps'). As it turned out, much of what happened next is not really about Bligh, it is about the people who confronted him and were determined to thwart him at every turn. Bligh's fault was to lack the guile to out-wit his opponents, or to bide his time until his enemies had over-played their hand. He certainly was not the first Governor to fail, and although the mutiny which occurred during his gubernatorial term was the worst confrontation between the parties, it happened simply because Bligh was determined to do the right thing – to impose law and order, to install an administration which served the entire community and not just the ruling class. Before Bligh, Governor Hunter had tried and failed to stand up to the stream of abuses endemic in the NSW Corps, and the irascible Governor King had failed absolutely to follow through on the reforms upon which he had insisted. The result was near anarchy. This was no society based upon democratic principles; here was a population divided into two main sections, the criminals and the captors, i.e. the NSW Corp. Apart from this there were a few people who had gone out to the colony of their own free will, many of them hoping for rich pickings. In practice, the only way they could gain those rich pickings was by assisting the NSW Corps. The Corps controlled the produce coming into the colony – they controlled the stores and they controlled the prices. They also controlled the sale of products grown or manufactured in the colony, and the members of the NSW Corps quickly became rich, aided and abetted by entrepreneurs and businessmen keen to bend the law, intimidate the justice system and bribe the administration.

This all coincided with a shortage of hard currency – there simply was not enough cash in circulation to manage the growing economy. Instead, a plethora of promissory notes was followed up by an exchange system linked to the value of various commodities, such as grain. The problem with grain is that it fluctuated greatly in value. A more reliable index was alcohol, particularly using rum, manufactured in India and imported into the colony, and supplemented by alcohol distilled in home-made stills by the early colonists. William Bligh was well aware that the British government insisted that the use of rum as a currency must be brought to an end, setting the scene for a head-on clash between any new Governor and the defenders of the status quo.

William Bligh knew that he would need a female companion to run his household and act as 'First Lady', and therefore it was agreed that he would take his eldest daughter, Mary, to accompany him. In 1805 she had married John Putland, an army lieutenant, and it was agreed that he would serve his new father-in-law as aide-de-camp. William and his daughter set off on board the transport ship *Sinclair* in February 1806, as part of a convoy led by Joseph Short on board HMS *Porpoise*. John Putland sailed on HMS *Porpoise* in what proved to be a most unhappy voyage with clashing personalities. Both Bligh and Short regarded themselves as expedition leaders, and when Bligh ordered a change of course, Short objected and ordered Putland to fire a shot across the bows of Sinclair. There would subsequently be various formal inquiries into such incidents when the ships finally reached their destination. Those inquiries reveal that Short was high-handed and a very awkward man to deal with, and that Bligh was quite possibly in the right – notwithstanding criticism by the Secretary of State.

After spending six months at sea, Bligh reached Port Jackson on 6 August 1806, and duly took up his appointment as Governor, amidst much pomp and ceremony, exactly one week later. While waiting for the formal ceremony to take place Bligh was made the beneficiary of three valuable land grants, conferred by the outgoing Governor King. The first grant was 'for a private residence near Sydney' and involved 240 acres, to be known as Camperdown. The second, 'for a private residence near Parramatta', comprised 105 acres, and was to be known as Mount Betham. The third, 'for a private residence between Sydney and Hawkesbury', consisted of a thousand-acre site to be called Copenhagen. Critics were not slow to point out that Bligh repaid the generosity within a few months by confirming a land grant in the name of Mrs Anna Josepha King, wife of the former Governor. The reciprocal arrangement was not necessarily corrupt but it certainly did not leave Bligh above suspicion.

It was to be another thirty-five years before the validity of these grants was challenged. By then the Bligh lands had passed into the hands of his six daughters, as co-heiresses, and in 1841 a deal was done whereby the 105 acres at Parramatta were surrendered to the Crown in return for the Crown agreeing not to challenge the other gifts.

Another example of how Bligh failed to ensure that he was seen as being above reproach concerned the farm which he developed at Parramatta on land which he bought and paid for but which he ran using state funding. The convict labour – some thirty men – working as farm labourers were fed and housed at public expense. The stock was provided out of the public purse. The buildings appear to have been put up without Bligh personally paying for the expenses. And yet he was not necessarily acting corruptly – merely unwisely – because he may well have intended to have repaid moneys out of subsequent profits, only to be denied the opportunity because his tenure was cut short by what is now known as the Rum Rebellion, but which at the time was termed The Great Rebellion.

Things really started to get complicated six months into Bligh's tenure when, on 14 February 1807, he issued a general order banning 'the exchange of spirits or other liquors as payment for grain, animal food, labour, wearing apparel or any other commodity whatever'. This may have been exactly what the British Government wanted Bligh to do, but it committed him to open conflict not just with the entire NSW Corps, but also with all the wealthier families in the colony, all of whom had a finger in the rum-trade 'pie' of corruption. In particular, it heralded the first major collision between Bligh's policies and the interests of a remarkable character called John Macarthur. Here was a man who had come out as soldier with the Second Fleet, in 1790, determined to make his way in the world by whatever means necessary. He held the position of lieutenant in the NSW Corps, in charge of sixty soldiers, and they quickly became central to the cartel controlling the import of spirits into the colony. At that stage the colony was governed by a man called Arthur Phillip and when the Governor ordered Macarthur to return a barrel of rum which he had 'liberated' from government stores, Macarthur refused point-blank.

Macarthur declined to cooperate in any way with Governor Phillip, and when the Governor returned to England in late 1792 Macarthur took his chance to consolidate his power base. The man put in interim charge of the colony was Francis Grose, commander of the NSW Corps. Grose not only appointed Macarthur paymaster of the NSW Corps but also made him Inspector of Public Works. In effect, he controlled all the finances of both the military and civil sections of the colony. Grose also awarded him some two hundred acres of prime agricultural land at Rose Hill near Parramatta, together with free labour in the form of convicts to work the land. It was here that he started to experiment with rearing Merino sheep on his land – sheep which had traditionally only been found in Spain but which turned out to be ideally suited to Australian conditions.

In 1794 Grose was replaced as Lieutenant Governor by Captain William Paterson – another member of the NSW Corps. He too was happy to reward Macarthur for being his chief racketeer, making him up to army captain, and in a short time, Macarthur could claim to be the wealthiest man in the entire colony, creaming off a percentage on virtually everything.

The following year (1795) John Hunter was appointed as Governor and immediately sought to separate out the civil and military functions of government, forcing Macarthur to give up his role as Inspector of Works. This caused huge resentment and Macarthur was not to be thwarted in his determination to frustrate and prevent any meaningful reforms. He was aided in this by the fact that the army controlled the courts – members of the NSW Corps made up a majority sitting as judges in all civil matters. It meant that in 1800 Governor Hunter was recalled to London, adjudged by his superiors as having failed to implement the reforms which he had been sent out to impose.

In his place came Governor King, Bligh's immediate predecessor. He soon had to deal with a problem when Macarthur shot and wounded one of his own commanding officers. King had Macarthur arrested but realised that there was no way that he was going to get a fair trial in front of judges made up from members of the NSW Corps. He therefore decided to send Macarthur back for trial before a court martial in England. In order to make the charges stick, King prepared a detailed dossier of all Macarthur's known transgressions and demonstrating how Macarthur's personal fortune of some £20,000 had been amassed by corrupt means. Both the dossier and Macarthur left for England on board the *Hunter* in late 1801 – but guess what? By the time the ship docked in London there was no trace of the dossier. The court martial never took place and all charges were dropped.

Macarthur wasted no time in using his return to England to press his claim for support from the British government for his venture in developing an Australian wool industry, based on importing and breeding Merino sheep. He was able to show that the wool taken from his small Merino flock was of the highest quality; he decided to 'think big', resigned his army commission, and petitioned the government for the grant of ten thousand acres of prime agricultural land to enable him to develop his sheep-rearing interests. In this, he was assisted by his patron Lord Camden, who occupied the position of Colonial Secretary.

Five thousand acres were granted immediately with a promise of a further five thousand on his return. He was also successful in acquiring nine Merino rams and a ewe from the royal flock at Kew. When Macarthur returned to New South Wales in June 1805, he had been away for almost four years. He immediately antagonised Governor King by demanding his second tranche of five thousand acres, in an area known as the Cowpastures. King declined to ratify the grant, stating in correspondence that 'one-half the colony already belongs to him, and it will not be long before he gets the other half'. For the time being, Macarthur had to 'make do' with the other five thousand acres, naming it Camden Park in honour of his main supporter back in England.

It was into this political minefield that Bligh stepped in 1806. He immediately declined Macarthur's demand for the remaining five thousand acres, thereby setting himself up for direct confrontation with Macarthur. The latter's resignation from the army had in no way diminished his influence within the NSW Corps. Those remaining in the Corps knew exactly which side their bread was buttered.

Bligh was so keen to oppose Macarthur at every opportunity that he arguably failed to follow due process. The pair were as bad as each other, but in the end it was Macarthur who came out as the clear winner.

Initially, the dispute concerned a civil case brought by Macarthur as he sought to enforce an existing promissory note expressed to be in terms of wheat prices. Sitting in the appeal court, Bligh dismissed Macarthur's case out of hand and without even giving him a chance to present his case. Bligh also had been conducting his own enquiries into the grant of various 'temporary' leases by Governor King, one of which was in favour of Macarthur and which involved land near St Phillip's Church. Bligh demanded that the leases should be forfeited and the land cleared. Another source of friction involved two stills, used in the production of spirits, which had arrived on board the *Dart*. Bligh demanded that the stills should be returned to Europe but Macarthur, for whom one of the stills was intended, refused to cooperate and managed to use a legal technicality to set aside the order for the still to be seized. Then there was the question of responsibility for an escaped convict by the name of John Hoare, who managed to leave the colony in June 1807 on board one of Macarthur's ships, the *Parramatta*, bound for Tahiti. Under the law, Macarthur, as owner of the vessel, was criminally liable for permitting the escape. He was summonsed, but refused to appear in court. Instead, he abandoned the schooner, informing the captain and crew of *Parramatta* that they would no longer be paid or be entitled to make use of provisions on board. Macarthur was eventually seized, brought before the magistrates, and bailed pending the criminal case which was due to be heard at the end of January 1808. Meanwhile, he used every trick in the book to evade justice; for instance, he objected to the appointment of Judge-Advocate Atkins. This was on the grounds that Atkins might be prejudiced against him because Atkins owed money to Macarthur.

Macarthur ranted about freedom of speech and complained that he was defending the rights and freedoms of the individual against tyranny. Above all, he was rallying the soldiers in the NSW Corps, who could see their privileges and illicit perks being eroded. As a rabble-rouser he was certainly more effective than Governor Bligh could ever hope to be. Keen to provoke Bligh, Macarthur also instructed his men to fence off the disputed plot near St Phillip's Church, inevitably prompting Bligh to order his men to pull the fence down.

The criminal court met on 26 January and consisted of Judge-Advocate Atkins and six military officers. Before the court was sworn in, Macarthur challenged the appointment of Atkins, insisting that his challenge should be decided on a simple majority of the members of the court. He was well aware that his case was unjustified in law and he must have been making the protest simply in order to force Bligh to retaliate. It worked. Bligh called on Major Johnston, in charge of the New South Wales Corps, to attend him at Government House. Johnston refused, claiming an injury prevented him from doing so. Macarthur was then arrested and thrown in prison, and later that same day the six military officers on the court panel wrote to Bligh objecting to Macarthur's imprisonment. Bligh's response was to summons the six to appear before him the following day, charged with treason and with usurping the government. Bligh again wrote to Major Johnston but the major maintained that he was 'otherwise indisposed'. Such indisposition did not, however, prevent the major from hurrying to the barracks, where he illegally assumed the title of lieutenant-governor and signed the warrant for the release of Macarthur from prison, where he had spent the day

Almost certainly this was all part of a pre-prepared plan and the soldiers were simply acting as stooges for Macarthur. Bligh had walked into the trap, and shortly after seven o'clock Government House was surrounded by upwards of three hundred soldiers, who had spent the afternoon drinking and celebrating. With bayonets drawn, they marched on Government House while the band played 'British Grenadiers', and proceeded to search the premises. Bligh's arrest was not without incident as the soldiers first had to cope with Mary, Bligh's daughter, yelling insults and curses at them, while brandishing her parasol at the armed soldiers. In later years her contemporaries called her 'the sauciest, daintiest and most determined little spitfire ever to preside at Government House'. She certainly wasn't short on courage, having been widowed in January 1808 when her husband died of tuberculosis.

After her father was arrested, the story was put out that he was discovered hiding under the bed and a cartoon depicting the scene was released. It has to be said, it was a most unlikely story since everything about Bligh shows that he never shirked from confrontation, never turned to run and never showed any sign of cowardice whatsoever. However, it suited the rebels to ridicule Bligh, who then had to endure house arrest, with his daughter, for a period of over a year.

Johnson's authority for assuming control had been a petition signed by a number of his officers, who claimed that such a step was necessary because 'insurrection and massacre' were imminent. The soldiers alleged that Bligh was planning 'to subvert the laws of the country', and 'to terrify and influence the Courts of Justice'. There was, however, no constitutional basis for the appointment of Johnston as lieutenant-governor. This could only come from a direct appointment by King George III. Also, the day after the armed insurrection, the judge-advocate, commissary, provost-martial and chief naval officer were all removed from post, a clear indication that the army wanted control of all aspects of colonial life.

At the same time, Macarthur was given the title of Colonial Secretary, a role which gave him power over all official appointments. He used this in order to pursue a personal vendetta against Bligh's supporters, and hence had the former provost-martial (William Gore) arrested on trumped-up charges of perjury, for which he was sentenced to seven years in prison. Likewise, any magistrates daring to oppose Macarthur were simply dismissed, while loyal supporters were rewarded with profitable appointments and significant land grants.

In April 1808 Johnston's time as lieutenant-governor came to an end with the arrival in Sydney of his commanding officer Jospeh Foveaux, who had been serving on Norfolk Island throughout the time of the rebellion. It marked the beginning of the end of this particular chapter in Macarthur's life. For now, his influence was in decline and it became increasingly clear that both Macarthur and various members of the NSW Corps, including Captain Johnston, were likely to be charged with treason and that any trial would be likely to take place back in England. Macarthur and Johnston accordingly set sail for England, determined to 'get their retaliation in first', before Bligh could get home to put his side of the story.

In the event, the authorities realised that whereas Macarthur may have broken the law in New South Wales, and could be tried there, he was not a member of the army at the time of the rebellion and therefore could not be charged with mutiny before a court martial. Not for the first time, all charges against him were quietly dropped. He was, however, unable to return to Australia for another seven years because there he still faced criminal charges.

During his time under house arrest Bligh came under increasing pressure to return to England but he steadfastly refused to do so, saying that he would not leave until a replacement had been appointed. In March 1809 he was compelled to sign a paper agreeing to go home on board HMS *Porpoise*, but as soon as he boarded the ship he reneged on the deal, saying that he owed it to His Majesty to break his word when it was given under duress. Father and daughter then sailed to Tasmania on *Porpoise*, and there became a thorn in the side of Lieutenant-Governor David Collins. Bligh was to remain moored up in the estuary near Hobart for a further year until the newly appointed Lachlan Macquarie arrived in Sydney to take over as Governor in January 1810. Macquarie, an army officer, was the first Governor of the colony not to be appointed from the ranks of the Royal Navy, and his arrival with the 73rd Regiment meant that he was able to disband the New South Wales Corps and thereby put an end to their illegal machinations.

Then, and only then, was Macquarie able to drive out the cronyism and corruption which had marked the earlier years of the colony.

Johnston and Macarthur reached England a full year before Bligh, who arrived back to England on 25 October 1810. Throughout the period after the rebellion, Bligh's wife Betsey had tirelessly campaigned on his behalf, writing countless letters to Sir Joseph Banks, and to the Board of Admiralty. It must have been an exhausting time for her, having to defend her husband from a continual stream of allegations. Stories had been circulating that Bligh had acted corruptly, had received benefits to which he was not entitled, and had profiteered by selling government supplies at inflated prices.

Bligh had barely arrived back in England before he was called to give evidence at the trial of Johnston. The Court Martial was held at Chelsea Hospital in London on Tuesday, 7 May 1811, under the presidency of Lieutenant-Colonel Keppel. It immediately became clear that it was, in effect, as much a trial of Bligh's conduct as it was a trial of Johnston, with the added piquancy that the man who should have been in the dock – the man who had pulled all the strings – was Macarthur, and he was not on trial. It would also appear that Bligh was not in any well hell-bent on seeing the prosecution of Johnston succeed, just as long as his own reputation was not attacked. In his own words, Bligh informed the court that his only interest was where it was 'connected with the vindication of my honour and reputation; and if Col. Johnston's innocence be consistent with that vindication, I shall be the first to rejoice at his acquittal'.

Bligh knew the importance of having his 'side' of the story put correctly, and to that end employed the brilliant 27-year-old lawyer Frederick Pollock as his legal adviser. Later, Pollock was to become Sir Frederick, First Baronet, and was eventually appointed Attorney General in the government of Sir Robert Peel, ending up as a member of the Privy Council. Anxious to make quite sure that the issues were reported correctly, Bligh also engaged the services of a court reporter by the name of Mr Bartrum. His report of the trial was subsequently published by Bligh in November 1811 and it contains detailed accounts of the evidence given not just by Bligh but also by Johnston, Macarthur and others. The report includes some interesting questions put to Bligh under cross-examination – such as, how many mutinies had he been involved in? How many times had he been the subject of a court martial? It must have made for an electrifying trial.

The charge before the court was:

> That Lieutenant-Colonel George Johnston, Major as aforesaid, did, on or about the 26th day of January, 1808, at Sydney, in the colony of New South Wales, begin, excite, cause, and join in a mutiny, by putting himself at the head of the New South Wales Corps, then under his command and doing duty in the colony, and seizing and causing to be seized and arrested, and imprisoning and causing to be imprisoned, by means of the above-mentioned military force, the person of William Bligh, Esq. then Captain-General and Governor in Chief in and over the territory of New South Wales.

Having heard all the evidence the court reserved its judgment until 2 July 1811. At that time it announced that:

> The Court having duly and maturely weighed and considered the whole of the evidence adduced on the Prosecution, as well as what has been offered in defence, are of opinion that Lieut.-Col. Johnston is guilty of the act of Mutiny as described in the charge, and do therefore sentence him to be Cashiered.

Much has been made of the fact that the sentence was extremely lenient – Johnston could, after all, have been sentenced to death for the crime of mutiny. It has also been suggested that the leniency of the situation was in part a criticism of Bligh. But what comes across from the evidence is that Johnston was very much caught in a trap – he was not the ring-leader, he was not the rebel-rouser, he was simply the man in charge of the army trying to respond to an impossible situation. Any implicit criticism was directed as much against Macarthur as it was against Bligh.

So, what is to be made of Bligh's tenure as Governor? He certainly was not a skilled political animal, using guile to out-manoeuvre his enemies.

He certainly antagonised and often bewildered people by his outbursts of temper and bad language. But at the end of the day, it was perhaps inevitable that he would end up on the wrong side of Macarthur and the members of the NSW Corps. And they were the ones who held the power and were determined to hold on to it.

The whole scenario was loaded against Bligh, because his brand of 'obedience to orders' could only work if he had military backing, and yet here he was in Sydney, with the army backing the law-breakers. For the average settler, Bligh had done his utmost to improve their living conditions. When he first arrived, the conditions – especially in Hawkesbury – were appalling due to heavy flooding and a poor harvest. Bligh worked hard to improve their living conditions and his efforts to quell drunkenness and to improve the standard of justice through the courts were certainly needed, as was his crusade against illegal housing development and against army corruption. The rich landowners may have hated him, the army may have thwarted him at every turn, but the average settler would have been sorry to see him go.

Aftermath

Mary did not return to Britain with her father; she remained behind to marry the considerably older Colonel Maurice O'Connell, Governor Macquarie's deputy. It was a union which William Bligh initially opposed, but the couple went on to have a large family, moving to Ceylon and then Malta before ending up back in Sydney in 1838. By then O'Connell had been knighted and was a major general, in charge of the army throughout the colony. He served in the New South Wales Legislative Council and for a short time in 1846 was Acting-Governor of New South Wales. He died in 1848 at which point his widow returned to Europe living mostly in Paris, before dying in London in 1864.

As for Johnston, he returned to New South Wales in 1813 to pursue his farming interests. These were based on several hundred acres of land where he had built his home known as Annandale House, in what is now the Sydney suburb of Annandale, along with an estimated seven thousand acres previously granted to him near Parramatta. In 1814 he finally got around to marrying Esther Abrahams, a Jewish girl who he had first met when she was a prisoner on the *Lady Penrhyn* which came out to Australia with Johnston's regiment in 1787. She had already given birth to seven of his children and the large family prospered. Eventually, his place in the army was restored and he became lieutenant-colonel before dying in 1823.

As for Macarthur, he stayed behind in England for several years, fearing to return to Sydney because he knew that Governor Macquarie had orders to arrest him. Throughout that time he kept up a steady flow of letters to his wife and nephew, telling them how to run his farming business, particularly by expanding his flock of Merino sheep. Finally, in 1817, he got an assurance that he could return free of the risk of arrest, given in return for a promise to accept no public office and to take no part in the administration of the colony. On his return he was immediately at loggerheads with Macquarie. As far as Macarthur was concerned, what this new world needed was for the rich to be given every encouragement to enable them to become still richer – because that would enable wealth to filter down to all levels. So, when an enquiry was set up to examine Macquarie's reforms, headed by John Bigge, Macarthur got Bigge to endorse his demands for more land to be given to entrepreneurs such as himself, and for cheap manual labour to be made available. Low agricultural wages meant higher farming profits, and when Macquairie was replaced by Thomas Brisbane, the new Governor happily adopted Bigge's findings. Before you knew it, he had also confirmed the grant to Macarthur of the five thousand acres which he had been promised two decades earlier. Before long Macarthur amassed a fortune, diversified into establishing the first vineyard in the country, moved into horse-breeding, and helped set up the Australian Agricultural Company. As director of the company, he helped secure a grant of a million acres of land north of Port Stephens, and promptly sold to the company many of his own Merino sheep for breeding purposes so that the land could be stocked. In 1826, he helped found the Bank of Australia. His application to become a magistrate was turned down (on account of his involvement in the Rum Rebellion) but he went on to serve on the New South Wales Legislative Council and campaigned vociferously against a free press – and also against the use of juries in criminal trials After seven years on the Council he was forced to retire due to his declining mental health. He died, insane, in 1834 and was buried on his Camden Park Estate. More recently he has been honoured on both postage stamps and Australian banknotes and remains a highly controversial figure in Australian history.

Chapter 17

Final Years and In Conclusion

100 Lambeth Road Lambeth London, with its blue plaque recording that this was the home of the Bligh family.

Final Years

The passing of time meant that William Bligh was made up to the rank of rear admiral at the end of July 1810, becoming vice-admiral four years later. His long-suffering wife Elizabeth was to die in April 1812, no doubt emotionally drained and worn out by the constant strain of having to defend her husband's reputation. He retired to the country, some twenty-six years after the mutiny on the *Bounty*, to his small estate at Farningham, Kent, where he lived with four of his daughters at the Manor House. The house was badly damaged by bombing during the Second World War but has since been restored and is described as being 'an elegant Grade II listed property set in magnificent park-like gardens and grounds'. A more detailed description is contained in *The Buildings of England* edited by Nikolaus Pevsner. Arthur Mee, in his *The King's England* writes:

> At the Manor House here lived Bligh of the Bounty who went around the world with Cook before he was 20, and at 25 was on a voyage to encourage the planting of the bread fruit in the West Indies…. He settled down after a career of much agitation and excitement to quiet days in Farningham Manor House.

Bligh died while walking down Bond Street, London, on 7 December 1817; he had cancer and had come up to London to see his surgeon. He was buried in the churchyard of St Mary-at-Lambeth in Lambeth Palace Road eight days later, alongside his wife. Their burial place is marked by an imposing piece of coade stone, topped by a carved image of an eternal flame (sometimes mistaken for an image of a breadfruit). The church and churchyard are nowadays home to the Garden Museum in Lambeth and the tomb bears the inscription:

> Sacred to the Memory of William Bligh, Esquire, F.R.S. Vice Admiral of the Blue. The celebrated navigator who first transplanted the bread fruit tree from Otaheite to the West Indies. bravely fought the battles of his country and died beloved, respected, and lamented on the 7th day of December, 1817, aged 64.

The structure is classified as a Grade II* listed building, with the official list entry reading: 'Tall, classical sarcophagus, pedimented on all four sides and with angle pilasters and *antefixae*. Large oval urn on top.' In a city where burial grounds are normally tightly packed and where individual tombs struggle to stand out, what is remarkable is that this particular mausoleum stands practically alone. Almost everything else has been cleared and although the graveyard is believed to have been used for the burial of upwards of 26,000 Londoners, only three memorials remain – this one, and two recording the burial of the two John Tradescant's, father and son, who were great plantsmen of the Elizabethan and Jacobean ages.

Early in the twenty-first century, workmen cleared the undergrowth of what had become something of a rubbish tip. In doing so, they moved the slab covering the four steps leading down to an arched brick chamber where the lead coffins holding the mortal remains of William and Elizabeth Bligh lay. At the back of the chamber two tiny coffins were found, one containing the bodies of the twin boys who had died on the day they were born, back in 1793. The other tiny coffin presumably contained the remains of a deceased grandchild, hence the inscription on the tomb:

> In this vault are deposited also the remains of William Bligh and Henry Bligh who died 21 March 1793 aged 1 day. The sons of M Elizabeth and Rear Admiral Bligh and also W Bligh Barker their grandchild who died Oct 22 1805 aged 3 years.

On the other side of the tomb are the words:

> Sacred to the memory of M Elizabeth Bligh the wife of Rear Admiral Bligh who died 13 April 1812 in the 60th year of her age.
>
> Her spirit soared to Heaven, the blest domain
> Where virtue only can its need obtain
> All the great duties she performed thro life,
> Those of a child, a parent and a wife.

The side panels show a coat of arms between a ribbon carved with the words '*In Coelo Quies*' – Latin for 'In Heaven is Rest'. And, goodness knows, William Bligh deserved his rest!

What others had to say

Shortly after Bligh's death his nephew Francis Godolphin Bond received a letter from George Tobin who, as mentioned, had served under Bligh. In it he offered this assessment of his old commander: 'he has had a long and turbulent journey of it, no one more so, and since the unfortunate

Mutiny on the Bounty, has been rather in the shade. Yet he was perhaps not altogether understood. He suffered much and ever in difficulty by labour and perseverance extricated himself.'

It was Bond who had written to his brother in 1792, after serving under Bligh during the second breadfruit voyage, saying: 'Yes, Tom, our relation had the credit of being a tyrant in his last expedition ... the chief part of his conduct must have arisen from the fury of an ungovernable temper.'

A fellow officer apparently said of Bligh that he was 'a very choleric gentleman, but at the same time, a very just man.'

In the opposite corner, his successor as Governor of New South Wales, Lachlan Macquarie, wrote to his brother saying: 'Governor Bligh certainly is a most disagreeable person to have any dealings, or public business to transact with, having no regard whatever to his promises or engagements however sacred, and his natural temper is uncommonly harsh and tyrannical in the extreme.'

Quite simply, Bligh was a Marmite-type of a person – if you did not like him, you loathed him.

Conclusions

Before drawing any conclusions about who or what caused the mutineers to take over *Bounty* it is worth setting it in context. This particular mutiny may be the one which the public best remember – probably the only one. Yet that is not to say that mutinies were especially rare during the late Georgian period. Indeed, during the reign of George III – and the twenty years which preceded it – there were around seventy such mutinies. Most occurred during wartime, onboard ships which were in or near harbour. They occurred in all parts of the globe and between 1740 and 1820 there were a dozen mutinies in the Mediterranean, seven in the West Indies, four in Africa and another four in the Pacific. Three occurred in North America. Some were over almost before they began. Others, such as the one on board HMS *Hermione* in 1797, had lasting effects. In that case, the mutiny resulted in the brutal massacre of the captain and nine of his officers. Woken by sailors brandishing axes, the officers were brutally chopped to pieces and thrown overboard, and the ship was then surrendered to the Spanish authorities and used in their navy against the British. In that instance, the rebellion appears to have been sparked by the callous and cruel behaviour of the captain – and in particular by his capricious use of punishments. He felt that the men were taking too long to furl and unfurl the topsails so introduced a punishment whereby the last two men to descend from the top mast would be flogged. That was utterly unreasonable given that those with the highest to climb would invariably be last down. In their haste to avoid punishment three men rushed, fell from a considerable height, and were killed. The incident did not save the two men who descended last from being flogged. The uprising quickly followed and it was not that the men opposed corporal punishment – it went hand in hand with life at sea – but that they expected it to be proportionate and fairly administered.

In that context, look at the floggings dished out by Bligh while on Tahiti. He was 'lenient' in only flogging the three deserters, when he could have applied the death penalty. But he was unfair in flogging others whose only offence was the misfortune of being in charge when items were stolen from under their noses by islanders.

Other mutinies arose because the punishments dished out were considered too severe for trivial offences. In 1797 the mutiny on board HMS *Beaulieu* was caused by this. Other rebellions occurred because of poor conditions on board – and poor levels of pay. This was what lay behind the mutinies at Spithead and on the Nore. Pay levels had been set back in 1658 and had been largely unaltered for over 125 years – and yet the last decade of the century saw rampant inflation and the erosion of earnings. To add to the feeling of being 'left behind', the sailors would have noted that their counterparts in the British army received significant pay rises in 1795. In the Spithead mutiny the mutineers set out their demands – and the order in which they put them is significant. There is very little evidence to suggest that the mutineers were republicans driven by a desire to emulate the French in overthrowing the monarchy – although later commentators have tried, rather unconvincingly, to suggest that the rebels were stirred into action by different factions – the Foxites, opposed to the government of Willim Pitt, the United Irishmen fighting for Irish independence, and so on. If instead one looks at the demands made by the Spithead mutineers it can be seen that their first demand was better pay; second, they wanted full rations, i.e. using a pound weight of sixteen ounces instead of some lesser measure used by unscrupulous pursers. It had become a widespread tradition that a pound would be treated as being fourteen ounces and the purser would then transfer the left-over two ounces into his own account. Third, they wanted improved pay for sick or injured sailors, together with better care for widows and orphans. They also asked for over one hundred officers to be sacked. These demands were indeed met by the Admiralty and in return the mutineers backed down on their fifth and sixth demands, namely, for higher pensions and for bigger shares of prize money when foreign ships were captured.

But more than anything else, mutineers objected to 'ill-usage'. Examples of ill-usage included tyranny, overwork and disregard for the welfare of the seamen, and was to be contrasted with 'proper usage', where the authority of the captain and his officers was conducted fairly, even-handedly and with due regard to naval practice and custom. The men liked to know 'where they stood' on matters of discipline. They also liked to know that their grog and food rations were not going to be withheld in a capricious manner – which is probably why there were murmurings of discontent on Bligh's second breadfruit voyage when the men felt that their daily allowance of fresh water was being cut, 'just in order to feed the plants'. And quite clearly, on the *Bounty* the men would have been angry at any idea of their daily allowance of yams being cut, just because one or more coconuts had gone missing.

It is also worth noting that the verb 'to strike' had a very specific naval origin. The first 'strike' was the London sailors' strike of 1768. The term referred to the act of striking – that is to say, dismantling the rigging and thereby backing up the sailors' refusal to set sail. And many of the eighteenth century mutinies were little more than 'strikes'. Only rare instances, such as *Bounty* and *Hermione*, led to the ship's command being taken over, and the majority of 'mutinies' involved a refusal to carry out orders until complaints had been met. A withdrawal of labour occurred on board HMS *Culloden* in December 1794. The ship was considered leaky and unseaworthy and was due to have a refit. Instead, the crew were ordered to sail for the Mediterranean, and in protest the crew barricaded themselves below decks. No leaders stepped forward to issue demands, so no individual sailors could be identified as being the instigators. This stalemate lasted for over a week until the crew gave in, but only after they had been given an assurance that they would not be punished. Events showed that they were unwise to believe such an assurance, because ten of the men were hauled before a court martial. Five were hanged and many of the subsequent events in the Spithead and Nore mutinies were shaped by this act of duplicity.

One particular mutiny on board HMS *Blanche* resulted in a court martial of the captain, Charles Sawyer, in 1796. He was dismissed from the navy because he had lost control of *Blanche* and had forfeited the respect of his crew because of his blatant homosexuality – and his partiality for certain members of the crew. Favouritism was a frequent cause of unrest, just as 'being picked on' was a catalyst for mutiny. Cruelty was also a cause and in 1806 the crew of HMS *Ferret* rebelled because the captain was considered to be too harsh. He regarded himself as a disciplinarian, fully justified in using punishments in order to get the men to work as a team. They disagreed, tried to attack him in his cabin, but were forced back at the sight of the captain, dressed only in his night shirts, brandishing a sabre and cutting down his attackers. Eleven were later court martialled and hanged.

Ill-usage was cited by the mutineers on HMS *Kingfisher*, who claimed that they were being treated 'more like Turks than Christians' in 1797. They got short shrift from Commander John Maitland, who regarded attack as being the best form of defence. He gathered his officers and available marines and attacked the mutineers with swords and cutlasses, killing and maiming several of the rebels. Bligh would no doubt have argued that if he had only had marines on board he too could have nipped his rebellion in the bud…

Horatio Nelson was particularly keen on punishing mutineers severely. At one stage he was put in charge of HMS *Theseus* (a ship which had been involved in the Spithead mutiny) when a mutiny occurred on board HMS *St George* off Cadiz. Four mutineers were court martialled in March 1797 and sentenced to death. Senior officers objected to the sentence being carried out on a Sunday – for religious reasons. John Jervis, 1st Earl of St Vincent, was Admiral of the Fleet and he ordered sentence to be carried out as planned, prompting Nelson to send his congratulations, with the words 'had it been Christmas Day instead of Sunday, I would have executed them'.

Sometimes mutinies occurred over relatively minor concerns. The crew on HMS *Defiance* objected to their grog being watered down in 1795, while the year before the crew onboard HMS *Orion* objected to the lack of shore leave. Sailors on HMS *Crown* felt that they had been equipped with inadequate and ragged clothing in 1764, and rebelled, while a mutiny on HMS *Berwick* in 1794 was all down to the poor quality of the beef. Sailors were particularly upset at any change to their customary privileges and therefore took exception when on board HMS *Minerva* because the captain insisted that they stop swearing and required them to be silent on deck. An added complaint was that he demanded that the men exercise by dancing to the fiddle – shades of Bligh and his compulsory dancing.

Turning to the mutiny on the *Bounty* it would be naïve to think in terms of only one cause. It would not have happened if the navy had not cut corners, or had sent two ships, or had allowed militia on board. It would not have happened if the men had not had an opportunity to 'go native' for weeks and weeks on end; if Bligh had been able to sail round Cape Horn he would not have missed the breadfruit propagation season and the crew would never have had a chance to lead such a settled existence on Tahiti.

In Bligh's view, it was simply a case that Christian and the other mutineers had become besotted by 'female connexions'. In his words, they 'flattered themselves with the hopes of a more happy life among the Otaheiteans than they could possibly enjoy in England', and perhaps that was true. England represented class distinctions, and for the average working man it meant poor living conditions, poor housing, poor health – and hard work. Tahiti represented the Garden of Eden, an island where a man did not have to labour on the land to grow the food he needed to support his family, where the sun shone every day, where the women were freely available and where there was no concept of riches based upon the coin of the realm.

Would the mutiny have occurred if Bligh had insisted that the entire crew had returned to the ship every night, rather than being allowed to live with the natives onshore? It is impossible to say. If Christian had not been unlucky in love with Isabella, his first choice, would he have been so determined to make a success of his relationship with Maimiti? If his father had lived, would he have been a lawyer in England rather than a sailor on a stinking, over-crowded ship sailing the Pacific? To this there is only one obvious answer: we cannot know.

What we do know is that the mutiny was not caused by some bullying tyrannical monster such as has been displayed on the silver screen. Bligh was not a cruel man, merely an insensitive one. He was a pompous little man, full of his own self-importance, but that doesn't justify the mutiny. Bligh probably was not helped by his own lack of stature. At a time when the average male was 5ft 3in tall, he was described as being 'small' – suggesting that he was probably no more than 5ft tall. By way of contrast, James Cook was over a foot taller. And size matters – Cook's height made it easy for him to have gravitas, to have a bearing of authority. Bligh had no such natural advantage. We talk of 'belittling' someone – Bligh was, by an accident of birth, 'belittled', and perhaps he made up for it by being so quick to detect any attempt to undermine his authority. He was irascible and used appalling language, to the extent that some recent biographers consider that he may have had Asperger's Syndrome – but that is simply putting him in a twenty-first-century pigeon-hole. What we can say is that he had a short fuse and a temper which could flare up and then die down as if nothing had happened. But the treatment of his crew on Tahiti made it easy for the men to succumb to the notion that they were in some way better off staying on Tahiti. His bombast, his constant belittling, his harping criticisms meant that there was no one who instinctively liked him and rushed to his defence. It perhaps explains why none of the officers actively tried to help Bligh when they saw the mutiny unfold. Bligh had been his own worst enemy – he was not a particularly likeable man. Months on shore had weakened the automatic bonds of discipline and loyalty, and certainly had dulled their reactions. And by the time they came to their senses, it was too late.

Out of loyalty to the traditions of the navy, Fryer would probably have led a counter-coup if he had stayed on board, but once he was led, forcibly, onto the longboat it was clear that there remained nobody on *Bounty* who was prepared to 'put their head above the parapet'. Bligh's account of the mutiny was certainly sanitised and self-serving, but if his account was 'economical with the truth' it was surely more accurate than the downright lies peddled by Edward Christian on behalf of his brother.

Fletcher Christian never planned a mutiny; he planned to run away. It was no noble search for Freedom with a capital F. It was running away – running from authority, running from squalor, running from 'duty'. He had not thought it through, he had not considered what life would be, permanently on the run and looking over his shoulder to see if the Royal Navy were after him. He had not garnered support for his scheme from any more than a small handful of the crew. His hare-brained scheme was hatched after a night of drinking, with barely three hours sleep, after the humiliation of being accused of theft by a man he had thought was his protector and mentor. That it succeeded was not down to his own force of character or to his minute planning – it was down to a series of coincidences which meant that Bligh was the wrong man, in the wrong pace, at the wrong time.

Fletcher Christian was, in many ways, someone who was desperate to find love; brought up from the age of 4 in a home without a father, with a mother who always had her hands full looking after his younger sisters. All his life, he never quite achieved what he thought was his entitlement. When he was promoted by Bligh to be his second in command, one suspects that he thought that he could continue being 'one of the boys', not realising that promotion brought responsibilities. It would then have been the final straw for him if he had then been demoted by Bligh, and forced to go back to being an Able Seaman. The fact that on his own admission he probably had 'liberated' one of the stolen coconuts probably accounted for much of his anguish. He felt suicidal, to the extent of apparently having packed a lead weight with his escape bundle of food and utensils – so that if he did not reach shore or was not picked up by friendly islanders, he could ensure a swift death by drowning. And then, while his mind was troubled in this way, he heard the words of George Stewart: 'The men are ripe for anything!' Stewart may simply have said those words to appeal to Christian not to do anything rash, because the ordinary seamen looked to him for leadership and guidance. But those words seem to have been a catalyst, intended or otherwise. To Christian it meant: 'You are not alone. You don't have to be the one to leave the ship.' Suddenly, Christian could see that there was a way out, a way he could escape, a way he could get back to a life without responsibilities. And when he broached his idea to his colleagues to cast Bligh adrift, they would simply have seen it as a chance to get away from a life in which they were threatened with near-starvation rations, back to an island where they could be as promiscuous and indolent as they wanted.

The fact that Fletcher Christian garnered support from his followers reflected the fact that young men, perhaps then as now, have concerns which are remarkably focused. It is no surprise that for the young males, sex was a hugely dominant concern. On board, the sailors could have looked forward to 'Nothing but rum, sodomy, prayers and the lash', as Winston Churchill is famously quoted as saying. Even once they got back home they would have had to pay for their sexual pleasures, and not every prostitute in every port would have had the inclination to offer 'the full menu', including both oral and anal sex. Yet even by Bligh's admission, both of these services appear to have been freely available on Tahiti. It must have been a total culture shock for the men on board *Bounty*, to find women eager to participate in the sort of sexual practices which back in England were regarded with horror. In England, society frowned on women who enjoyed sex, to the extent that the word 'whore' did not necessarily mean a woman who charged for sex – it simply meant a woman who enjoyed sex. As Dr Johnson put it in his *Dictionary of the English Language*, it could simply mean 'A woman who converses unlawfully with men; a fornicatress; an adultress; a strumpet.'

In Britain, 'whore' had a clearly pejorative meaning – and yet in far-off Tahiti the men discovered women who enjoyed giving and receiving sexual pleasure but who were never looked down upon in Tahitian society. Discovering such a lack of hypocrisy must have been truly amazing, even if subsequent events on Pitcairn showed that the Europeans never actually believed in sexual equality. The women were chattels just as much as they would have been in Britain, 'belonging' to a man. It was a concept utterly foreign to the Tahitians.

Christian's libido may well have been the main cause of the mutiny – Bligh certainly thought so. And it is a contention borne out by Edward Lamb, Commander of the *Adventure*, who wrote to Bligh in October 1794 in support of Bligh's *Answer to the Appendix*. Commenting on the time all three had served on the same vessel (*Britannia*) during Bligh's time in the merchant navy, Lamb wrote:

> When we got to sea, and I saw your partiality for the young man, I gave him every advice and information in my power, though he went about every point of duty with a degree of indifference, that to me was truly unpleasant; but you were blind to his faults, and had him to dine and sup every other day in the cabin, and treated him like a brother, in giving him every information. In the Appendix it is said, that Mr Fletcher Christian had no attachment amongst the women at Otaheite; if that was the case, he must have been much altered since he was with you in the Britannia; he was then one of the most foolish young men I ever knew in regard to the sex.

That final sentence suggests that while in the Caribbean, Christian had been unable or unwilling to exercise any self-control. Presumably he was so busy indulging his sexual desires in the many brothels in Jamaica that his behaviour was noted by his fellow-sailors. Fast forward to Tahiti and it is easy to imagine that Christian found himself in a sexual heaven. Here was a man heavily influenced by his libido, and faced with the prospect of many months of confinement on a crowded ship with a complete absence of female company, he was driven to foolish decisions and reckless actions.

To finish with, it may be worth recalling the words of Dr Samuel Johnson, as re-told by James Boswell:

> No man will be a sailor who has contrivance enough to get himself into jail; for being in a ship is being in a jail, with the chance of being drowned … A ship is worse than a jail. There is, in a jail, better air, better company, better conveniency of every kind; and a ship has the additional disadvantage of being in danger.

Johnson might as well have added: 'No sailor will therefore stay in a ship without seeking to escape from his jail.' And that is what Fletcher Christian did – escape. Leaving William Bligh to carry the blame …

Chapter 18

The Story According to Hollywood

Advertisement from 1933 for *In the Wake of the Bounty*.

Nearly a century after the actual mutiny took place, writers started to come up with fictional accounts based on the mutiny. Back in 1879 Jules Verne had written a short novel entitled *Les Révoltés de la Bounty*, looking at the story very much from the point of view of Bligh adrift in his longboat. With its exotic setting, its story of Polynesian life, bravery and sailing skill, and with the conflict between two men leading to an inevitable climax, it was never going to be long before the new-fangled motion picture industry got hold of the story.

Way back in 1916 there was a New Zealand silent movie entitled *Mutiny of the Bounty*, starring George Cross as Bligh and Wilton Power as Fletcher Christian. The film was directed and co-written by Australian Raymond Longford, with writing assistance from Lottie Lyell. The latter also appeared in the film as Nessie Heywood, sister of Peter, the man found guilty of mutiny but subsequently pardoned. The filming mostly took place at Rotorua and on Norfolk Island and, at the time, it was thought to be the most expensive film commissioned in Australia. It is considered 'a lost film', but records suggest that it was reasonably faithful to historical events and was fair in its depiction of William Bligh.

A rather curious film appeared seventeen years later under the title of *In the Wake of the Bounty*, directed by Charles Chauvel. The makers described it as 'not a drama. It is the first of a series of great travel films to be produced by Expeditionary Films Ltd, depicting strange incidents, strange places, and strange peoples. Each travel feature will contain the thread of a story based upon a true-life drama.' In the film a purported former crew member of the *Bounty* tells the story of what happened on Tahiti and Pitcairn, and the film then cuts to a documentary about modern-day (i.e. 1932) island life. Reviewers said that they had 'never seen anything like it', and described most of the acting as 'very, very, bad'; the film is famous for one reason and one reason only: it marked the acting debut of a certain Errol Flynn, playing the part of Fletcher Christian against Mayne Lynton's William Bligh. Claiming to be a descendant of one of the *Bounty* mutineers, Flynn hammed it up impressively – and so he should, for a purported salary of three pounds ten shillings. The film was partly made on location, so at least that was accurate, but the film makers ran into problem with the censors because of the use of bare-breasted women in the native dance scenes. The paying public were perhaps rather more concerned with the appalling dialogue and poor acting. In any event, the film never really made it beyond the shores of Australia. It can, however, be seen online on the kanopy.com site. The film, or rather the documentary sections of it, enjoyed a brief reincarnation when it was reissued in 1935, with contributions from various descendants of Fletcher Christian, under the title of *Pitcairn Island Today*. This time around, Errol Flynn's contribution was left on the cutting-room floor in its entirety, but even that did not save the documentary from total obscurity.

The original film of *In the Wake of the Bounty* did, however, give Errol Flynn bragging rights over Clark Gable, who was thereby merely 'reprising' the role of Christian in the 1935 film *Mutiny on the Bounty*, which starred the irrepressible Charles Laughton as the irascible, tyrannical and thoroughly unpleasant William Bligh. Laughton was at his towering best, in a film brilliantly directed by Frank Lloyd and filmed largely on Santa Catalina Island, around Monterey Bay, and in San Francisco's South Beach Harbor. The film crew did venture as far as Tahiti, with a rumoured one hundred tons of equipment, but the footage shot on location was only used for background scenes since none of the main actors left US waters. The film was shortlisted for numerous awards, but in the event only won one Oscar, for Best Picture. It was the highest grossing US film of 1935, and went on to be one of the most successful films of the decade.

What makes the film is the magnetic performance by Clark Gable, and the counterpoint between his portrayal of the heroic, oppressed but invincible character of Christian, and the violent, sadistic Bligh. The characters were one dimensional in the sense that Bligh is shown as having no redeeming features whatsoever – his sadism knows no bounds – while Gable, armed always with a boyish grin, portrays Christian as a perpetually popular 'good guy'. One feels he should be wearing a big white Stetson at all times, just to remind us how nice he is. How ironic that in practice Gable loathed working with Laughton because he despised homosexuals. One suspects that he also hated having to shave off his moustache for the film, since the film's one concession to historical accuracy was to emphasise that moustaches were banned in the British navy in the eighteenth century.

The plot is ludicrous and makes little attempt to be faithful to historical events. For instance, it starts in an English Tavern, where five men are being press-ganged to serve on *Bounty*. That did not happen. From the outset, Bligh is shown punishing his men unreasonably – Bligh never flogged a dead man. He also never ordered a keel-hauling, in which a man was dragged under the hull of the ship before being hauled back on board, half-drowned and with this flesh ripped to pieces on barnacles. Bligh also never deliberately starved his men – although the film would have you believe that he had previously transferred all manner of groceries and dried goods to the cellar of his own home, knowing full well that his men would go hungry as a consequence. The film shows that Fletcher Christian's child was born while he was on Tahiti – some going, given that Christian was only there for five months. And when Bligh finally gets back to England after his remarkable voyage as a castaway, lo and behold the navy sends him straight back to Tahiti, as captain of *Pandora*! This is done purely to be able to show Christian sneaking away on the *Bounty* en route to the Pitcairn Islands, just as Bligh hoves into view.

It is a complete travesty, but a travesty which was hugely enjoyable and extremely effective, to the extent that the 'Bligh was an absolute bastard' portrayal has become the accepted truth. Hollywood has never been too bothered with the truth – after all, it would say in great innocence, 'we are here to entertain not educate'. The fact remains: the film contains enough historical inaccuracies to sink a battleship, let alone the *Bounty*.

So where did the screenwriters get this twisted version of history from? The script was written by Talbot Jennings, Jules Furthman and Carey Wilson, but the ideas, the characters and the plot were taken straight from the trilogy of novels written by Charles Nordhoff and James Norman Hall in 1932, entitled *Mutiny on the Bounty*. Nordhoff and Hall were American flying aces serving in the First World War, as members of the Lafayette Escadrille. After the War they collaborated on various books, mostly linked to the recent war, and for a time shared a rented house on Martha's Vineyard. When commissioned by *Harper's Magazine* to write travel articles set in the South Pacific, they travelled to Tahiti to carry out background research but ended up staying, Nordhoff for twenty years, Hall for the rest of his life. In Nordhoff's case he married a Tahitian woman and had six children. It was Hall who came up with the idea of the *Bounty* trilogy. The pair then jointly mapped out the characters and storylines and it was Nordhoff who wrote the Polynesian chapters, while Hall covered the chapters based in England.

The story was told through the eyes of a fictitious observer called Roger Byam – loosely based on the character of Peter Heywood, and it was this first-person narrative that helped convince readers that the story which unfolded was based not just on real events, but on real characters, accurately portrayed.

It certainly made for a good yarn and the film's success prompted Universal Studios in 1940 to try and persuade director Frank Lloyd to make a film about the life of Bligh, starring either Spencer Tracy or Charles Laughton in the title role. It was never made. Five years later MGM announced that it would make a sequel to be called *Christian of the Bounty* starring Gable in the title role, but again, it failed to materialise.

Filmgoers had to wait until 1962 before a remake, still based on the Nordhoff-Hall novels, hit the silver screens under the title of *Mutiny on the Bounty*. MGM must have regretted its decision to cast Marlon Brando as Fletcher Christian almost immediately. He proved to be almost impossible to direct because he was constantly demanding changes to the script. The film benefited from being a widescreen, full Technicolour masterpiece, running to more than three hours. Filming took place on Bora Bora, on Tahiti and on Moorea, and there was no denying its beautiful photography. The production was beset with problems and budget over-runs. The original director (Sir Carol Reed) was replaced by Lewis Milestone. Brando kept insisting on changes, and on appearing in an extraordinary array of garments. He also insisted on casting his girlfriend Tarita Teriipaia (who he later married) to play the part of Maimiti, the daughter of the Tahitian king Hitihiti. Brando was previously married to the Mexican-American actress Movita Casteneda who, by an interesting coincidence, had played the part of Fletcher Christian's love interest in the 1935 film. Tarita, born on Bora Bora, was nominated for a Golden Globe award for her portrayal of Maimiti and went on to have two children by Brando before the couple divorced in 1972, after ten years of marriage.

Rewrite after rewrite was ordered and writer Eric Ambler reckoned that he submitted some fourteen drafts. In practice, only the first third of the film was written by Ambler, with other scriptwriting credits going to William Driscoll, Borden Chase, Howard Clewes and Charles Lederer. Talk about writing by committee!

Then there were the delays, in part necessitated by the fact that the replica *Bounty* took an additional three months build and then sailed to Tahiti. Some two hundred hotel rooms on the island were taken over by the cast and film crew. Then the rainy season started and island filming had to stop. This was when the studio sacked director Reed. Then Brando started to insist on ever more major plot changes, apparently disliking the way that Bligh was being portrayed in too favourable a light. It appears that if he did not like the lines he was given, he would simply refuse to say his words. Costs mounted until the overrun reached $10 million, and in all the film was a financial disaster, losing an estimated $6 million. It was also a critical flop, with filmgoers put off by Brando's absurd accent, odd foppish mannerisms and strange acting. The film echoed its 1935 predecessor by showing Bligh, played by Trevor Howard (a late replacement for Peter Finch) as a vicious tyrant. All in all, it seems to have ended up as a vanity project for Brando. He may have been MGM's great hope, but it was to be another ten years before his star status was fully restored in *The Godfather*.

In 1984 the film industry had another go at portraying the Bounty story. This time it was based on the book *Captain Bligh and Mr Christian* by Richard Hough, with screenplay by the renowned Robert Bolt. Directed by New Zealander Roger Donaldson, the film was called *The Bounty* and starred Mel Gibson as Christian, with Anthony Hopkins as Bligh. At an earlier stage it had been intended to cast Oliver Reed as Bligh and Christopher Reeve as Christian. It is generally considered to be the most historically accurate of the various films, and featured Laurence Olivier in one of his last films, appearing as Admiral Hood in the court-martial scenes. Daniel Day-Lewis, who went on to win multiple Oscars, played the part of Sailing Master John Fryer, while the then unknown Liam Neeson appeared as the thuggish Churchill.

The film starts with the Bligh court martial and proceeds via a series of flashbacks. It tries to establish some sort of tension by suggesting that there was a risk that Bligh would be found guilty, whereas in reality a finding of innocence was never in doubt. It does, however, show Christian as basically a good person and therefore by definition has to cast Bligh as being less good. It plays as much on class differences between the two, with Christian as the better-bred dreamer, up against the stubborn, rule-bound Bligh. In its favour, the film shows more of the rough-and-ready aspects of life at sea, in contrast with the 'jolly tar' portrayal in earlier films. Bligh is shown as a man of his times – a disciplinarian who uses corporal punishment whenever he deems necessary. It isn't because he enjoys flogging his men, it is because discipline is necessary to get the job done.

It might be interesting if the next remake of the story shows Christian as a man who thoughtlessly casts a boatload of men adrift to face an almost certain death; who selfishly pursues his own voyage of discovery; who leaves his followers high and dry by having no considered proposals as to how they could succeed; a man who is a racist and a misogynist and who kidnaps islanders to use as sex slaves. Then, perhaps, it could leave room to show Bligh as the good guy. It would not be the complete story – any more than the historically inaccurate films made to date. But at least it would act as a counterbalance to the absurd one-dimensional characters shown in the films made in the last century.

Acknowledgements and Credits

Text image 1: *A detailed drawing of the different parts of the breadfruit Tree* by Sir W. Johnston, shown in *Encyclopaedia Britannica*, Ninth Edition.

Text image 2: *The Western Prospect of His Majesties Dock-Yard near Plymouth* by Samuel and Nathaniel Buck. Via British Library, in public domain.

Text image 3: Detail from an engraving of Captain Cook by Thornton. In public domain, Scottish National Portrait Gallery.

Text image 4: Engraving by C.E. Wagstaff based on Official portrait of Sir Joseph Banks as President of the Royal Society, painted by Thomas Phillips in 1812. National Portrait Gallery Australia.

Text image 5: *Illustration of a ship-building operation*, by Jospeh Mulder. Author's own collection.

Text image 6: The plan and elevation of HMS *Bounty* showing the 'Garden' with its spaces for hundreds of plant containers. From the Project Gutenberg e-Book of A Voyage to the South Sea, by William Bligh.

Text image 7: *View of Tahiti*, 1777, by Daniel Nikolaus Chodowiecki, after Friedrich Georg Weitsch. Rijksmuseum.

Text image 8: Robert Dodd's picture of the mutiny on the *Bounty*, National Maritime Museum.

Text image 9: Bligh's original logbook, held by the State Library, New South Wales.

Text image 10: *Rough Seas and a dangerous landing place* showing the landing place of HMS *Blossom* in 1825. Credit: Mitchell Library, New South Wales.

Text image 11: Engraving purporting to be a likeness of Fletcher Christian, held in the Rijksmuseum.

Text image 12: HMS *Pandora* in the act of foundering, 29 August 1791. Etching by Robert Batty from an original sketch by Peter Heywood published in *The Eventful History of the Mutiny and Piratical Seizure of HMS Bounty: Its Causes and Consequences*. In public domain, Wikimedia Commons.

Text image 13: Extract from the portrait of Admiral Lord Hood, by James Northcott. In the public domain, per Wikipedia.

Text image 14: *William Bligh* by John Webber painted in 1775. Public domain, per Wikipedia.

Text image 15: A breadfruit tree growing on Papeete next to an ancient temple. Author's own photograph.

Text image 16: Richard Parker shown in an etching from July 1797. In public domain.

Text image 17: Newspaper cutting dated 1790. Shown courtesy of New South Wales State Library.

Text image 18: *The Battle of Camperdown*, engraving by Thomas Hellyer after Thomas Whitcombe. Rijksmuseum.

Text image 19: *The arrest of Governor Bligh*, by an unknown artist. National Museum Australia.

Text image 20: 100 Lambeth Road, Lambeth, London per Wikimedia Commons courtesy of Joe MiGo CC BY-SA 3.0

Text image 21: Advertisement from 1933 for *In the Wake of the Bounty*. Universal Pictures.

Text image 22. The 1960 replica of the Bounty sinking in rough seas during Hurricane Sandy in October 2012. Picture, by US Coast Guard, in public domain.

Text image 23: *Sailors in Argument*. Published by P Roberts c1795. Lewis Walpole Library.

Plate 1. *Portrait of Bligh* shown courtesy of the National Library of Australia

Plate 2. *Portrait of Elizabeth Bligh* painted by John Russell, R.A. in 1802, shown courtesy of the James Cook Memorial Museum, Whitby.

Plate 3. Rear Admiral Bligh in 1814. State Library of New South Wales.

Plate 4. A ship's carpenter by Thomas Rowlandson. In public domain, per Wikimedia.

Plate 5. Ship's cook by Thomas Rowlandson. In public domain, per Wikimedia.

Plate 6. '*Transplanting of the breadfruit trees from Otaheite*' by Thomas Grosse, 1796. Original in State Library of New South Wales and shown courtesy of Wikimedia.

Plate 7. The Cape of Good Hope. In the public domain and with the original held by the National Maritime Museum (per Wikipedia).

Plate 8. *A scene in Tahiti 1769*. ©The British Library Board

Plate 9. *Portrait of Mrs William Bligh* by John Webber

Plate 10. *Portrait of William Bligh* by an unknown artist. In the public domain (per Wikipedia).

Plate 11. Chart of Tahiti from an etching by I.S. Klauber in 1794. Rijksmuseum.

Plate 12. *Coconut Trees* engraved by J. Nieuhof in 1682, shown courtesy of the Wellcome Collection.

Plate 13. List of mutineers in Bligh's handwriting held by the National Library of Australia (per Wikimedia Commons).

Plate 14. *Captain Peter Heywood* by John Simpson, c.1822, In public domain (per Wikipedia).

Plate 15. Caricature of Sir Joseph Banks by James Gillray. In public domain (Library of Congress).

Plate 16. Caricature from 1803 by James Gillray entitled *Germans Eating Sour-Kraut* shown courtesy of the Lewis Walpole Library, Yale University.

Plate 17. Caricature by Isaac Cruikshank published by S.W. Fores in 1797, shown courtesy of the Lewis Walpole Library at Yale University.

Plate 18. *Going on board the 'Hector' of 74 guns* by Thomas Rowlandson. In public domain per Wikimedia Commons (original at National Maritime Museum Greenwich).

Plate 19. Tiger cowrie – in public domain.

Plate 20. *Deux Tahitiennes* by Paul Gauguin, 1899, shown courtesy of the Metropolitan Museum in New York. In public domain.

Plate 21. *Mary Putland* painted by an unknown artist in 1803. Original held by New South Wales State Library. In the public domain per Wikipedia.

Plate 22. Silhouette of John Macarthur circa 1834. In public domain.

Plate 23. *Portrait of Lt. Col. George Johnston*, by Robert Dighton painted in 1810. Public domain per Wikimedia Commons.

Plate 24. *Government House, Sydney* possibly painted by George William Evans. Original held by New South Wales State Library. In the public domain per Wikipedia.

Plate 25. 'Distress' by Thomas Rowlandson. In public domain, per Wikimedia Commons.

Plate 26. William Bligh's tomb. per Wikimedia Commons. Photograph by Miranda Hodgson CC BY-SA 2.0

Plate 27. *The Botanic Macaroni* by M Darly. In public domain, per Lewis Walpole Library at Yale University.

Plate 28. *Sydney from the western side of the cove* painted by G.W. Evans. In public domain (original in the State Library of New South Wales).

Plate 29. *Portrait of Governor Philip Gidley King c.1800*. In public domain (original held by the State Library of New South Wales).

Plate 30. Proceedings of the Court Martial of Lt.-Col. George Johnston, 1811. In public domain.

Plate 31. Photograph of 100 Lambeth Road, Lambeth, London, by spudgun67 per Wikimedia Commons.

Plate 32. *Mutiny on the Bounty* poster from 1935, Metro Goldwyn Mayer Pictures.

The name *Bounty* has not been an auspicious title for a ship. Here, the final moments of the replica Bounty, built in 1960 and sinking in a storm in 2012.

Bibliography

There have been literally hundreds of books written about Bligh, Christian, the mutiny, *Pandora*, the Courts Martial and so on. These are some of the more important ones and in the case of many of the earlier books they are also available online

e.g via Project Gutenberg – including https://gutenberg.net.au/

Also highly recommended are the websites such as those operated by:

Famous Trials at famous-trials.com/bounty

Whalesite at https://whalesite.org

Mitchell Library – The State Library New South Wales at https://www.sl.nsw.gov.au/contact-us/mitchell-library

Pitcairn Islands Study Centre at https://library.puc.edu/pitcairn/index.shtml

Books

Alexander, Caroline, *The Bounty: The True Story of the Mutiny on the Bounty* London: Harper Collins, 2003

Barrow, Sir John, *The Eventful History of the Mutiny and Piratical Seizure of HMS Bounty* London 1831 (available in electronic format).

Bartrum, J., P*roceedings of a general court-martial for the trial of Lieut.-Col. Geo. Johnston* Sherwood, Neely and Jones, London,1811.

Beechey, F.W., *Narrative of a voyage to the Pacific and Beering's Strait, to co-operate with the polar expeditions performed by HMS Blossom* Colburn & Bentley, London,1831

Belcher, Lady Diana Joliffe, *The Mutineers of the Bounty and Their Descendants in Pitcairn and Norfolk Islands* London, John Murray 1870. Available in electronic format.

Bligh, William, *A Narrative of the Mutiny on the Bounty* 1790

Bligh, William, *A Voyage to the South Sea* 1792

Bligh, William, *An Answer to Certain Assertions Contained in The Appendix to a Pamphlet, entitled...* etc., etc G Nicol, Pall Mall, 1794. Available online via Google books.

Bligh, William, *The Log of the Bounty*, Owen Rutter (ed.), Golden Cockerel Press London 1937.

Bligh, William, *Miscellaneous letters* Mitchell State Library of New South Wales. Available online.

Bonner Smith, D., 'Some Remarks About the Mutiny of the Bounty', *Mariner's Mirror*, vol 22, no 2, Apr 1936.

Bonner Smith, D., 'More Light on Bligh and the Bounty', *Mariner's Mirror*, vol 23, no 2, April 1937.

Bougainville, Comte de, A Voyage Round the World Exshaw, et al., Dublin, 1772. Available online in digitised format.

Bruce, Julia, 'Banks and Breadfruit', *RSA Journal* Vol. 141, No 5444 (November 1993).

Byron, Lord, *The Island, or Christian and his Comrades* John Hunt, London, 1823.

Callum, E., *A social and economic history of the 1797 fleet mutinies at Spithead and the Nore* Trinity College, University of Cambridge, 2020.

Christian, Edward, *A Short Reply to Capt. William Bligh's Answer*. J Deighton, Grays Inn, London, 1795. Available online via the National Library of Australia.

Christian, Glynn, *Fragile Paradise: the discovery of Fletcher Christian, Bounty mutineer* London, Hamish Hamilton, 1982.

Cook, James, *Journal – First Voyage* London 1893. Available via Project Gutenberg.

Cook, James, *A Voyage Towards the South Pole and Round the World* London, 1777.

Cook, James, *The Three Voyages of Captain Cook Round the World* A. & R. Spottiswoode, London, 1821.

Dampier, William, *A New Voyage Round the World* London, 1697. Available online via Project Gutenberg.

Delano, Amasa, *Narrative of Voyages and Travels in the Northern and Southern Hemispheres* Printed by E.G. House, Boston 1817. Available in digital format via Google Books.

Dening, Greg, *Mr Bligh's Bad Language: Passion Power and Theatre on the Bounty* Cambridge University Press, 1992.

Du Reitz, R., *The Causes of the Bounty Mutiny*, Almqvist & Wiksell, Uppsala, 1965.

Evatt H.V., *Rum Rebellion* Angus & Robertson, Sydney, 1938.

Gesner, Peter, *Pandora: An Archaeological Perspective* Brisbane: Queensland Museum, 1991.

Gesner, Peter, *HMS Pandora Project* Brisbane, Queensland Museum, 2000.

Hamilton, George, *A Voyage round the World, in His Majesty's Frigate Pandora* W. Phorson and B. Law and Son, Berwick and London, 1793.

Hough, Richard, *Captain Bligh & Mr Christian: The Men and the Mutiny London* Hutchinson, 1972.

Kennedy, Gavin, *Bligh* London, Duckworth, 1978.

Kennedy, Gavin, *Captain Bligh the man and his mutinies* London, Duckworth, 1989.

King, James, *A Voyage to the Pacific Ocean: performed under the direction of Captains Cook, Clerke, and Gore in the years 1776, 1777, 1778 1779, & 1780* W. & A. Strahan, 1784.

Ledyard, John, *A Journal of Captain Cook's Last Voyage* Hertford, Connecticut, 1783.

Mackaness, George, *The Life of Vice-Admiral William Bligh R.N., F.R.S.* Sydney, Angus and Robertson, 1931.

Mackaness, George (ed.) *A Book of the Bounty* London: J. Dent, 1938.

Mawe, John, *The voyager's companion, or shell collector's pilot* Longman, Hurst, Rees, Orme, Brown, and Green, London, 1825.

Maxton, Donald A., *The Voyages of the Pandora and Matavy* McFarland, 2020.

McFarland, Alfred, *Mutiny in the Bounty! and story of the Pitcairn Islanders* Sydney, J. J. Moore, 1884.

McKay, John, *The Armed Transport Bounty* Naval Institute Press, 1989 and available online.

Morrison, James, *After the Bounty – a Sailor's account of the Mutiny and Life in the South Seas* Potomac Books, USA, 2010.

Mee, Arthur, *The King's England* Hodder & Stoughton, London, 1936.

Nordhoff, C. & Hall, J. N., *The Bounty Trilogy (Mutiny on the Bounty, Men Against the Sea, Pitcairn's Island)* Little, Brown & Co. Boston 1934.

Oliver, Douglas L., *Return to Tahiti: Bligh's Second Breadfruit Voyage* 1988, University of Hawaii Press.

Pevsner, Nikolaus and Nairn, Ian, *Buildings of England*, Sussex. Penguin Books, London, 1965.

Rawson, Geoffrey, *Bligh of the Bounty* London, Philip Allan, 1930.

Renouard, David, *Voyage of the Pandora's Tender* (1791) Available on the National Library of Australia website.

Rickman, John, *Journal of Captain Cook's Last Voyage* London, 1781.

Schreiber, Roy E., *The Fortunate Adversities of William Bligh* P Lang, Wisconsin University, 1991.

Shapiro, H.L., *Heritage of the Bounty: The story of Pitcairn through six generations* London. Victor Gollancz, 1936.

Swainson, William, *A catalogue of the rare and valuable shells which formed the celebrated collection of the late Mrs. Bligh* W. Smith, London, 1822, (available in digital format online).

Taylor, A.H., '*William Bligh at Camperdown*', *Mariner's Mirror*, vol 23, no 4, Oct 1937.

Thomson, Basil, (ed.), *The voyage of HMS Pandora* London, Francis Edwards, 1915.

Sailors in Argument.

Index